T0194655

# TOLKIEN, MYTHOLOGY,

## Imagination and Spiritual Insight:

*The Enduring Power of The Lord of the Rings*

**LUIGI MORELLI**

TOLKIEN, MYTHOLOGY, IMAGINATION
AND SPIRITUAL INSIGHT:
THE ENDURING POWER OF THE LORD OF THE RINGS

Editor: Kristine Hunt
Image source: Adobe Stock
Book Cover: Megan Pugh

iUniverse books may be ordered through booksellers or by contacting:

iUniverse
1663 Liberty Drive
Bloomington, IN 47403
www.iuniverse.com
1-800-Authors (1-800-288-4677)

ISBN: 978-1-5320-8071-5 (sc)

Print information available on the last page.

iUniverse rev. date: 08/22/2019

# CONTENTS

# INTRODUCTION

This book departs somewhat from what I have written in previous years. The intention of writing about J. R. R. Tolkien came out of a time of rest, from a deliberate attempt to place everything of a research nature on hold. And that is what I did. For two to three months I abandoned myself to the pure delight of reading, or rereading, first *The Hobbit*, then *The Lord of the Rings*. During any free time I had, I returned to the reading of Tolkien's opus; it formed an oasis out of time, a magical space in itself; it modified the quality of my days, weeks, and months. A wonderful soul cloak protected me from the cares of the world, and yet allowed me to meet those cares more fully, making me wholeheartedly agree with W. H. Auden that "No fiction I have read has given me more joy." Putting the book down was partly an occasion of grieving.

I remember my previous experience of reading the book some thirty years ago as a youth of twenty-six. I had explored a lot of science fiction or fantasy (Madeleine L'Engle, Lloyd Alexander, and Ursula K. Le Guin stand out among them). Still, I read *The Lord of the Rings* only at my sister's insistence. And I remember the engrossing effect of reading it, and the sense of completion in putting the book down after the last page. I happened to have finished it just as my bus arrived at its destination in the mountains of Santa Cruz, California. I was still enveloped in a cloak of peace and awe. I got down from the bus and raised my gaze to the tall redwoods all around me, in a way that I felt meant looking at the "real" world, after having finished being in another world. And my mind was living in this contrast and telling me something like, "You are returning to this world, but you have just been in a world that is more real than this external one."

It was a pleasure to immerse myself in this space of otherworldly inspiration and delight for a second time. Concluding this second reading, I remembered reading Tolkien's biography two years earlier. I told myself that surely there is something more that Tolkien knew, or "something more that he was," that made it possible for him to write such a masterpiece; that conviction grew and found confirmation as I looked more deeply into his biography and work. It became only natural to try to honor such beauty by, well, . . . researching it, and hopefully offering some new insights about this celebrated author and his enduring legacy.

No doubt the first Tolkien experience nourished further my love of myths and inspired me later to work on North and South American legends. I still carry this feeling in relation to the Iroquois *White Roots of Peace*, a legend that keeps informing my life, and about the confrontation of the Twins in the realm of Xibalba as we know them from the Mayan *Popol Vuh*.

And yet there is a substantive difference between what I mention above and the world Tolkien invites us into. The North and South American legends mentioned above are a legacy of the past, of other forms of consciousness remote from ours. What happens in Iroquois and Mayan myths or legends baffles the consciousness that is bound to the senses and purely material world, because it comes from a completely different form of consciousness than our postmodern worldview, the more so the further we go back in time. Tolkien, a contemporary, has written a legendarium to which the minds of many are inclined to give as much credence as to the world of ancient Native Americans, ancient Greeks, or modern native populations. His goal was to offer England the mythology he felt it was missing. He seemingly failed at this project, only to succeed instead in offering us a modern mythology accepted in all corners of the world.

Another attempt has accompanied me in what I have written, from the love of biographies. I have delighted in delving into the lives of famous people; delving until, hopefully, something emerges that is more than a flat portrayal on a two-dimensional page. until something emerges from between lines and words, at least for me. I would call it rising to a living imagination of the individual in the biography. Those are individuals who are not either quickly glossed over or exhaustively understood and shelved. Oftentimes these biographies arise from looking at a life from many angles; what comes from a certain biographer forms one facet while other views add yet other aspects. And if everything works effectively, something more than the sum of the parts emerges.

At times a controversy around an individual becomes the very key of entrance into his biography. One clear example of this met me in the biography of Black Elk, the Lakota Sioux chief and medicine man. How could so many clamor that his was an authentic and exclusive Lakota spiritual faith—and others be equally convinced of Nick Black Elk's commitment to the Christian Catholic faith? The answer is, "Well yes, both/ and." And that is why his personality is fascinating: because in himself he tried, and managed to quite an extent, to reconcile the terms of what is normally seen as an opposition at a cultural level. In his breast no such opposition existed. Such is the case of Tolkien too, as we will see him emerge from this essay. He was an avowed Christian, very much aligned with the Roman Catholic faith. And yet one cannot help but think that the label "Catholic" confines the grandeur of Tolkien. His mythology covers much of what is considered the pre-Christian or pagan worldview, in which he seems to be fully at home. At any rate, much of Tolkien's imaginations and insights break free of dogma and cultural restrictions of one kind or another.

Tolkien seems to gather in himself a bundle of contradictions. A Christian, he is yet loved by many who have a New Age or pagan worldview, not to mention people with more secular affiliations. A traditionalist, even medievalist, yet he is the author of the myths that most grip the modern mind because of the relevance, even urgency of their themes. *The Lord of the Rings* could not have been written at another point in history; it could not better fit the cultural mood of the "end of history" as we perceive it all around us. Tolkien's is not only one of the most read body of legends in modern times; people who read him do not tire of reading him over and again. I know one reader who has read the series forty times. It is true that, just as Tolkien has many admirers, he has very clear detractors as well. He does not take a comfortable middle-of-the-road position. Reading Tolkien requires, after all, the challenge of entering what he called a secondary reality, a created world with laws of its own. We readers must leave this comfortable reality of our senses to enter a new, challenging reality—but in another sense, we escape to better be able to return. His books are not for everyone; they require the willingness to step across a threshold, at least if one doesn't love the epic literary genre at first.

What many don't know is that Tolkien was as much a scientist in his scholarly pursuits in philology as he was a well-known author of fiction. And this, I would argue, as others have, is one of the major strengths of his work. Science—as applied to his understanding of language, myth, and culture—is allied to art to create something that is larger than either. And Tolkien was as much of a visionary as he was an "experiencer." In other words, what he communicated was very often what he perceived in his mind's eye. It may sound perplexing to hear from him that he mostly did not *invent*, and that such was his best work. What did he mean by that?

Why has Tolkien's work endured to such an extent that even today, much to the chagrin of the critics of his "escapist" literature, he comes at the top of the list of the most-read works of English literature? Why have *The Hobbit* and *The Lord of the Rings* movies become such box-office hits? Partly because Tolkien's work could be compared to a new sacred text, minor though it may be in comparison to ancient tradition. Still, one can read Tolkien on many levels; on the surface we can delight in the characters, the magic, the otherworldliness, the beauty of landscapes, the accompanying challenges, action, triumphs against all odds, and so forth. A second and third reading will show that there is unsuspected depth, a clever intricacy in the interlacing of events in chapters and books; there are amazing symmetries and connections; there are encompassing views of the ages of Middle-earth, and so forth. So, how could Tolkien achieve all of this?

Looking back at the success of *The Lord of the Rings*, Tolkien commented that

> it was written slowly and with great care for detail, and finally emerged as a Frameless Picture: a searchlight, as it were, on a brief period in History, and on a small part of our Middle-Earth, surrounded by the glimmer

of limitless extensions in time and space. Very well; that may explain to some extent why it "feels" like history; why it was accepted for publication; and why it has proved readable for a large number of very different kinds of people.[1]

Further reflecting "on the wholly unexpected things that have followed its publication," he adds with what seems to have been a touch of surprise:

I feel as if an ever-darkening sky over our present world had been suddenly pierced, the clouds rolled back, and an almost forgotten sunlight had poured down again. As if indeed the horns of Hope had been heard again, as Pippin heard them suddenly at the absolute *nadir* of the fortunes of the West. But *How?* And *Why?*[2]

We will return to this puzzling letter at the end of our explorations.

*The Lord of the Rings* as a timely inspiration offered to humanity through an ideal, though certainly imperfect, instrument as J. R. R. Tolkien, summarizes everything I will present here. I am calling this book *Tolkien's Lord of the Rings: Mythology, Imagination, and Spiritual Insight* because I want to add something to what we know of Tolkien that appears only tangentially here and there in his letters, in various essays, or through Tolkien's fictional characters. Tolkien could talk to the spirit of the time only in the way that spirit talks to spirit; an author needs a deep spiritual perception to lead people to a spiritual accomplishment of the size of *The Lord of the Rings*. And he needs to have a dimension of personal spiritual experience in order to put it onto paper in a convincing way. This book's main intent is to shed light on the sources of Tolkien's spiritual perceptions and the discipline with which he pursued them. It is the spiritual dimension of Tolkien's work that makes it a universal legacy.

Tolkien's biography acquires a whole new dimension when we fully examine what we know of his spiritual experiences. Some of those appear in his letters; others in veiled but highly consistent terms in his writings, especially some unpublished ones. So this is the first stage of

[1] Carpenter, *Letters of J. R. R. Tolkien*, 413.
[2] Carpenter, *Letters of J. R. R. Tolkien*, 413.

looking at some phenomena: Tolkien's work as a scientific philologist and as a fiction writer forms another aspect; his deep perception of the link between languages, mythology, and culture; his clear understanding of what the human being can receive from the life of dream (big dreams, mind you), visions, and artistic inspiration; his discipline in working with all of these; and because it was an inner experience, what he carried from previous lives (at least one), however uncomfortably it lived next to his Catholicism.

Once we understand these foundations—the phenomena in Tolkien's life and work—then we can start to characterize what is present in his body of imaginations: the eons of earth existence and how they succeed each other; the Light and the Word and their role in the creation of the world. And then the endless sets of contrasts: the deathless Elves and the mortal men; Morgoth and Sauron; the varying ways time flows in the Shire, in Tom Bombadil's domain, in Rivendell, and in Lórien. Why is Tolkien so painstakingly specific in the way his created world works? Why does he go to such lengths in attaching appendices and cross-referencing all the parts of his creative work? Was it just what he admitted, a part of his exacting and pedantic nature? Or was there more?

There is definitely more if one looks to the work of Tolkien from the perspective of modern understanding of the spirit. There is genuine spiritual insight into deeper dimensions and connections of existence. Tolkien's work is deeply mystical or even esoteric, though he himself, quite rightly, would have shunned the term *esoteric*. His work was primarily a consistent and coherent artistic creation; something self-contained. After all, he detested allegory and detested bringing the primary world (which includes religious views), into his created world. So maybe he just couldn't help but perceive more deeply into the depths of existence, all the while in pure artistic fashion. One of his reader's expression of appreciation particularly touched Tolkien. In his words,

by a strange chance, just as I was beginning this letter, I had one from a man, who classified himself as "an unbeliever, or at best a man of belatedly and dimly dawning religious feeling ... but you," he said, "create a world in which some sort of faith seems to be everywhere without a visible source, like light from an invisible lamp."[3]

This feeling could be echoed by many.

Exploring this mystical sphere is the last aspect of this work. There is a clear reason for the mark that Tolkien has left on people's hearts and minds. He puts us in touch with deep archetypes of existence. We may not know these, but we cannot fail to sense the deeper reality of what comes from Tolkien's work. Toward the end of the book we will explore how Tolkien leads us from artistic imaginations to deeper spiritual insights. There is so much that Tolkien has allowed us to fathom about the nature of free will and fate; life and death; evil and its role in the shaping of the world; the initiation toward the spirit, as in the examples of Gandalf and Saruman; the nature of the spiritual world. This attempt will be a way to marry art and science once more. After all, art and science were the foundation of Tolkien's work. And art and science can help us shed light on its furthest reaches.

To conclude, a word of thanks. This work was rendered possible partly through the life-long dedication of professor Verlyn Flieger to Tolkien's opus. Of all the references to Tolkien's work, all her books and articles have been central to my understanding, both of Tolkien and of *The Lord of the Rings*. They have directed me toward many additional lines of personal inquiry.

---

[3] Carpenter, *Letters of J. R. R. Tolkien*, 413.

# PART I

# J. R. R. TOLKIEN

# CHAPTER 1

# *THE LORD OF THE RINGS*: SUCCESS AND PARADOXES

---

> Above all [Tolkien's vision] leaves us knowing deeply that
> there is more to be found in his fiction than meets the eye, that
> something wonderful and mysterious and deeply significant
> lies just beyond our rational perception, and that if we were to
> be given only a little more time, we would be able to see it.
> —Verlyn Flieger

In this chapter we will look at how Tolkien's trilogy seems to be everything to everyone. It has been seen as fitting all religious and spiritual leanings, and clearly speaks to those who would shy away from the word "religion" and call themselves humanists. Most interesting of all, *The Lord of the Rings* equally satisfies Pagans as well as traditional Christians. How this is possible is actually the goal of this exploration and book to surface.

The above is not the only apparent contradiction in Tolkien's work. *The Lord of the Rings* has all the trappings of an ancient, bygone world, and Tolkien's personality would seem to fully support this tendency towards constantly looking back. And yet, in many other ways, it is thoroughly modern, and this is why it can speak as effectively as it does to the yearnings of modern humanity.

# THE SUCCESS OF *THE LORD OF THE RINGS*

*The Lord of the Rings* rode the crest of the 1960s in America and Europe. Ever since then it has remained one of the most beloved fiction books of the 20th century. And the movement did not abate in the following decades. A 1999 Amazon poll found *The Lord of the Rings* to be the Amazon's customers "book of the millennium."[4] Beyond the English-speaking world Tolkien has fans worldwide. A 2003 Big Read Survey confirmed the book as the UK's "best loved novel."[5] A 2004 German survey discovered 250,000 who ranked the book their first choice.[6] And at present *The Lord of the Rings* remains one of the greatest world literary successes, with over 150 million copies sold.[7] Harper Collins has counted almost 40 languages for which translations of *The Hobbit* and/or *The Lord of the Rings* exist. In Russian, Swedish, Norwegian, German, Polish, and Slovenian there is more than one translation.[8]

In America, inspired by the hippy movement, branches of the Tolkien Society formed everywhere in the sixties, extending eventually into the Mythopoeic Society which added the works of C. S. Lewis and Charles Williams. Eventually Tolkien's work became the subject of theses and dissertations. Before being discovered by the hippies *The Lord of the Rings* was mostly read within Christian circles. In Denmark a book has been published that refers to biblical motives in *The Lord of the Rings* and is used in preparing children for their confirmation.[9]

---

[4] Andrew O'Hehir, "The Book of the Century," *Salon*, 4 June 2001. https://web.archive.org/web/20060213000712/http://www.salon.com/books/feature/2001/06/04/tolkien/.

[5] BBC, "The Big Read," April 2003. https://web.archive.org/web/20121031065136/http://www.bbc.co.uk/arts/bigread/top100.shtml.

[6] Krysia Diver, "A Lord for Germany," *Sydney Morning Herald*, 5 October 2004. https://web.archive.org/web/20070817074109/http://www.smh.com.au/articles/2004/10/04/1096871805007.html.

[7] Vit Wagner, "Tolkien Proves He's Still the King," *Toronto Star*, 16 April 2007. https://www.thestar.com/entertainment/2007/04/16/tolkien_proves_hes_still_the_king.html.

[8] The Children of Hurin, "Frequently Asked Questions." https://web.archive.org/web/20070530043707/http://www.tolkien.co.uk/faq3.aspx.

[9] Skogemann, *Where the Shadows Lie*, xxi.

The fame acquired by *The Lord of the Rings* was a surprise to Tolkien. The enduring success of the epic delights the fans and infuriates the advocates of more "serious" and realistic literature. But this is only one part of the enigma that surrounds this modern masterpiece. Let us look at some of these aspects.

## TOLKIEN BETWEEN THE MIDDLE AGES AND MODERN TIME

Tolkien's personality and literary works attract scrutiny from a variety of perspectives. They are the sources of many conundrums. Tolkien is very modern in his interests and outlook, but spent most of his life looking back to the past of language and mythology. Tolkien himself felt that he, and his fellow Inklings—the literary circle that included C. S. Lewis, Barfield, and C. Williams—were somehow out of step with their time. "We [Inklings] were born in a dark age out of due time (for us). But there is this comfort: otherwise we should not *know*, or so much love, what we love. I imagine the fish out of water is the only fish to have an inkling of water."[10] Anchored in the past but with a keen eye on the present—this insight may prove an important one to follow.

An example of the above: Tolkien expressed in interviews that after reading a medieval work he felt impelled to write something similar but modern "in the same tradition." And he did take on the medieval tradition in more than one way, noticeably in the structure of the book. Richard C. West reminds us that one of the early reviews of *The Lord of the Rings* called it "perhaps the last literary masterpiece of the Middle Ages."[11] Tolkien was somewhat amused by all these interpretations and conflicting kinds of appreciation.

Contrary to what he quotes above, West himself takes another angle on the book: "The Lord of the Rings is not the last masterpiece of the Middle Ages, but it was, if nothing more, a just instinct that led Tolkien to choose a medieval technique for his modern masterpiece."[12]

---

[10] Pearce, *Tolkien, Man and Myth*, 61.

[11] West, "The Interlace Structure of *The Lord of the Rings*," 77.

[12] West, "The Interlace Structure of *The Lord of the Rings*," 91.

West sees it as a right choice to use a structure that is reminiscent of medieval times—the interlace—particularly used in romances of the 13th century, among which is the Grail legend tradition. *The Lord of the Rings* is also a mix of old and new. It is a novel that obviously speaks to the consciousness of our apocalyptic "end of times." And yet, its inner structure harkens back many centuries; fulfilling Tolkien's desire to write something modern "in the same tradition."

Modern "organic unity" calls for a narrative with a single major theme, which can eventually be connected to a limited number of collateral themes, all clearly subordinated to the main one. The main theme is stated in the introduction, develops organically in the middle section, and comes to a resolution in the epilogue. In contrast, the medieval interlace was of such complexity that until modern times the critics could not detect a coherent design in medieval romances. The peak of this tradition was reached in medieval romances of the 13th century, the time of the Grail legends.

Richard C. West has detected in *The Lord of the Rings* a very expert use of medieval literary devices.[13] In the interlace, in contrast to modern organic unity, everything seems to happen at once; the narrative calls our attention in the direction of many events, characters, and themes. Any one of these can dominate at a given point. The paths of the various characters separate, merge, and diverge again without any apparent coherence. However, the attentive reader may realize that there is a structure because no part of the story can be altered or removed without causing damage to the whole. Often later sections are announced earlier on, and earlier events reecho in later ones. Themes return with repetitions and variations, whose patterns can be discerned. There are numerous causes for a given event, as we can notice in real life, contrary to the seemingly powerful single causes we find in organic unity.

In the interlace there is no clear-cut beginning or end because the story is generally a section of a larger whole. This was also the case for *The Lord of the Rings*, which needed an appendix in order to document the connections of the stories with Tolkien's mythology of *The Silmarillion*, which was only published after his death.

---

[13] West, "The Interlace Structure of *The Lord of the Rings*."

Alongside Tolkien's use of the medieval interlace is his creation of a comprehensive mythology. The Romantics of the 19th century developed an interest in folk and fairy tales in the forging of a national cultural identity. In Germany this had been the work of the Brothers Grimm. In many ways Tolkien behaved in England like the last of the Romantics.

In college after reading the Finnish *Kalevala* Tolkien wrote: "I would that we had more of it left—something of the same sort that belonged to the English." Some years later he wrote:

> Do not laugh! But once upon a time (my crest has long since fallen) I had a mind to make a body of more or less connected legend, ranging from the large and cosmogonic, to the level of romantic fairy-story—the larger founded on the lesser in contact with the earth, the lesser drawing splendor from the vast backcloths— which I could dedicate simply to: to England; to my country . . . I would draw some of the great tales in fullness, and leave many only placed in the scheme and sketched. The cycles should be linked to a majestic whole, and yet leave scope for other minds and hands, wielding paint and music and drama. Absurd.[14]

Tolkien's grandiose intention did not fulfill the promise of an English mythology; he seemingly missed the mark, but not by much, or he even exceeded it. One can confidently say there is no modern mythology that speaks to the human soul as does *The Lord of the Rings*. It is, one could argue, the epitome of a story for times of great transition. Though clothed in all the accoutrements of past times, *The Lord of the Rings* brings forward themes that are utterly modern.

There is something of a mix of the old and the new in the narrative itself of *The Lord of the Rings*. We can find some of these elements in the contrast between Aragorn and Frodo. Aragorn gathers in his essence much of the bigger-than-life hero; Frodo unites in himself all the contradictions of the utterly human. Aragorn is the hero of the

---

[14] Tolkien, *The Silmarillion*, xv.

quintessential ancient epic story. He has to fight against all odds and show the qualities and consistence of a legendary hero. The story makes it clear that he is a holdover of the past, of a time in which the king was a fighter and a healer. For any person of our time it is hard to identify with such a paragon of perfection and constancy.

Frodo is a hero in spite of himself. He is drawn into the story almost against his wishes. He continues the quest because there is nobody else who can take his task and relieve him. He is a Hobbit, or a smaller-than-life human being, with all the love of comfort and the tug-of-war feeling life that is the lot of modern human beings. Aragorn is first set on a quest for the defense of the land against Sauron, and then in search of the restoration of a kingdom. The romantic aspect of his quest is only thinly alluded to; his daring feat leads to the happy ending of his reunion with the beloved Arwen. Frodo is the hero of an anti-quest, as Verlyn Flieger often points out. He has to enter deeply into the belly of the dragon, not to retrieve or conquer, but to rid humanity of the Ring that chains it to Sauron, to the one who is its deepest adversary. He has to wrestle through mud, heat, and despair, experience thirst and hunger, and can only succeed out of sheer will and determination, but almost in spite of himself.

The villain of Tolkien's romance—Sauron—never shows anything else than his roving eye. The only other visible dragon (the villain of medieval romances) is Gollum, and in many ways he is Frodo's shadow or double, here too an element that was not known to or incorporated in medieval romances.

The epic ending is not the happy ending of the fairy tales of old. Frodo's riddance of the Ring is all but straight and unequivocal. But it is in keeping with our modern consciousness. His epilogue, however, is the outcome of a life well lived and a worthy goal pursued with courage: "[Like Beowulf and Arthur] their stories end not happily but fittingly, and that is as it should be," concludes Flieger.[15]

Once more it is Flieger who points out that Tolkien is more effectively and naturally postmodern than many of his contemporaries. On the way to Mordor, on the steps to Cirith Ungol, Sam and Frodo realize that they are part of a story just like the heroes of old whom they

---

[15] Flieger, *Green Suns and Faërie*, 158.

admire and whose stories they have read or heard countless times. And they wonder whether they will end up as part of a story themselves. Sam wants to know whether future generations will read out of "a great big book with red and black letters, years and years afterwards. And people will say: 'Let's hear about Frodo and the Ring!'"[16] Here Tolkien is completely self-referential; he is talking about the story that the reader has in his own hands; and which in the collector's edition is written "with red and black letters." At the point in which Sam utters the words of course the story is still waiting to be written. It's as if Tolkien were playing with the notions of quantum physics. This goes a step further into musings about stories in general and the way each individual perceives his role in them. Sam wonders, "Why, even Gollum might be good in a tale . . . and he used to like tales himself once by his own account. I wonder if he thinks he's the hero or the villain?"[17] It is C. S. Lewis, one of Tolkien's closest friends, who rightly intuited the book's links with past traditions and its utter modernity when he reviewed the trilogy thus: "in the history of Romance itself—a history which stretches back to the *Odyssey* and beyond—it makes not a return but an advance or revolution: the conquest of a new territory."[18]

## TOLKIEN BETWEEN CHRISTIAN AND PAGAN

Another interesting debate has involved many minds in the academic world with the question "How did Tolkien's opus reflect his Catholic Christianity?" And therefore "Was Tolkien really a Catholic?" If so, how could have he written *The Lord of the Rings* and *The Silmarillion*? It is clear to anybody who has visited his work that Tolkien did not write any of his stories as a Christian allegory. He simply wrote it from genuine artistic inspiration. Only later did he pause to reflect on how it fit with his own theology. He deliberately wanted to avoid being a Christian apologist in the vein of C. S. Lewis or George MacDonald.

---

[16] Tolkien, *The Two Towers*, 321.

[17] Tolkien, *The Two Towers*, 322.

[18] Carpenter, *Tolkien: A Biography*, 219.

Ronald Hutton argues that Tolkien "was anxious to defend two very different positions at once" and by that he meant the Christian and the Pagan.[19] As an example he invokes the author's defense of the Elves' reincarnation in an unpublished letter, and Tolkien's position on magic producing real physical change.

Hutton sees in Tolkien's positions "Christianity with a particular twist . . . Neoplatonism." And he argues that this Neoplatonism incorporates both Christian and Pagan elements. Among the Pagan elements: a love of faery and deities, though he admits these do not intervene in the affairs of human beings.[20] Hutton argues that, after his youth (or sometime later in his work), Tolkien returned to a Christian Platonism. But, on the other hand, he continued to reelaborate his youthful material late in life. Thus Hutton concludes: "If it was Christian, then it was a Christianity so unorthodox, and diluted, as to merit the term heretical. It could be made orthodox only by discarding many of its most characteristic earlier elements." And further: "As [the non-Christian elements in his mythology] represented about two thirds of the ingredients that made up his imagined universe, they are not incidental, or mischievous, part of it. They are part of the essence of the work, and therefore of the man, and that is how I justify my choice of title ['The Pagan Tolkien']."[21] In another article Hutton, replying to N. I. Agøy, adds: "I still think that we can have a 'pagan' Tolkien. I also think that we can have a Christian one."[22] This amended view sums up best Tolkien's being, in my opinion.

Tolkien's own words bring this truth to bear in a very refreshing way. Discussing *The Lord of the Rings*'s "theology" in a letter of 1958, he wrote, "Theologically (if the term is not too grandiose) I imagine the picture to be less dissonant from what some (including myself) believe to be the truth."[23] With these words Tolkien implies he is surprised at the concordance between his mythology and orthodox Christianity. This means that he never set out to be in accord with doctrine in the

[19] Hutton, "The Pagan Tolkien," 69.
[20] Hutton, "The Pagan Tolkien," 62–63.
[21] Hutton, "The Pagan Tolkien," 69.
[22] Hutton, "Can We Still Have a Pagan Tolkien?" 103.
[23] Carpenter, *Letters of J. R. R. Tolkien*, 283.

first place. And further in the same direction, to Father Robert Murray, who pointed out to Galadriel as a Mary figure, he replied:

> I have been cheered specially by what you have said . . . because you are more perceptive, especially in some directions, than anyone else, and have even revealed to me more clearly some things about my work. I think I know exactly what you mean by the order of Grace; and of course by your references to Our Lady, upon which all my own small perception of beauty both in majesty and simplicity is founded.[24]

Yet, others could argue with success that Tolkien's Christianity shines through the pages of his trilogy. Tolkien offers another inkling into the evolution of his cosmology in the same letter above to Robert Murray: "*The Lord of the Rings* is of course a fundamentally religious and Catholic work; unconsciously so at first, but consciously in the revision." He further explains that he had removed all references to institutional theology in *The Lord of the Rings* so that his work would remain theologically orthodox, so that the "religious element is absorbed into the story and the symbolism." This may be the reason why many perceive the presence of the Christ in the opus. Stephen R. Lawhead says, "What an extraordinary thing I thought: though Tolkien makes never so much as a glancing reference to Jesus Christ in a single paragraph of all *The Lord of the Rings*' thick volumes, His face is glimpsed on virtually every page."[25]

Magic, gods, traces of reincarnation, references to the initiations of old times—in Gandalf and Saruman—all border on heresy if Christianity is to be defined through the lens of Catholicism, or of any other Christian denomination for that matter. And yet Tolkien's trilogy has achieved the feat of navigating this seemingly huge contradiction. As a story of Pagan times it is entirely Christian in a deeper sense; or rather, it does not set Pagan against Christian worldviews but rather sees the two from a higher vintage point that embraces and includes.

---

[24] Carpenter, *Letters of J. R. R. Tolkien*, 172.
[25] Quoted in Pearce, *Tolkien, Man and Myth*, 82.

Moreover, it is a story of a fictional past, rooted in Tolkien's deep taste for mythology and times gone, and yet timeless and modern. From this perspective it can speak to all who have at least some spiritual yearning in their soul, no matter how weak or undefined.

I have come more and more to realize that there are unplumbed depths in Tolkien's opus. It is the intention of this book to dig deeper in this direction. With this in mind we will first look at the deeper aspects of Tolkien's biography and being, then immerse ourselves in the images of *The Lord of the Rings*.

CHAPTER 2

# BLENDING SCIENCE AND ART: LANGUAGE AND LITERATURE

It occurs to me that in all externals [Tolkien] resembles the
archetypal Oxford don, at times even the stage *caricature* of a don.
But that is exactly what he is not. It is rather as if some strange
spirit had taken on the guise of an elderly professor. The body
may be pacing this shabby suburban little room, but the mind is
far away, roaming the plains and mountains of Middle-earth.
—Humphrey Carpenter

While looking at Tolkien's biography we have no illusion that we will
find an explanation of the opus in the life of the author. This is not
the way Tolkien would have seen his opus, for he knew that often the
author of a work that speaks for the time conveys something that goes
beyond his own personality. The personality, plagued by its flaws and
shortcomings, cannot serve as the sole substratum upon which posterity
can understand the legacy. Humphrey Carpenter, his biographer, points
out that even in relation to Tolkien's very first legends, his work "passes
beyond this [fusion of Icelandic and Finnish traditions] to achieve a
degree of dramatic complexity and subtlety of characterization not
often found in ancient legends."[26] The seeds of something exceptional
were already present in the early days. This chapter and the next will

---

[26] Carpenter, *Tolkien: A Biography*, 96.

highlight what was out of the ordinary in Tolkien's personality, even when it was covered up by his shortcomings.

No matter how limited the personality of an author is in relation to his or her literary legacy—especially great literature—nevertheless such works will illuminate something about their creator. This chapter will point out that we have not finished unearthing all of Tolkien's personality, which can only be done through Tolkien's words themselves. It will be our attempt to show that there is more than has been surmised heretofore about Tolkien's personality.

Tolkien was critical of psychologizing authors and artistic creations, saying "Only one's guardian Angel, or indeed God Himself, could unravel the real relationship between personal facts and an author's works." And further, "I should not suppose that artistic work proceeded from the weaknesses that produced them, but from other and still uncorrupted regions of my being."[27] It is from this perspective that we will look at the phenomena in his life. Let them reveal to us here and there some of the symptoms that point to the uncorrupted regions of Tolkien's being.

As to what were the major influences in his life, Tolkien offered us three categories of facts:

1. Really significant facts: his birth in 1892, living his early years in "the Shire" in a premechanical age (the four years spent in the cottage in Sarehole); his being a Catholic Christian; his relationship with his mother (he felt he owed his faith to her)
2. Significant facts: his academic vocation as a philologist at Oxford University; his taste in languages
3. Insignificant facts[28]

In what comes next we will try to build an imagination of Tolkien, working as closely as possible to how the author would have produced the imaginations in his work. We are aiming at letting Tolkien the man live in our imagination. To do this we will look at his life's turning points, his character and personality, and lastly and most importantly

---

[27] Carpenter, *Letters of J. R. R. Tolkien*, 288.
[28] Carpenter, *Letters of J. R. R. Tolkien*, 288.

his unusual faculties. In the next chapter we will deepen the picture looking at the many-faceted aspects of Tolkien's inner life.

## BIOGRAPHICAL TURNING POINTS

When we look at the intensity of Tolkien's life, some particularly difficult trials stand out as the challenges that created the conditions for the unfolding of his personality.

Tolkien was born in Bloemfontein, South Africa, on January 3, 1892, and was christened John Ronald Reuel. At that time it was a rather small town with some hundred buildings. The predominant Afrikaner didn't mix much with the local English population. Having returned to England at age three, Tolkien had very few recollections of his birthplace: a few words in Afrikaans, memories of the barren landscape, some dramatic but minor events.

His father, who was still in South Africa, soon entered a phase of poor health due to rheumatic fever and died in early 1896. His investments bequeathed a meager inheritance to the family. Left to her own resources Tolkien's mother looked for a house a mile south of Birmingham, in the hamlet of Sarehole. One anecdote struck the boy's mind growing up: a willow tree he used to climb was cut down for no apparent reason, and without being put to use. The adult Tolkien never forgot it.

Since she had teaching skills, Mabel Tolkien started educating both Ronald, as Tolkien was called by his family, and his brother Hilary in Latin, French, and German. She soon recognized her son's ability with languages. Among the early literary influences for which Tolkien gained respect, were *Alice in Wonderland*, the Curdie books by George MacDonald, and the fairy books of Andrew Lang—in the latter particularly the tale of Sigurd, the slayer of the dragon Fafnir. Reminiscing about these early tales Tolkien stated, "I desired dragons with a profound desire. . . . the world that contained even the imagination of Fafnir was richer and more beautiful, at whatever cost of peril."[29] In contrast Tolkien disregarded popular children's literature

---

[29] Carpenter, *Tolkien: A Biography*, 22–23.

such as *Treasure Island, The Pied Piper,* or the tales of Hans Christian Andersen.

At her husband's death Christianity had started to play an important role for Mabel. She started to bring her children to a Catholic church in the slums of Birmingham, and subsequently converted with her sister in the spring of 1900. Both met with the outrage of their Anglican family. Mabel remained faithful to her faith in spite of the added financial strains that the choice caused, due to the distancing of her father, who withdrew financial help. Ronald himself converted at age eight, in what became a lifelong commitment.

After four years in the cottage in Sarehole, which the youth called "the longest seeming and the most formative part in my life,"[30] Mabel rented a house in Moseley, closer to the city's center. They stayed there only briefly because the house was due for demolition, until they moved close to the Catholic church of St. Dunstan. Ronald was very unhappy about leaving "the Shire" behind.

In 1902 the family moved again to Edgbaston, close to the Birmingham Oratory where Father Xavier Morgan, a valued friend of Mabel who was going to play an important part in Tolkien's life, served as a priest. Soon Mabel had to enter a hospital, where she was diagnosed with diabetes. Her condition quickly deteriorated, and she died after a coma in November 1903. Mabel had appointed Father Xavier to be the guardian of her two sons. She had left him very little, but Father Francis contributed to the children from his own pocket and arranged for the sons to go live with their aunt Beatrice, not far from the Oratory.

The Oratory became Ronald's real home. Here he had to conform with strict religious observance, including daily attendance at Mass and Communion. His religious sense was very much formed in these years, strengthened by Tolkien's conviction that his mother had been a martyr for the faith. At this point in his life, Tolkien had a cheerful disposition with a zest for life, sense of humor, and friendliness, yet accompanied by bouts of profound despair from which he felt he could see no way out.

In 1903 Ronald entered the prestigious King Edward's School thanks to a grant. The library at King Edward's was administered by senior boys. Here Tolkien first met Christopher Wiseman and Rob

---

[30] Carpenter, *Tolkien: A Biography*, 32.

Gilson, with whom he formed the TCBS (Tea Club Borrovian Society), which was later joined by Geoffrey Bache Smith, the youngest of the four. What the youths had in common was a thorough knowledge of Latin and Greek literature. To the group Tolkien also introduced *Beowulf, The Pearl*, and *Sir Gawain and the Green Knight*, Anglo-Saxon and medieval works that he explored deeply later in life.

The most important meeting of the TCBS for Tolkien took place during the Christmas vacation of 1914 on a weekend spent talking together. They were starting to formulate plans for some common work and felt they were "destined to kindle a new light." The meeting led Tolkien to decide that he was a poet. He later claimed "I have always laid that [to write poetry] to the credit of the inspiration that even a few hours with the four brought to us."[31] He wrote one of the first of his poems, interestingly written in a "nonsense fairy language"—of which more will be said later—in November 1915.

Tolkien wanted to finish his studies before volunteering in the British forces in World War I. He obtained his degree magna cum laude in English language and literature in 1915 and was commissioned soon after as a second lieutenant in the Lancaster Fusiliers, together with Bache Smith. The first seeds of what would become *The Silmarillion* entered his mind just before and during his engagement in World War I. As a signals officer he became a Morse operator and learned to operate visual signals and a field telephone. It seems he was extending his passion for language to every possible form of it that he could encounter.

Destiny brought Tolkien to one of the nightmares of modern warfare: the Battle of the Somme fought in the trenches. On the first day of the battle the British troops suffered 19,000 casualties and 60,000 wounded, the greatest war loss in a single day. Among the casualties was Rob Gilson. Tolkien was crushed by the news. The same fate engulfed Bache Smith soon after.

The allied armies had miscalculated what they thought would be a relatively easy effort to dislodge the Germans. Tolkien's battalion had been held in reserve at Bouzincourt on the first day, and was not mobilized until a week later, when the battlefield had turned into a slaughterhouse. And there he remained for months afterwards, either

---

[31] Carpenter, *Tolkien: A Biography*, 73.

in the front lines or in rest areas. The British and Germans suffered some 600,000 total casualties. Daniel Grotta aptly summarizes this war episode: "An entire generation of the best and brightest was shattered for a few yards of mud."[32] Most of Tolkien's school and university friends had been killed or wounded, and not necessarily from enemy fire; many froze to death while others died of influenza or trench fever. Trench fever is a form of rickettsia, whose symptoms are closely related to typhus and flu. It is rarely fatal, but can last for months and reappear long after the first onset and healing. Tolkien suffered a particularly strong attack of the illness, lasting some eighteen months.

Tolkien could not have written while in the trenches; but he started as soon as he was hospitalized, writing the first significant drafts of *The Silmarillion* between 1915 and 1918.[33] What Tolkien called the First Age of his mythology had been completed, and he had begun to develop the Second Age of Middle Earth and the rise of the central figure of Sauron.

Tolkien was finally released from active duty in October 1918. By some dispensation of destiny Tolkien was exposed to the knowledge of man's most ferocious brutality (he called it "animal horror"), but then also spared from it by a providential illness, which likely played a part in releasing and bringing to the surface of consciousness what lived in his unconscious, and formed the first seeds of *The Silmarillion*. In a 1938 Andrew Lang lecture Tolkien estimated that "a real taste for fairy stories was wakened by philology on the threshold of manhood, and quickened to full life by war."[34]

Tolkien's strong friendships played an important role in encouraging Tolkien the writer. When he wrote to Bache Smith to say that the TCBS was dead (after the death of Gilson), the latter replied: "The T.C.B.S. is not finished and never will be."[35] Before dying he wrote again to Tolkien that

> there will still be a member of T.C.B.S to voice what
> I dreamed and what we all agreed upon. . . . Death

---

[32] Grotta, *Biography of J. R. R. Tolkien*, 57.

[33] Carpenter, *Tolkien: A Biography*, 231.

[34] Tolkien, "On Fairy-Stories," in *Monsters and the Critics*, 135.

[35] Carpenter, *Tolkien: A Biography*, 84.

can make us loathsome and helpless individuals, but it cannot put an end to the immortal four! *A discovery I am going to communicate to Rob before I go off tonight. . . .* Yes, publish. You, I am sure, are chosen, like Saul among the children of Israel. . . . May God bless you, my dear John Ronald, and *may you say the things I have tried to say* long after I am not there to say them, if such be my lot.[36] (emphasis added)

Note that the above is not conveyed as a vague feeling by Smith but as a truthful insight, a "discovery." One can surmise he had a foreboding of his coming death and a resulting sense of urgency in communicating his insight.

Humphrey Carpenter concludes that Smith's words were a call for Ronald to begin his great work. And Wiseman likewise intuited that this was the desire of Tolkien, writing to him, "You ought to start the epic."[37] In 1918 Tolkien, encouraged by Wiseman, published a collection of Geoffrey Bache Smith's poems *A Spring Harvest*. Smith had encouraged Tolkien to turn towards a wider spectrum of poetic expression in the English language, recommending the likes of Browne, Sidney and Bacon. It is remarkable to note that one of the poems of Smith talks of the longing for the West, and of an island in the western sea, both themes that were to become central to Tolkien's opus. In fact the poem is reminiscent of Tolkien's own *The Sea-Bell*:

> *Now the old winds are wild about the house,*
> *And the old ghosts cry to me from the air*
> *Of a far isle set in the western sea,*
> *And of the evening sunlight lingering there.*
> *Ah! I am bound here, bound and fettered,*
> *The dark house crumbles, and the woods decay,*
> *I was too fain in life, that bound me here;*
> *Away, old long-loved ghosts, away, away!*[38]

---

[36] Carpenter, *Tolkien: A Biography*, 86.
[37] Carpenter, *Tolkien: A Biography*, 89–90.
[38] Flieger, *Interrupted Music*, 223.

Could this be one of the themes that Bache Smith tried to develop, of which he said *may you say the things I have tried to say*?

Before reaching age thirty Tolkien had faced the death of both his parents and of two of his closest friends, and known poverty first-hand. He had turned with some yearning to religion and experienced the deepest horror of which the human soul is capable in the European trench warfare. He had awakened his love of language, mythology, and writing, and had already started to write parts of the opus that he would not publish during his lifetime. There was a clarity of purpose in the young man that manifested in manifold variations and themes. We will turn to these now.

## CHARACTER AND PERSONALITY: THE "EPIC MOOD"

There were two predominant moods in Tolkien: by nature, Carpenter tells us, he was a "cheerful almost irrepressible person with a great zest for life."[39] His easy sense of humor and social disposition allowed him to make friends easily. On the other hand was a melancholy that could plunge him into great depths of despair.

In his college days Tolkien immersed himself in every opportunity that the world offered him, regardless of the fact that socially speaking he was the underdog. He was thirsting for experience and life. He achieved success in rugby, making up for what he lacked in body weight with aggressiveness. In fact rugby caused him injuries, breaking and slightly deforming his nose, and cutting his tongue. He made it onto the school team, curiously ascribing his success to "the impulse of chivalry": "Having the romantic upbringing, I made a boy-and-girl affair serious, and made it the source of effort."[40]

In his college days he also joined the Essay Club and the Dialectical Society and started his own club, the Apolausticks (those devoted to self-indulgence). He enjoyed places where there was "good talk, plenty of

---

[39] Carpenter, *Tolkien: A Biography*, 31.
[40] Carpenter, *Tolkien: A Biography*, 48.

tobacco . . . and male company."[41] His sociable disposition brought him anywhere something lively was happening; predictably, he neglected his school work. For a time he became lazy, played tennis, ordered tailor-made suits, and turned stylish.

The worldly side of Tolkien's character was balanced by bouts of deep despair in which he felt engulfed by the weight of the world, so to speak. He would see no way out for a time. However, he always maintained the ability of looking at himself and the world around with detachment and humor. The extremes of his moods subsisted in old age, even though he kept up his gregarious and social side. His late diaries show us great depths of gloom, even if only temporary. On the other hand, Tolkien could not be cynical; he could neither be half-hearted nor deny commitment to what mattered most to him. He tended to take matters to heart. One could detect in these dramatic heights and depths the "epic mood" that is most strongly reflected in Tolkien's writings.

Something else was present that could cause a surprise in one so at home with the word, written or spoken, what Carpenter calls his "swift speech" and that Tolkien himself called "congenital and incurable."[42] It underlined and pointed to another important facet of his personality. Tolkien knew that he was the butt of jokes among his Oxford colleagues. About this Carpenter comments, "True often: due in part to having too much to say in too little time, in larger part to diffidence, which such comments [of his colleagues] increased."[43] He adds, "Words come out in eager rushes. Whole phrases are elided or compressed in the haste of emphasis."[44] When meeting someone interested in his work, Tolkien would talk and move in a restless fashion, lighting a pipe then leaving it aside and hardly smoking from it. Once the listener got past Tolkien's mannerisms, one could understand him at least at the literal level; but one could easily be left behind by the rapidity of his intellectual arguments or the nature of his allusive speaking. For all of these shortcomings Tolkien was able to recite poetry with greatest clarity.

---

41  Carpenter, *Tolkien: A Biography*, 53.
42  Carpenter, *Letters of J. R. R. Tolkien*, 372.
43  Carpenter, *Letters of J. R. R. Tolkien*, 396.
44  Carpenter, *Tolkien: A Biography*, 5.

Something else could be fathomed by a keen ear in Tolkien's voice. Carpenter describes his voice as strange, deep, but without resonance and "with some quality in it that I cannot define, as if he had come from another age or civilization."[45] This elusive quality seems to reflect Tolkien's feeling that not only himself but the other Inklings were born out of time.

It is somehow curious that Tolkien's speech was not very clear since Tolkien's life revolved around the word, written or spoken, in every possible aspect ever since his earliest days. And Tolkien's love for language in all its forms was awakened in him from early childhood.

At age seven after he started writing his own dragon story, his mother pointed to one linguistic matter: that you can only say "a great green dragon" instead of what he wrote, "a green great dragon." Characteristically for what will follow in his biography, he stopped writing and turned to the study of language. This would be the first recorded time in which the question of "language or literature" took center stage in Tolkien's biography. It would become a leitmotif, a central theme around which his life revolved.

Tolkien was later exposed to many literary influences, to which he responded in truly unique ways. About English literature he said: "[I] never found much there in which to rest my heart (or heart and head together). I was brought up in the Classics, and first discovered the sensation of literary pleasure in Homer."[46] Part of his enjoyment he found in "any aesthetic pleasure that I am capable of from the *form* of words (and especially from the *fresh* association of word-form with word-sense)."[47] And this is something he found most in a foreign language—which he first met in Latin and French—or one that sounded foreign because remote in time, such as Anglo-Saxon.

Tolkien was as much interested in the sounds of the words as in their meaning. In contrast music held little interest for the child. In fact words seemed for Tolkien to replace music. He relished listening to words, repeating them, whether he knew their exact meaning or not. And

---

[45] Carpenter, *Tolkien: A Biography*, 5.
[46] Carpenter, *Letters of J. R. R. Tolkien*, 172.
[47] Carpenter, *Letters of J. R. R. Tolkien*, 172.

already in his school days when part of the Debating Society he was able to offer a full address in Greek or in fluent Gothic or Anglo-Saxon.

Ronald could already read by age four. He learned to write from his mother, whose handwriting was apparently rather unconventional. Tolkien learned calligraphy at the same time that he learned drawing, taking inspiration mostly from a book published in 1906 that based itself on 10th- and 11th-century models. And he found himself supremely interested in this craft, a natural parallel to his language interests. C. S. Lewis noticed, in what may have been a slight exaggeration, that "he had a different style of handwriting for each of his friends."[48]

Alphabets were only a natural outgrowth of this series of interests. Later in life he invented alphabets along with his languages, including the *certar* or *cirth* for his runic characters. This script was supposedly developed by the Sindarin elves of his books. It is used in Thror's map and in the inscription above the Doors of Durin in *The Lord of the Rings*. He also developed a beautiful script that he called *tengwar* for his elves. At the time of writing down his first of *The Lost Tales* he invented "the Alphabet of Rúmil" and even composed his diary entries in this alphabet.

Tolkien recognized his love for language thus:

> It was an inevitable, though conditionable, evolvement of the birth-given. It has always been with me: the sensibility to linguistic pattern which affects me emotionally like colour or music; and the passionate love of growing things; and the deep response to legends (for lack of better word) that have what I would call the North-western temper and temperature.[49]

His love for the word was to develop both in the direction of the scientific aspect in philology, and in the artistic aspect of what he called "trivial literature," according to the judgment of academia. Verlyn Flieger, who has studied Tolkien's work thoroughly, concludes, "Language came first, and his development of it forced him to realize

---

[48] Carpenter, *Tolkien: A Biography*, 57.
[49] Carpenter, *Letters of J. R. R. Tolkien*, 212.

that there can be no language without a people who speak it, no people without a culture which expresses them, no culture without a myth which informs and shapes it."[50]

Already in his youth Tolkien spent considerable time in evolving two fictitious languages, later codified as Quenya and Sindarin. Thus for Tolkien, as we will see later, the study and invention of languages became a foundation. The "stories" were made to provide a world for the language rather than the reverse. And this is a paradoxical aspect of his personality that will need further elucidation. How in effect could Tolkien say "To me a name comes first and the story follows [in a footnote he explains that this is exactly what happened with his "Hobbit inspiration."] I should have preferred to write in Elvish"?[51]

After working out the rudiments of Quenya, a language based on Finnish, Tolkien began working on his vast legendarium, of which the Trilogy forms the conclusion, in a first attempt to "reorganize some of the Kalevala, especially the tale of Kullervo the hapless, into a form of my own."[52] Tolkien traces his first attempts back with this language to the years 1912–13.

## SOME SPECIAL INTERESTS

Tolkien's interest in the literary world directed him towards language rather than literature, as Oxford categorized the two fields of inquiry. Everything up to Chaucer was studied primarily with a scientific eye to the evolution of language. The name *literature*, and by extension everything of an artistic nature, was given primarily to everything that followed. In a unique fashion Tolkien considered medieval literature from an artistic perspective as well as a scientific one. The scientific perspective interested him under the lens of the evolution of consciousness, under which the word only made sense when it could be perceived in the living context of a culture vastly different from the present. He could immerse himself so deeply into the imagery of the

[50] Flieger, *Splintered Light*, 60.
[51] Carpenter, *Letters of J. R. R. Tolkien*, 219.
[52] Carpenter, *Letters of J. R. R. Tolkien*, 214.

ancient legends and myths, as few probably could in his time. He did not doubt their intended artistic quality.

Together with his medievalist frame of mind, Tolkien also had a very unique perspective on history, one that had evolved from the elaboration of the ages of Middle-earth in *The Silmarillion*. Through one of his characters in the unfinished *The Notion Club Papers* Tolkien tells us that the mythic Atlantis (his Númenor) was the dividing line between myth and history.[53] *The Lord of the Rings* then corresponds to the beginnings of the historical period, and in talking about it Tolkien explains to his biographer the necessity of his extensive correspondence with the readers and his extensive reelaboration of the material: Tolkien saw his book not as a work of fiction but as a chronicle of actual events, and himself "not as an author who has made a slight error that must now be corrected or explained away, but as a historian who must cast light on an obscurity in a historical document."[54]

Exhausting all the facets of the Tolkien being takes time. His love for the literary world and for history went hand in hand with a deep appreciation for the natural world, even a true participation within it, as we already saw from the importance that he gave to the four years spent in Sarehole, the fragile preserved environment at the edge of the encroaching city.

From early on Tolkien had developed skills in drawing, especially landscapes and trees. Carpenter adds, "And though he liked drawing trees he liked most of all to be *with* trees."[55] Over the years Tolkien underlined ever and again his love for nature and his loathing for technology and its encroachment on the natural world. In many ways in his letter he reminds us of his love for "the Shire" and his experience of the premechanical age in early childhood.

Not surprisingly Tolkien had been very interested in natural history since childhood; it was very important to him to draw accurately from nature, as many of his attempts show. This interest carried on in later life, although quite subdued by his other priorities, and it manifested in a gift for careful observation. Three examples will illustrate it.

---

[53] Flieger, *Interrupted Music*, 103.
[54] Carpenter, *Tolkien: A Biography*, 4.
[55] Carpenter, *Tolkien: A Biography*, 22.

Tolkien had turned with interest towards botany, particularly towards matters of taxonomy in the *Scrofulariaceae* family. He was interested in a plant whose affiliation with the family was not so obvious. He introduces his interest thus: "They [variations] rouse in me visions of kinship and descent through great ages, and also thoughts of the mystery of pattern/design as a thing other than its individual embodiment, and recognizable."[56] He was interested in a plant that is a "missing link" somewhere between figwort and foxglove, and in general to the links between the branches of the family, which are not commented upon in botany books. In a second instance in his letters he turned his interest to the changes that the cultivated daisy type (*Bellis perennis*) undergoes when it seeds a lawn and has to compete with the grass, or when the latter's seeds find a fertile spot and then develop "four times the size with a flower the size of a half-crown."[57] He also kept over the years very precise observations about trees such as oak and ash, which over the years he saw "wakening" one very close to the other. But then in 1971 he noticed that the oaks were among the first to "be leafed" while the ashes followed only a month later.[58]

Tolkien's views on nature or human sciences rest, as in all his other domains of inquiry, upon a gift for precise observation, and the capacity for accompanying this with his artistic touch in painting. Likewise, in the realm of psychology, he stands in contrast to the prevailing materialistic trends. In looking at the way the psychological tendency sees the work of an author, he criticizes it thus: "Not that this attitude of mind has my sympathy: as should be clearly perceived in Vol. I, p. 272: Gandalf: 'He that breaks a thing to find out what it is has left the path of wisdom.'"[59] This was said about psychology, but it applies just as well to natural sciences. In a later letter he calls the tendency "this destructive process," going a step further in the characterization of his more phenomena-based approach to art.[60] In the contrast Tolkien is referring to the science of Saruman as opposed to that of Gandalf. The

[56] Carpenter, *Letters of J. R. R. Tolkien*, 402.
[57] Carpenter, *Letters of J. R. R. Tolkien*, 403.
[58] Carpenter, *Letters of J. R. R. Tolkien*, 408.
[59] Carpenter, *Letters of J. R. R. Tolkien*, 414.
[60] Carpenter, *Letters of J. R. R. Tolkien*, 424.

science of Saruman is that which pursues purely immediate goals; the sum of "the ends justify the means." Gandalf's approach is that one of science marrying art that resembles magic, or that effortlessly produces magic.

An all-around interest—artistic and scientific—in the word was matched in Tolkien with the same attitude in natural sciences, though this one did not find as great an unfolding as did his philological studies or his literature. Tolkien does more than appreciate nature; he wants to participate in its being and life. Here too this is achieved through an unsuspected and little-reported scientific interest, matched by his other natural artistic capacities. We will turn to this aspect of his activity to highlight how Tolkien the writer was accompanied and supported by Tolkien the painter. All in all we have a man who lives as a matter of fact in the world of imagination. Imagination itself serves him to characterize the world; in his scientific/analytic work it supports and complements his precise, fact-based understanding of any subject matter.

## TOLKIEN THE PAINTER

From the days of his adolescence Tolkien had enjoyed drawing from nature. Even during his studies Tolkien did not give up this artistic interest; he soon started to draw more and more from what arose in his imagination and in fact inventing landscapes. The sea played a great part in his inspiration, and most of his illustrations were concerned with the imaginations arising in his writings.

Much of what Tolkien incorporated in his body of myths and legends came in strong visions or dreams. This is part of what enables the reader to enter his invented worlds and while in them feel part of a world that evokes a lasting sense of wonder. For Tolkien some of these visions had such a compelling presence and strength that writing was a means of laying them to rest. This is what he specifically told friends about his "Great Wave dream," which he jokingly called his "Atlantis complex" in a jibe to the psychologists. To W. H. Auden he wrote: "I mean the terrible recurrent dream (beginning with memory) of the

Great Wave, towering up, and coming in ineluctably over the trees and green fields. (I bequeathed it to Faramir.) I don't think I have had it since I wrote 'Downfall of Númenor' as the last of the legends of the First and Second Age."[61] Arguably many of Tolkien's abstract or most imaginative paintings served the same purpose.

Soon after extensively drawing from nature, and before entering the world of his own visions and dreams, Tolkien undertook a series of early drawings on abstract themes, including *Before*, *Afterwards*, and *Wickedness*. Particularly interesting is a painting entitled *Thought* (1912), which portrays the theme as a mythical being. Wayne G. Hammond and Christina Scull believe it could be someone like the Valar called Manwë in *The Silmarillion*.[62] In *The Lost Road* we are told that "Manwë, greatest of the Valar, sat now long in thought, and at length he spoke to the Valar, revealing to them the mind of the Father."[63] What is fascinating, according to Hammond and Scull, is that the painting antedates the earliest *Silmarillion* writings by two years. And the authors conclude, "Tolkien's art [illustrations] foreshadowed his texts."[64] It is my contention that the themes of these paintings were far from abstract experiences or artistic inventions. We will return to them.

Another two abstract paintings were titled *Undertenishness*, in which one can see both a forest and the outline of a symmetrical butterfly, and its companion *Grownupishness*. One cannot help feeling that Tolkien is exploring polarities. Another painting called *Other People* points to Tolkien's feelings that other people were preventing him from walking his path. A more optimistic painting, its seeming polarity, is that of a figure happily walking off a cliff towards a shining sun, stars, and moon under the horizon. These are part of what Hammond and Scull call some twenty "visionary pictures" that Tolkien painted between 1911 and 1913. He collected them in an envelope that was labeled "Earliest Ishnesses," probably referring to pictures drawn from the imagination, rather than from nature and life.

---

[61]  Carpenter, *Letters of J. R. R. Tolkien*, 213.

[62]  Hammond and Scull, *J. R. R. Tolkien*, 37.

[63]  Quoted in Hammond and Scull, J. R. R. Tolkien, 37.

[64]  Hammond and Scull, *J. R. R. Tolkien*, 37.

Of particular interest to our explorations are two other paintings: *The Land of Pohja* and *Water, Wind and Sand*, of 1915. *The Land of Pohja* gives a flavor of future directions since it is inspired by a *Kalevala* theme. And the *Kalevala* would soon draw Tolkien into Finnish studies, and the creation of the Quenya language and the mythology of *The Silmarillion*. From the time of this work, with few exceptions, nearly all of Tolkien's paintings refer to his own writings. They mirror the explosive unleashing of his imagination.

The painting *Water, Wind and Sand* of 1915 is an illustration for the poem "Sea Song of an Elder Day," which was reelaborated in three versions. It was at least partly inspired by Tolkien's visit to Cornwall's Lizard peninsula—the most south-westerly point of the British mainland—which left a deep impression on his soul. The second version, "Sea Chant of an Elder Day," dates to March 1915. The third version, "The Horns of Ylmir [Ulmo]," became the song Tuor sings to his son Eärendil in their exile following the fall of Gondolin, another of *The Silmarillion* themes. The illustration, Hammond and Scull deduct, must have been executed for one of the first two versions of the poem.[65] Of great interest is a little figure enclosed in a white sphere at the foot of the painting, pointing to someone being transported into the scene out of his body. It could point in fact to Tolkien himself experiencing the scene in a vision. The authors conclude, "Tolkien's creativity sometimes worked in advance of his consciousness, and the painter occasionally preceded the poet." It is as if Tolkien both saw and heard simultaneously the elements of his mythology.

Another painting of the epoch is the one called *Tanaqui*, which does not correspond to the form of the mountain that Tolkien calls Taniquetil. It seems that *Tanaqui* is more closely associated with the poem "Kôr," written also in 1915. The name *Kôr* refers to both the Elven city and the hill upon which it was built. In later times Tolkien called it Tirion upon Túna.

Tolkien's imagination lived in the word and in the inner wealth of images that surfaced in his consciousness through dreams and visions. But it went beyond, to permeate all of his worldview.

---

[65] Hammond and Scull, *J. R. R. Tolkien*, 46.

# TOLKIEN AND THE IMAGINATION

Tolkien felt very at home in the world of ancient legends and myths. Because they still spoke with clarity to his consciousness, he was alarmed that most people would not take heed of the importance of fairy tales and myths. To Tolkien they spoke of eternal truths.

Over the years the characters of Tolkien's stories, many of which literally irrupted in the content of his legendarium, took a life and a reality of their own in his psyche and life. As an example of many, to Rayner Unwin (son of his publisher) he wrote: "I feel, if I may say so, that our relations are like that of Rohan and Gondor [two kingdoms from *The Lord of the Rings*], and (as you know) for my part the oath of Eorl will never be broken, and I shall continue to rely in and be grateful for the wisdom and courtesy of Minas Tirith."[66]

Above, as in so many other instances, Tolkien makes his point with an image. Following the image, one can sense the lawfulness of his thinking. Such is his parallel of the Catholic Church with the growth of a plant:

> "My church" was not intended by Our Lord to be static or remain in perpetual childhood; but *to be a living organism (likened to a plant)*, which develops and changes in externals by the interaction of its bequeathed divine life and history—the particular circumstances of the world into which it is set. *There is no resemblance between the "mustard-seed" and the full-grown tree.* For those living in the days of its branching growth the Tree is the thing, for the history of a living thing is part of its life, and the history of a divine thing is sacred. The wise may know that *it began with a seed, but it is vain to try and dig it up, for it no longer exists, and the virtue and powers that it had now reside in the Tree.* Very good: but in husbandry the authorities, the keepers of the Tree, must look after it, according to such wisdom as they possess, prune it, remove cankers, rid it of parasites, and so forth.[67]

---

[66] Carpenter, *Letters of J. R. R. Tolkien*, 379.
[67] Carpenter, *Letters of J. R. R. Tolkien*, 394.

He ends his imaginative appraisal by pointing out that those who want to go back 'to the seed' (early Christianity) will do damage because nature cannot go back, and because they do so naively believing that that stage was free from evils. The images allow Tolkien to livingly enter the realm of polarities, the yins and yangs of existence that cannot be too strictly defined; only livingly apprehended.

Let us continue with a very telling example of Tolkien's recourse to imagination as a way to perceive reality around him. Tolkien had been interested in many schools of painting and experimented with them in his youth. In coming across Surrealism he qualified it as "a state similar in quality and consciousness of morbidity to a high fever, when the mind develops a distressing fecundity and facility in figure-making, seeing forms sinister or grotesque in all visible objects about it."[68] Here too it is interesting that his assessment is given with an image.

Two of Tolkien's essays are devoted to light and darkness: "Beowulf," written in 1937 and "On Fairy-Stories" of 1939. In "Beowulf" Tolkien characterizes the attitude of modern researchers, when it comes to understanding myth or fairy tales, with a little parable. He compares English words to stones and the heritage of myth and legend to an old hall. He further compares the living language of a poet to a house that borrowed some of the stones of the old hall.[69] The poet builds a tower with some of the stones of the old hall as well, from which he can see far off over the sea. The scholarly attitude of the time corresponds to that of pushing the tower over in order to see if they can find something under it, such as old inscriptions, while all along believing that only an odd fellow would have built such a tower in the first place. These scholars will not entrust themselves to the structure and vision of the poem and thus miss the opportunity to be carried beyond themselves, which is exactly what Tolkien attempts: to engage his imagination and let it be moved in order to participate in the consciousness from which the *Beowulf* poem sprang.

In the case of *Beowulf* Tolkien wants the reader to understand that it is death by the forces of darkness that gives the poem its meaning. It is for this reason that monsters, not other human adversaries, intervene.

---

[68] Hammond and Scull, *J. R. R. Tolkien*, 11.

[69] Tolkien, *Monsters and the Critics*, 7–8.

And Tolkien perceives that the enemies that the fairy stories portray live both outside of and within the human being.

In view of all the above it is not too surprising that Tolkien had a certain ability for acting. In his youth he took the part of Hermes in Aristophanes' *The Peace*, and later the central role of Mrs. Malaprop in Sheridan's *The Rivals*. His performances were praised. Before the war he had impersonated Chaucer in the "Summer Diversions" that took place in Oxford. One year he recited by heart the *Nun's Priest's Tale*, the next one *The Reeve's Tale*. Tolkien also took advantage of these acting skills when teaching. They would allow him to bring his subject to life, as when he would impersonate an Anglo-Saxon bard, leading the writer J. I. M. Stewart to comment, "He could turn a lecture room into a mead hall in which he was the bard and we were feasting, listening guests."[70]

In closing this preliminary exploration of Tolkien's inner world, we would be amiss not to look at Tolkien's uniquely individual relationship to Christianity. After all, he indicated that this was one of the very important influences in his life. This too rested on strong imaginative foundations.

## TOLKIEN AND CHRISTIANITY

Various authors have linked Tolkien's Christianity too strongly to the death of his mother, whom he considered a martyr to the faith. To see it from this perspective alone would be limiting. Tolkien clearly indicates in which way this faith was peculiarly his own. We can detect at least two elements in it: a clearly devotional aspect linked to the practice of Communion, and a unique imaginative understanding of the life of Christ as a myth, though a historically enacted myth. Let us look at both.

Mabel Tolkien appointed Father Xavier to be the guardian of her two sons. She arranged for them to live with their aunt Beatrice, not far from the Oratory. The Oratory became young Ronald's real home, where his religious views were formed in these years. He was very attached to offering his confession before Communion. In instances when he felt

---

[70] Carpenter, *Tolkien: A Biography*, 133.

unable to go to confession he would deprive himself of Communion as well. At those times, Carpenter indicates, he would experience "a pathetic state of spiritual depression."[71] In reverse, Communion could often bring him to a state of great spiritual joy. This may be why Tolkien called Communion "the only cure for sagging or fainting faith."[72]

Tolkien related to the Old and New Testaments as he did to myths. To C. S. Lewis expressing early on that myths are lies, Tolkien energetically countered that they weren't. He conveyed that they "reflect a splintered fragment of the true light, the eternal truth that is in God."[73] And in Tolkien's estimation the story of Christ is both a true myth and a historical event. Tolkien felt that what had only been announced in the images of the resurrection of the gods in old myths became historical in the Crucifixion and Resurrection of Christ. While a historical event, the deed of Golgotha also retained the quality of myth:

> The Gospels contain a fairy-story, or a story of a larger kind which embraces all the essence of fairy-stories. They contain many marvels—peculiarly artistic, beautiful, and moving: "mythical" in their perfect, self-contained significance. . . . But this story has entered History and the primary world; the desire and aspiration of sub-creation has been raised to the fulfillment of Creation. The Birth of Christ is the eucatastrophe [contrary of catastrophe] of Man's history. The Resurrection is the eucatastrophe of the story of the Incarnation. This story begins and ends in joy. It has pre-eminently the "inner consistency of reality."[74]

To relate to much of Tolkien's meta-historical understanding of the world, we must place the human being amid the condition of Eden, the

---

[71] Carpenter, *Tolkien: A Biography*, 128.

[72] Carpenter, *Letters of J. R. R. Tolkien*, 337–39.

[73] Walter Hooper, interview with Joseph Pearce, Oxford, August 20, 1966, quoted in Pearce, *Tolkien, Man and Myth*, 58.

[74] Tolkien, "On Fairy-Stories," *Monsters and the Critics*, 155–56.

Christian Fall, and the event of Christ's Crucifixion and Resurrection. Talking about Eden, Tolkien tells us:

> I do not now feel either ashamed or dubious on the Eden "myth." . . . certainly there was an Eden on this very unhappy earth. We all long for it, and we are constantly glimpsing it: our whole nature at its best and least corrupted, its gentlest and most humane, is still soaked with this sense of "exile."[75]

This tension between Fall and Resurrection informs much of Tolkien's worldview and imagination, even though he never allowed his faith to enter the world of his creation.

In Tolkien's view humankind has been alienated from its divine origin through the biblical Fall. To this Fall Tolkien attributes the strange fate and guilt that weighs on the human condition. The need to escape—that Tolkien effected in his myths and stories—offers the possibility to return; to overcome human separation and experience re-union, communion. And the final "great escape," the greatest consolation offered by the happy ending, is the escape from death, an experience of Christ's Resurrection. For Tolkien the Christian story offers the final consolation; it promises re-union and absolves from guilt. Everything that Tolkien called *sub-creation*—under which he included all literary creation—echoes the primary experience of the resurrection.

Tolkien's life trials allowed him to know the most tragic dichotomies and open wounds of the modern soul—such as abandonment, hunger, and death—and the trials of the 20th century at large—social inequality, the ravages of industrialization, and the most devastating destruction that war could bring.

From very early on he had a strong relationship with, and love for language, which evolved in as many directions as possible: from the creation of new languages to the yearning for an English mythology, to the pursuit of the understanding of how language has evolved and consciousness changed with it. Thus, he brought together science and art, even though at heart he was first and foremost an artist.

---

[75] Carpenter, *Letters of J. R. R. Tolkien*, 109–10.

Indeed, Tolkien was an artist through and through. He had a gift for keen observation of natural phenomena, which naturally verged into the artistic. This led him to drawing and painting, over which he had some degree of mastery and which supported him in his literary pursuits.

What appears in the "external" Tolkien is mirrored in the "inner" Tolkien, as it were. Tolkien had an uncanny ability, or rather preference, for expressing himself in fully artistic and imaginative terms. Whether he referred to matters of religion or modern events, he saw in them a reality that could not be encompassed with the simple, often strong opinions of which his contemporaries in times of deep polarization, such as the world wars, seemed most fond. Rather, he felt that the nuances of a complex reality could only best be captured with an encompassing, often provoking image.

We have attempted to circumambulate Tolkien's being from 360 degrees, as it were, and offered different and complementary perspectives. We will now attempt to bring these together, to show how the whole is more than the sum of the parts.

# CHAPTER 3

# A DEEPER LOOK AT TOLKIEN

Before him stood the Tree, his Tree finished. If you could say
that of a Tree that was alive, its leaves opening, its branches
growing and bending in the wind that Niggle had so often felt
and guessed, and had so often failed to catch. He gazed at the
Tree, and slowly he lifted his arms and opened them wide.
"It's a gift!" he said.
—J. R. R. Tolkien, *Leaf by Niggle*

We have just finished looking at the historical, external side of Tolkien's
personality. This chapter will attempt to explore Tolkien's rich inner
life. What special qualities were present in such a large soul? How did
Tolkien see the world, and what were the formative experiences that
reflected and laid the foundation for being able to write *The Lord of the
Rings*? We will call them "living in the word," "living in the dream,"
and "living in Faery."

We will thus explore what made Tolkien's relationship to language
unique. First, his love for language already appeared in very early days; it
somehow marked out Tolkien for his destiny and task. Second, Tolkien
had spiritual experiences, which were like the exposed tip of the iceberg
of his personality. Chief among them was what appears to me to be a
previous-life experience in so-called Atlantis, which opened up for him
an understanding of the life of big dreams and visions. Finally, the way
itself in which Tolkien was launched into his legendarium could be seen

as an extension of his spiritual experiences, or at least give us indications about a very unique kind of literary inspiration.

# LIVING IN THE WORD

From an early age Tolkien was interested in words for their own sake, fascinated by their sound and musicality. He loved to recite words regardless of their meaning, so much so that one can start to gain a feeling that they took the place of music in the child's mind. Languages fascinated him. During his days at King Edwards, while learning Greek, he was enthralled by the contrast between its fluidity, its hardness, and its "surface glitter." In his college days he took up the study of Old Welsh, whose sound he deeply appreciated, just as a child he stood spellbound by the Welsh place names on coal trucks: Nantyglo, Senghenydd, Blaenrhondda, Penrhiwceiber.

**Invented Languages**

When referring to his writings Tolkien once said that

> it is not a hobby [writing and publishing fairy-stories and romances], in the sense of something quite different from someone's work, taken up as a relief-outlet. The invention of languages is the foundation. The "stories" were made rather to provide a world for the language than the reverse. To me a name comes first and the story follows. I should have preferred to write in Elvish.[76]

Statements like these are not isolated. In fact something of this very same nature was stated by Tolkien in relation to *The Lord of the Rings*. And when, around 1930, Tolkien jotted down almost without thinking, "In a hole in the ground there lived a hobbit," he was writing a sentence that only later would take him in the direction of the celebrated *The Hobbit*. At the time he still had to discover the nature of a Hobbit.

---

[76] Carpenter, *Letters of J. R. R. Tolkien*, 219.

To see how all of this is possible, let us take a look at Tolkien's love affair with languages. During secondary school while immersed in the official Greek and Latin studies, he turned his interest to Gothic, Anglo-Saxon, and Welsh. This study fed his early taste for inventing his own idioms, particularly his early Elvish language, about which one of his eulogist comments, "This was no arbitrary gibberish, but a really possible tongue, with consistent roots, sound laws, and inflexions, into which he poured all his imaginative and philological powers."[77] It is very indicative that Tolkien first developed languages for his beings (particularly the Elves) and then developed a mythology for them. Verlyn Flieger, who has devoted much of her life to an understanding of Tolkien, concludes, "Language came first, and his development of it forced him to realize that there can be no language without a people who speak it, no people without a culture which expresses them, no culture without a myth which informs and shapes it."[78]

The reader will remember that Tolkien first wrote his own dragon story when he was seven. His mother pointed out that he could not say "a green great dragon" but only "a great green dragon." This puzzled him and moved him from stories to language. On a later occasion, upon reading the *Crist* he came across two lines about Earendel: "Hail Earendel, brightest of angels / above the middle-earth sent unto men." Referring to the time of the discovery Tolkien later commented, "There was something very remote and strange and beautiful behind these words, if I could grasp it, far beyond ancient English."[79] This offered him the motivation to start working on his own *Lay of Earendel*.

In order to understand the importance of Tolkien's invented languages, we will first look at his biography and letters, then to some of his unfinished work. He delivered his lecture *A Secret Vice* to the Johnson Society, Pembroke College, Oxford, in 1931.[80] It could be argued this was the first time Tolkien spoke publicly, though in a very veiled fashion, about his work in "sub-creation." Tolkien calls his secret passion both a "new game" and a "new art."

---

[77] Quoted in Pearce, *Tolkien, Man and Myth*, 33.
[78] Flieger, *Splintered Light*, 60.
[79] Carpenter, *Tolkien: A Biography*, 64.
[80] Tolkien, *A Secret Vice*, xii.

In chronological order Tolkien first mentions Nevbosh (the "New Nonsense") a language that he invented together with his cousin Marjorie Incledon. The language phonetically distorted words from common languages (English, French, Latin); it was closer to a code than an invented language and was only shared by the two inventors.

Soon after Tolkien turned his energies to Naffarin, based on Latin and Spanish. He felt it was a step forward because through it he attempted to fulfill "the instinct for linguistic invention—the fitting of notion to oral symbol, and *pleasure in contemplating the new relationship established.*"[81] At the time of the lecture he outlined what he thought were the essential elements for language invention:

- the creation of aesthetically pleasing sound forms
- a sense of fitness between symbol and meaning
- an elaborate and ingenious grammar
- a fictional historical background that gives "an illusion of coherence and unity to the whole"

There had been various invented languages before Tolkien. Examples include those of Thomas More, Bishop Godwyn, Cyrano de Bergerac, and Jonathan Swift. Specimens of invented languages also appeared in the works of Edward Bulwer (Lord Lytton), Edgar Allan Poe, and Percy Greg. In addition, the late 1920s and early 1930s saw the development of so-called International Auxiliary Languages and language experimentation in art, mainly through the literary movement of Modernism. Among the International Auxiliary Languages were Volapük, Ido, Novial, and the more well-known Esperanto. Interestingly, Tolkien was a patron of the 24th British Esperanto Congress in 1933. Although he lent his support to the development of the language, he judged the newly invented language, and all the other ones, dead because thoroughly deprived of a past, real or fictional.[82]

Tolkien finally broke through to a more productive experiment when he turned his attention to what would become Quenya, which had much of its rooting in Finnish. The language was in Tolkien's mind

[81] Tolkien, *A Secret Vice*, 15–16.
[82] Tolkien, *A Secret Vice*, xlvii.

derived from an earlier form—from which a second Elvish language was later added—and used by the Elves of Middle-earth. A second language, Sindarin, was more closely modeled around Welsh.

Tolkien set the basis for his Quenya language in the spring of 1915 in his *The Quenya Lexicon* and the *Quenya Phonology*. The language was inspired by Tolkien's love of Finnish and his reading of the *Kalevala*. Here too love of language and mythology go hand in hand: Quenya was used at length in *The Book of Lost Tales*. And by 1920 Tolkien had completed his *Quenya Grammar*. Tolkien expressed that in Quenya he found his "own most normal phonetic taste."

Sindarin was originally called Gnomish or Goldogrin. It was associated with the Elves exiled from Valinor, also originally called Gnomes or Noldoli. Tolkien used Welsh sounds to build the second language. He used a system of mutation (how words are affected when they are close to other words) almost identical with Welsh mutations. This second language also appeared in *The Book of Lost Tales*. It was finally called Sindarin, the language often used in *The Lord of the Rings*. Tolkien associates Quenya with the highest Elven race, and with the highest and purest of his imagined beings. Quenya had more open vowels, as in Finnish, than his Sindarin.

Around 1937 Tolkien wrote *The Lhammas* ("Account of the Tongues") in which he created a "Tree of Tongues" showing how each language is related to older ones and contemporary ones, and how the language of Elves related to that of Men and Dwarves.[83] Out of an original root language he derives twelve Elvish languages or dialects. The splintering of these languages occurred when the Elves went separate ways. At first some decided to join the Valar (the gods) in the West, and others remained behind. Later some of the Elves left the West to return to Middle-earth. The language splintered at each step of the way.

## Tolkien's Love of Language

In his legendarium Tolkien took great care in the determination of his names. He gave a lot of attention to them and wrote with a certain pride

---

[83] In *The Lost Road*, quoted in Tolkien, *A Secret Vice*, xxix.

to Stanley Unwin his publisher: "Personally I believe (and here believe I am a good judge) they are good, and a large part of the effect. They are coherent and consistent and made upon two related linguistic formulae, so that they achieve a reality not fully achieved to my feeling by other name-inventors (say Swift or Dunsany)."[84]

Humphrey Carpenter, Tolkien's biographer, has retraced how the author would form the names with great care by first deciding on a meaning, then developing the form first in one language then in the other (most often he used Sindarin as the last version). At other times, however, he would construct a name that seemed appropriate to the character without regard to linguistic roots. Over time Tolkien came to look upon his languages as real ones. In this mood he would approach contradictions or unsatisfying names not as problems to be fixed, but something to be discovered, leading Carpenter to conclude, "In part it was an intellectual game of Patience . . . and in part it grew from his belief in the ultimate *truth* of his mythology."[85]

So much for the official Tolkien. Something more appears from the Tolkien of fiction, the Tolkien that speaks through his characters, especially in two works of science fiction, or rather time-travel, that remained incomplete: *The Lost Road* and *The Notion Club Papers.*

*The Lost Road*, which meanders through various historical ages, was to end with the hero at the drowning of Atlantis. Time travel is what occurs in consciousness through the intermediary of unusual personal experiences, rather than resorting to time machines or other technological devices. The book spans epochs of time through the thread of serial identity of father-son pairings. A closely tuned father and son pair dream themselves back in time and carry the thread of their folk memory, through serial identity of their preceding ancestors. In other words there is a collective memory running through the bloodlines.

The book was initially meant to have a series of historical settings, culminating backwards in the Atlantean episode. Among these: a Lombard story, a "Norse story of ship-burial," a "Tuatha-de-Danaan story," a story concerning "painted caves," and others before the flood of Númenor. The book's narrative is interrupted at the fourth chapter,

[84] Carpenter, *Letters of J. R. R. Tolkien*, 26.
[85] Carpenter, *Tolkien: A Biography*, 95.

39

at the place in which the main characters would have entered the exploration of the fall of Númenor. Carpenter estimates that Tolkien's *The Lost Road* was written sometime after the completion of the legend of Atlantis/Númenor, which corresponds to "Akallabêth," a part of *The Silmarillion.*[86] We will return to the importance of Atlantis soon.

Tolkien's son Christopher indicates that *The Lost Road* is a kind of idealized autobiography.[87] It is in this attempted time travel that Tolkien portrays the history professor Alboin who hears words rise in his consciousness "that seem to be fragments of ancient and forgotten languages."

The father and son pair, Oswin and Alboin, are the main characters in the first part of the plot, and Alboin closely conveys much of the autobiographical flavor. The dates penciled in for his birth—February 4, 1890/1891—correspond to only one or two years earlier and one day after Tolkien's birthdate.[88]

Like Tolkien, Alboin has to learn Greek. However, on his own he decides to study Old English, Norse, Welsh, and Irish, though these are not encouraged in his curriculum—another autobiographical parallel. "Alboin liked the flavour of the older northern languages, quite as much as he liked some of the things written in them. . . . sound-changes were a hobby of his, at the age when other boys were learning about the insides of motor-cars."[89] And he had an intuitive grasp of these languages, of what he calls "language atmosphere":

> You get echoes coming through, you know, in odd words here and there—often very common words in their own language, but quite unexplained by the etymologists; and in the general shape and sound of all the words, somehow; as if something was peeping through from deep under the surface.[90]

[86] Carpenter, *Tolkien: A Biography*, 170.
[87] Tolkien, *The Lost Road and Other Writings*, 53.
[88] Tolkien, *The Lost Road and Other Writings*, 53.
[89] Tolkien, *The Lost Road and Other Writings*, 39.
[90] Tolkien, *The Lost Road and Other Writings*, 40.

At one point Alboin tells his father: "But I got a lot of jolly new words a few days ago: I am sure *lomelinde* means *nightingale*, for instance, and certainly *lome* is *night* (though not *darkness*)."[91] Notice here that the words come, and then they are interpreted as for their meaning; contrary to the process of artificially creating a language. It seems that Tolkien is revealing here—in the comfort of an unpublished book—something more about his passion for languages.

We get a feeling of how the themes of mythology, culture, and language are part and parcel of the whole search of Alboin, who says "I like to go back—and not with race only, or culture only, or language; but with all three."[92] Surveying his life Alboin says something that Tolkien could have related to: that the purpose or mood of his life has been one of traveling back in time, an experience that he equates to walking on long-forgotten roads, echoing the title of the book.

*The Notion Club Papers* portend to report the meetings of an Oxford discussion group called the Notion Club, that resembled in spirit much of the Inklings. Many of the members of the club carry parts of Tolkien's persona. The published part of the story revolves around Númenor/ Atlantis, or Tolkien's Great Wave dream.

Among the characters who bear some resemblance to Tolkien are Ramer, professor of Finno-Ugric philology; Alwin Arundel Lowdham, interested in Anglo-Saxon, Icelandic, and comparative philology; and Wilfrid Trewin Jeremy, who specializes in escapism and writes about time travel and imaginary lands. An interesting addition is that of Rupert Dolbear, who acts a little like Tolkien's consciousness, alerting us when something relevant is about to happen, or offering seemingly far-off, but quite to the point, insights.

In the story Lowdham, who receives words in his sleep consciousness, explains:

> Most of these "ghost-words" . . . began to come through as I said, when I was about ten: and almost at once I started to note them down. . . . But later on, when I was older and I had a little more linguistic experience,

---

91  Tolkien, *The Lost Road and Other Writings*, 41.
92  Tolkien, *The Lost Road and Other Writings*, 40.

> I began to pay serious attention to my "ghosts", and saw
> that they were something quite different from the game
> of trying to make up private languages.[93]

Note that here Tolkien brings together two elements; the desire to craft a private language, and the inspiration through which he receives words in his sleep. This too seems to mirror Tolkien's evolution in relation to languages that he first invents and later discovers.

Further in what becomes very interesting in relation to Tolkien's life, the same Lowdham states:

> As soon as I started looking out for them, so to speak,
> the ghosts began to come oftener and clearer; and when
> I had got a lot of them noted down, I saw that they were
> not all of the same kind: they had different phonetic
> styles, styles as unlike as, well—Latin and Hebrew. . . .
> Well, first of all I recognized that a lot of these ghosts
> were Anglo-Saxon, or related stuff. What was left I
> arranged in two lists, A and B, according to their style,
> with a third rag-bag list C for odd things that didn't
> seem to fit in anywhere. But it was language A that
> really attracted me; just suited me. I still like it best.[94]

The question of language preference too has a very biographical echo.

Concerning languages A and B Lowdham then realizes that they are related neither to any language ever heard nor with the languages he invented at an early stage. And then he adds that

> they came through made: sound and sense already
> conjoined. I can no longer niggle with them than I can
> alter the sound of the word *polis* in Greek. . . . Nothing
> changes but occasionally my spelling. . . . In other words
> they have the effect and taste of real languages. But one

---

[93] Tolkien, *Sauron Defeated*, 238.
[94] Tolkien, *Sauron Defeated*, 238.

can have preferences among real languages, and as I say,
I like A best.[95]

Lowdham calls the two languages Avallonian and Adunaic, and
marks his preference for the older one of the two, Avallonian. Adunaic
is in consciousness closer to the present. "But *Avallonian* . . . Seems to
me more august, more ancient, and, well, sacred and liturgical. I used to
call it Elven-Latin. The echoes of it carry one far away. Very far away.
Away from Middle-earth altogether, I expect."[96] The characterization
of Elven-Latin renders Avallonian reminiscent of Tolkien's official
Quenya, which he preferred over the later Sindarin.

**Language: Science and Art**

In his first attempt at college in 1913, Tolkien did not achieve First
Class Honour Moderations (only a Second Class) but nevertheless
achieved a "pure alpha" or a practically faultless paper in Comparative
Philology. After being discharged from the army Tolkien's first job
occupied him for a time at putting the finishing touches at one of the
most comprehensive efforts ever to craft an English dictionary. Dr.
Bradley, who supervised the work, said of Tolkien: "His work gives
evidence of an unusual mastery of Anglo-Saxon and of the facts and
principles of the comparative grammar of the Germanic languages.
Indeed I have no hesitation in saying that I have never known a man of
his age who is in these respects his equal."[97]

In his early days at Oxford Tolkien wanted to reduce the gap
between what were called Language (philology) and Literature. There
were many factions and strong animosities. Undertaking this task was
natural for Tolkien since his love for philology was firmly grounded
in appreciation for literature. By 1931 he had achieved a remarkable
success—thanks in part to the support of C. S. Lewis. He was the
recognized architect of a revised syllabus that achieved a great deal of
rapprochement between Language and Literature.

---

[95] Tolkien, *Sauron Defeated*, 240.
[96] Tolkien, *Sauron Defeated*, 241.
[97] Carpenter, *Tolkien: A Biography*, 101.

---

We have already explored Tolkien's Beowulf essay. In another essay, titled "Sigelwara Land," Tolkien concentrates on the meaning of the Old English word *Sigelwaran* or *Sigelhearwan* to stand for something like "black people living in a hot region." To recapture meaning and understanding of the consciousness of the times, the scholarly attitude has to be accompanied by a willingness to stimulate the imagination to enter a lost dimension of consciousness. Tolkien's scholarship allies here great precision with imaginative penetration. On the basis of all the above Carpenter characterizes Tolkien's philological writing as "forceful in its imagery . . . however abstruse or unpromising the subject might seem."[98] Thus Tolkien combined a scrupulous and painstaking concern for accuracy with an uncanny ability for unearthing patterns and relationships.

The same attitude of scholarship and imagination penetrates all his fiction work. *The Lord of the Rings* is a *Beowulf* in reverse; here the artistic part takes the front seat, but the researcher isn't that far off, accompanying his characters and geography of Middle-earth with digressions, maps, and appendices. Here again the estimation of Verlyn Flieger is worth quoting in full:

> Research into early forms and uses of words, the search after lost meanings and nuances—a scientific study in the truest sense of the word—led him through science into art, and from art into an almost spiritual realm wherein the word was the conveyer of primal truth, the magic vehicle not just of communication but of genuine communion. As such, words were for Tolkien not just a window onto the past but the key to that lost relationship between man and God of which our sense of the Fall is our only memory.[99]

We will return to this aspect of Tolkien's genius.

Tolkien was keenly aware of how words have lost great part of their meaning and magic in present time. He felt that farmers and tradesmen

---

[98] Carpenter, *Tolkien: A Biography*, 134.
[99] Flieger, *Splintered Light*, 9.

of old lived so fully in the experience of the word that they "savoured words like meat and wine and honey in their tongues. Especially when declaiming. They made a scrap of verse majestically sonorous: like thunder moving on a slow wind, or the tramp of mourners at the funeral of a king." They were able to pronounce them each in such a way as to evoke an experience from nature or from life. Tolkien was trying to complement modern scientific consciousness with the artistic perspective. This was not a return to the past, but an evolution that mirrored at a new level what was true in much earlier times. When he referred to the ancient times of his legendarium, Tolkien says, "The light of Valinor (derived from light before any fall) is the light of art undivorced from reason, that sees things both scientifically (or philosophically) and imaginatively (or sub-creatively) and 'says that they are good'—as beautiful"[100] It is this determination to newly unite science and art that forms a constant thread in Tolkien's work.

At the end of his life Tolkien's scholarly work was rewarded with a 1972 honorary Doctorate of Letters from Oxford University. It was specifically for his contribution to philology, not for *The Lord of the Rings* or other writings. And Carpenter goes as far as to say that he almost founded a new school of philology. How is this claim justified? In *On Fairy Stories* Tolkien argues against the positions of philologists like Max Müller and George Dasent and from evolutionary anthropology against the positions of Andrew Lang. He counters Müller's assertion that mythology was a disease of language thus: "Mythology is not a disease at all. . . . It would be more near the truth to say that languages, especially modern European languages, are a disease of mythology."[101] What he said in jest he then moderated by saying that language, myth, and the correspondent culture arose together and formed an indivisible whole. Dasent had focused on race. Tolkien countered by focusing on the story itself, rather than its cultural background. To Lang who argued that fairy tales in their savageness belonged to something like an infancy of human development, Tolkien replied that fairy stories were not for children alone, though not all adults may appreciate them. This is something he knew first-hand, since he had such a deep appreciation

---

[100] Carpenter, *Letters of J. R. R. Tolkien*, 148.
[101] Tolkien, "On Fairy Stories," in *Monsters and the Critics*, 121–22.

for them. In the same essay Tolkien predicates that the fairy tale is not an escape because it does not deny the reality of sorrow and failure; it just denies its final defeat. Tolkien was the first scholar of stature to concern himself with the theme after the brothers Grimm; both sustained the validity of the fairy tale genre. Until then the entire subject had been dismissed out of hand.

Part of this deep penetration of the Word came to Tolkien from innate faculties, and what amounted to spiritual experiences that accompanied the early part of his life, as we have seen more closely from his two time-travel books. Another important part came to him through the work of and acquaintance with Owen Barfield.

Verlyn Flieger points to Tolkien sharing very close lines of thought with Barfield, another member of the Inklings. Although he also wrote fantasy, Barfield shines most as a creative thinker and philosopher; one of his early and persistent interests lay in the relationship between myth and language. And his related thoughts on the matter seem to have had a lasting influence on Tolkien's outlook.

We know of the direct effect of Barfield's theories about language on Tolkien from a letter that C. S. Lewis sent to Barfield:

> You might like to know that when Tolkien dined with me the other night he said, *a propos* of something quite different, that your conception of the ancient semantic unity had modified his whole outlook, and that he was always just going to say something in a lecture when your concept stopped him in time. "It is one of those things," he said, "that when you've once seen it there are all sorts of things you can never say again."[102]

Note that Tolkien was not only taking in Barfield's ideas, but he was always casting other ones aside for good as the consequence of this. They deepened his scholastic perceptions.

Although Tolkien and Barfield saw each other, they were both better friends of C. S. Lewis. Tolkien and Barfield shared a common interest in the history of language in relation to its myths. And Barfield

---

[102] Flieger, *Splintered Light*, 35–36.

felt that Tolkien's idea of sub-creation was very close to his "poet as world-maker," closer than Lewis had been to him. There is no evidence that Tolkien knew of the other works of Barfield. But for the two of them words were the instruments allowing the sub-creator to reunite with the divine.

In *Poetic Diction* Barfield considered the evolution of words and the evolution of their meaning in the relations of perception to word, and word to concept. He proposed that three things are completely enmeshed into each other: language, myth, and the human being's perception of his world.

In language's infancy there was no separation between a literal and a metaphoric meaning, between abstract and concrete. There was in fact no such thing as a metaphor when the human being both perceived phenomena and lived in a kind of mythic participation within them. And words in the early stages of language enveloped a world of meaning, many interpenetrating layers. Thus, for example the world *pneuma* in Greek stood for wind, breath, and spirit all at once. The modern human being, when translating the word, by necessity splinters the meaning by considering only one aspect of the whole.

Over time, with human feeling separating from the phenomena, there was a greater differentiation of the phenomena themselves, with a consequent fragmentation of perception and word meaning. More percepts led to more words, and these led to the ability to perceive more differentiation and generate more words—a self-sustaining cycle.

Tolkien could see words as fragments of the Logos and part and parcel of how the human being sees the world. Tolkien wrote his essay "Sigelwara Land" six years after reading Barfield, and this explains how he could now immerse himself imaginatively in the reality that permeates and conditions the experience of the word. And Barfield could not have affected Tolkien the scholar without affecting Tolkien the sub-creator. In fact the whole of *The Silmarillion* exemplifies the process of splintering of language and perception, which Verlyn Flieger has so aptly brought to light.

Tolkien's sub-creation takes its departure from the lived experience of language. Tolkien characterizes the fantasy writer as the creator of the Secondary World, who does, on a minor scale, what God does with the Primary World. And words are the tools for this sub-creation; words which are an expression of the Logos. As one of many examples, in his essay "On Fairy Stories" Tolkien marvels at what it meant for the evolution of language to arrive at the concept of adjective thus:

> The mind that thought of *light, heavy, grey, yellow, still, swift*, also conceived of magic that would make heavy things light and able to fly, turn grey lead into yellow gold, and the still rock into a swift water. If it could do the one, it could do the other; it inevitably did both.[103]

In his unfinished poem *Mythopoeia*, Tolkien writes:

> *Man, Sub-creator, the refracted light,*
> *through whom is splintered from a single White*
> *to many hues, and endlessly combined*
> *in living shapes that move from mind to mind.*
> *Though all the crannies of the world we filled*
> *with Elves and Goblins, though we dared to build*
> *Gods and their houses out of dark and light,*
> *and sowed the seed of dragons, 'twas our right*
> *(used or misused). The right has not decayed.*
> *We make still by the law in which we're made.*

Tolkien sees the human being capable to create by the same law "in which we're made." And the law is the Word, the Logos, which once was whole. The material through which the sub-creator creates is now light, as Flieger points out, rather than the word. And Tolkien sees in this shift from word to light, a shift from literal to metaphoric. This harkens to Barfield's ancient semantic unity. It is in the nature of the word to try to reach for "metaphors of light." Both light and word are agents of perception allowing us to see phenomena. We say "clarifying an argument" or "we see" for we understand; a change in wording can "put things under a different light." For Tolkien the word is light, enlightenment, as we will see later on.

---

[103] Tolkien, "On Fairy Stories," in *Monsters and the Critics*, 43.

It is interesting to note that *fantasy* and *phenomena* come from the same root; *phenomena* comes from *phainesthai*, "to appear"; *fantasy* from *phantazein*, "to make visible." And their root is in the Greek *phainein*, "to show." Here is another example of the fragmentation of word and light. This indicates that there was a time when "appearances perceived" closely matched "appearances shaped by the imagination." And further linguistic research shows the linkage between "to speak" and "to shine," between light and word, in the Indo-European *bha*. Tolkien thus sees the origin of truth, light, and word in God. And the sub-creator makes manifest fragments of this original truth.

**Language and Mythology**

It is very indicative that Tolkien first developed languages for his beings (particularly Elves) and then developed a mythology for them. It's as if the mythology was the justification and follow-through of the preceding languages.

The prevailing theories of language of the time derived myth from language, not vice versa. The leading German philologist, Max Müller, argued that mythology was a "disease of language." Tolkien argued for the contrary: language as a "disease of mythology." By *disease* he meant dis-ease or discomfort, one that leads to consciousness and from that to language.

In *The Silmarillion* we see the fragmentation of Elvish language from the perception of the whole to many views reflected in languages, illustrating the splintering process of light and word. From this splintered light arise all the colors in their beauty through greater variety and narrower, more precise expressions. From unified light we move to colors; and from Word (Logos) to words. "The Logos [Word] is ultimately independent of the verbum [word]."[104]

In *The Silmarillion* language arises with the awakening of the Elves in Cuiviénen, when their history begins. When the Elves awaken they behold the stars, saying "Ele!" which means "behold." *Ele* is a primary percept on the way to becoming metaphor, as the Elves use it to shape and characterize their culture (Eldar). The primary act of speech is a

---

[104] Carpenter, *Letters of J. R. R. Tolkien*, 269.

response to the perception of the light of the stars, to the percept "to shine." And from *quen* for "say, speak" comes their characterization of themselves, since they are the first ones to speak: the Quendi, "those that speak with voices." The speech comes in response to the light [of the stars]. But the Valar gods see the Elves as *Eldar*, or "people of the stars," a name that originates from light and speech, from *el*, related to *ele*.

Tolkien's scholarly work informed his artistic literary output down to the minutest details, as in the uses of regional, sociocultural variations of language in his characters: the more city-minded language of the Tooks and Bagginses in contrast with the rural dialect of Gamgees and Cottons. Or the musicality of Elvish language in contrast to the guttural and harsh sounding Orc speech. Even in things as subtle as the difference between the enamored Eowyn addressing Aragorn with "thou" and the distant Aragorn responding with "you."[105]

Tolkien illustrated all these ideas about language in both an artistic and scientific fashion in his literary opus. He had understood first intuitively, then more consciously, through Barfield that poetry and science can be made to converge in the artistic creation.

Verlyn Flieger offers some examples, which follow, from *The Lord of the* Rings, the first of which concerns the understanding of the nature of Tom Bombadil. Frodo asks Goldberry, "Who is Tom Bombadil?" And Goldberry simply answers, "He is." But she is not answering Frodo in the sense of "I am that I am." She is meaning that "he is as you have seen him." She adds, "He is the Master of wood, water and hill."[106] And Frodo misunderstands that all in Tom's domain belongs to him, to which she replies negatively. Thus, the term *master* does not desire for possession; it is intended as "teacher" and "authority." Then Frodo asks Bombadil directly, "Who are you, Master?" And Tom answers, "Don't you know my name yet? That's the only answer."[107] At the Council in Rivendell Elrond calls Tom "Iarwain Ben-adar," oldest and fatherless. *Iarwain* means "old-young" in Sindarin. *Ben-adar* means "without

---

[105] See Flieger, *Splintered Light*, 4–8, and "The Mind, the Tongue, and the Tale," in *Green Suns and Faërie*, 242–49.
[106] Tolkien, *The Fellowship of the Ring*, 122.
[107] Tolkien, *The Fellowship of the Ring*, 129.

father." Since Tom has his origin before what is known as history, he can only be associated with himself. He existed before language itself. "Tom was here before the river and the trees. . . . He made paths before the Big people, and saw the little people arriving. . . . He knew the dark under the stars when it was fearless." This explains that in the end one can only simply say that he is.[108]

In the book Tolkien also explores how experience and word interconnect and develop each other in the instance of Treebeard. The Ent lives in the consciousness that knowing someone's name means being able to dominate them. He does not want to tell the Hobbits his name because it would take too long, and his name is growing all the time because "it is like a story." Just as the Hobbits are hasty and so is their language, the reverse is true of the Ents. This means that they live in different worlds and perceive the world's unfolding in diametrically different ways.[109]

Still within the context of fiction, Tolkien offers us another insight about language: a changed experience can preserve the word but obscure the meaning. Language can expand as well as contract. Lórien is also called Lothlórien, or in the longest terms *Laurelindórenan linderolendor malinorélion ornemalin*.[110] The full name means "The valley where the trees in a golden light sing musically, a land of music and dreams; there are yellow trees there, it is a yellow-tree land."[111] When shortened we arrive at *Laurelinórenan*, "The land of the Valley of the Singing Gold." The still shorter *Lothlórien* stands for "Dreamflower" and *Lórien* simply means "Dream." Thus Lórien stands for the opposite of what we carry in our waking consciousness. The shortening of the name reflects the regressing relationship of the place towards time and change. It is a remnant of an old state of consciousness and is on its way out; for the time being it is artificially preserved, and in its shores time seems to be at a standstill. The Ents have another name for Lórien that means "There is a black shadow in the deep dales of the forest." It's a predictive

[108] Tolkien, *The Fellowship of the Ring*, 129 and 258–59.
[109] Flieger, *Green Suns and Faërie*, 247.
[110] Tolkien, *The Two Towers*, 456.
[111] Carpenter, *Letters of J. R. R. Tolkien*, 308.

name for what Lórien is on the way to becoming. This relates to the fact that the Elves try to embalm time and therefore stop change.

Time, and with it cultural change, can also change shape and sound and erode the meaning of a word. Gandalf cannot properly read what appears on the Doors of Moria: *pedo mellon a minno*. He first interprets it as "Speak, friend, and enter."[112] But the meaning is only revealed by the possible variations of the word *speak* and how the punctuation is used. If instead of *speak* we use the word *say* the whole becomes "Say friend, and enter." Which is to say that language depends on context for meaning. At a time of great cultural distress "friend" has acquired a less perceptible and immediate meaning.

The last example of how Tolkien mixes science and art in his *The Lord of the Rings* shows that the disappearance of the object can deprive language of the word. Loss of the thing leads to loss of the experience of the thing, and therefore of the word that expressed it. In referring to this example Tolkien expressly turns to Barfield's ideas. In chapter 12 of *The Hobbit* Tolkien refers to Bilbo's encompassing reaction to the sight of the dragon, an experience no longer to be had by those who cannot experience dragons: "To say that Bilbo's breath was taken away is no description at all. There are no words left to express his staggerment, since Men changed the language that they learned of the Elves in the days when the world was wonderful."[113] In being faithful to Barfield's ideas that he made his own, Tolkien comes up with the fictionally old word "staggerment" to express that for which there are no more words to express.

In all the above examples Tolkien has shown rather than explained to readers all the anomalies to which language is exposed when conveying consciousness that is different, belonging to the past, extinct, or otherwise modified.

## Living in the Word

Tolkien's research into the evolution of words blended science and art to a high degree. Science and art ultimately led him to the realm of the Word/Logos, which conveys ultimate truths. This research became for

[112] Tolkien, *The Fellowship of the Ring*, 300.
[113] Tolkien, *The Hobbit*, 198.

Tolkien the avenue for an almost spiritual communion. Through words Tolkien returned to the Word, to the primeval relationship between the human being and God.

Listen to Tolkien comparing the synonyms *silver* and *argent*, taken as an example of how words could be taught in early education. He argues that the meaning of the words cannot be made obvious. And he recommends that people first learn to listen to the sound and realize that they don't have the same meaning, not only because they sound different. If one were to hear *argent* in a poetic context first, then "there is a chance then that you may like it for itself, and later learn to appreciate the heraldic overtones it has, in addition to its own peculiar sound, which 'silver' has not." And his conclusion is quite remarkable:

> I think that this writing down, flattening, Bible-in-basic-English attitude is responsible for the fact that so many older children and younger people have little respect and no love for words, and very limited vocabularies—and alas! little desire left (even when they had the gift which has been stultified) to refine or enlarge them.[114]

The above is a concrete illustration of the love for the musicality of the word that was inborn in Tolkien.

C. S. Lewis recognized Tolkien's "unique insight at once into the language of poetry and into the poetry of language." This led him to look at early texts both from the perspective of study of language and literature worthy of appreciation. Seeing this mastery over all aspects of language, Lewis saw what distinguished Tolkien from other philologists in the fact that "He had been inside of language."[115]

This insight is confirmed and expanded upon by a certain Simonne d'Ardenne, one of Tolkien's Oxford students, who later became a philologist. At one time she asked Tolkien, "You broke the veil, didn't you, and passed through?" And she wrote that he recognized this assertion as true. This was meant in relation to language. This

[114] Carpenter, *Letters of J. R. R. Tolkien*, 311.
[115] Carpenter, *Tolkien: A Biography*, 133–34.

denotes that for Tolkien the word was the avenue to the perception of supersensible reality. In a sense, according to Flieger, the "word was the light through which he saw."[116]

# LIVING IN THE DREAM

As was pointed out earlier on, Tolkien lived in full imaginations that came to him in dreams or visions. Some of those were so vivid that the young Tolkien could capture them in paintings with accompanying poems. Of great interest and uniqueness to him was his "Great Wave" dream, to which we will turn now.

## Tolkien and the Idea of Reincarnation

When we look at Tolkien's life experiences, or the ways in which his characters undergo past life memories (or "serial longevity"), a consistent pattern emerges that matches evidence that has surfaced in the literature of the last twenty to thirty years. No such literature about spontaneous previous life recollections existed in Tolkien's lifetime. This makes the correspondence between Tolkien's narratives and present reports all the more remarkable.

In a letter to W. H. Auden in which he talks about his "sensibility to linguistic pattern which affects [him] emotionally like colour or music . . . the deep response to legends (for lack of better word) that have what I would call the North-western temper and temperature," Tolkien also mentions his "Atlantis complex" thus:

> I mean the terrible recurrent dream (beginning with memory) of the Great Wave, towering up, and coming in ineluctably over the trees and green fields. . . . I don't think I have had it since I wrote "Downfall of Númenor" as the last of the legends of the First and Second Age.

---

[116] Quoted in Flieger, *Splintered Light*, 9.

In another letter he called it the "Atlantis haunting," which took the form of a recurrent dream of a great wave that threatened to engulf him, and from which he awakened "gasping out of deep water."[117] Note that his use of the term *complex* is meant to taunt the psychologists of his time, with good reason. Very few in his time could have seen anything else than a projection or complex in such a recurrent dream. Lastly Tolkien mentions that his son Michael also shared a similar dream. Númenor was the name that Tolkien most often used in relation to the lost continent.

That Tolkien had memories of what could only have been the moment of death, or felt like death, in Atlantis is not exceptional; it's rather close to the norm. Many spontaneous recollections are associated with the final years, months, or days before death. Death itself is often very clearly remembered. Ian Stevenson, who has conducted extensive studies on cases of reincarnations occurring shortly after the previous death, concludes that memories are the most precise in relation to the proximity to the moment of death than in relation to possible length of association with particular individuals, and even close relatives.[118]

It is important to underline that Tolkien comes to the Atlantis tradition from inner experience:

> [The legends of *Númenorë*] are my own use for my purposes of the Atlantis legend, but not based on special knowledge, but in a special personal concern with this tradition of the culture-bearing men of the Sea, which so profoundly affected the imagination of peoples of Europe with westward–shores.[119]

Christopher Tolkien has a telling comment about the "Great Wave" dream. "By 'beginning with memory' I believe that my father meant that the recurrence of the dream went as far back in his life as his memory reached."[120] In Tolkien's personal letters the dream is amplified with

---

117 Carpenter, *Letters of J. R. R. Tolkien*, 213, 347.
118 Stevenson, *Children Who Remember Previous Lives*, 172–73.
119 Carpenter, *Letters of J. R. R. Tolkien*, 303.
120 Carpenter, *Letters of J. R. R. Tolkien*, 217.

historical elements belonging to Númenor as these are experienced by Tolkien: "They built a great temple . . . on the high hill . . . and they there sacrificed unspeakable offerings on an unholy altar. . . . Thus came death-shade into the land of the Westfarers and God's children fell under the shadow."[121] Tolkien goes thus from knowledge of the Flood to at least some of the underlying causes. Tolkien called this part of his mythology *Akallabêth* or *Atalantie*, indicating that both words mean "the downfallen"—the first in Númenorean, the second in Adûnaic.

In *The Lost Road*, Tolkien hypothesizes the Atlantis dream as a race memory and a family inheritance that is maintained through generations. The idea of reincarnation posed more than one moral dilemma to the Catholic Tolkien. Still, it was not something that he was willing to let go all that easily. And in his writings it pokes its head up shyly or coyly more than once. Let us turn to these.

When reincarnation appears, it seems Tolkien is cognizant of how it pierces through the veil of consciousness, now that we can compare his experience with many of those that have become popularized in the literature. At other times this reference to reincarnation takes even what looks like a purely gratuitous form, one that seemingly does not add anything to the plot, as is the case in the episode of the Barrow-downs in *The Lord of the Rings*.

The first draft of the event of extrapersonal memory narrated in the Barrow-downs episode dates from near the end of 1938, two years after the uncompleted *Lost Road* and before the unfinished *The Notion Club Papers*. After being made captive in the Barrow-down and upon recovering his senses, Merry exclaims: "Of course I remember. . . . The men of Carn Dûm came upon us at night, and we were worsted. Ah! The spear in my heart!"[122] Immediately after he clutches at his breast, then chases off the memory as nonsense or dream. In the published version details are offered about the battle, the death, the experience of pain.

The experience in the barrow is preceded by Merry's tactile experience of the "golden circlet" on his head. The phrase "we were worsted" underlines his journey through time since it is archaic and

---

[121] Carpenter, *Letters of J. R. R. Tolkien*, 258.
[122] Tolkien, *The Fellowship of the Ring*, 140.

formal English, which indicates a change of identity in Merry. Memories of the moment of death have been illustrated in the literature pertaining to spontaneous recollection, without any need to refer to the dubious remembrances induced through past-life regressions. Once more, as was mentioned earlier on, memories of the moment of death are some of the most common spontaneously induced memories of previous lives. The so-called phenomenon of xenoglossy—speaking in other languages than the ones known in everyday consciousness—has been observed in cases of children who are recalling a previous life. Xenoglossy can refer to a different language, or the language or dialect spoken in a neighboring region to the child's original one.[123]

Flieger rightly invokes that what Tolkien so innocently drops in the narrative can be explained by neither "serial longevity" nor "hoarding memory," to which he refers in his *The Lost Road* or *The Notion Club Papers*. In Appendix A of *The Lord of the Rings* we are told that Carn Dûm was the main city of Angmar, a kingdom ruled by a witch-king— the later Lord of the Nazgûl—who had been defeated by Cirdan and Glorfindel at the battle of Fornost. Furthermore, the barrows were built during the First Age as grave mounds of the Dúnedain; successively they were haunted by the "evil spirits out of Angmar."[124] And the Appendix adds that Hobbits were present at the battle—however, not at the present barrow but rather some hundred miles further north (at Fornost).

The particular mound of the story was the burial ground of the last prince of Cardolan (a Dúnadan, or descendant of Atlantis survivors) who also fell in the war against Angmar. Thus Merry is reliving the painful memory of someone who could not have been his ancestor (no ancestral memory or serial longevity is possible). Interestingly the episode is quite disconnected from the plot and seems to add nothing of significance to it other than the chance of introducing a new phenomenon. It belongs, however, quite lawfully to the episode of the Barrow-downs, as we will see later.

Some element of explanation is offered by Tom Bombadil, who tells the Hobbits that the blades in the barrow's treasure were forged by Men of Westernesse who had been slain by the evil king of Carn Dûm

---

[123] Hardo, *Children Who Lived Before*, chapter 5.
[124] Tolkien, *The Return of the King*, Appendix A.

in Angmar. Tolkien's linchpin to Merry and to the story's credibility is the golden circlet on Merry's head. On this basis it can only lead to the possibility of memories of previous lives, indicating that Tolkien continued to struggle with the possibility, that "Tolkien did at least not disbelieve in reincarnation."[125] We will return to this episode and see how it actually corresponds to deeper spiritual insight in Chapter 6.

As we saw earlier Tolkien tried his hand at two time-travel science fiction stories: both of them aborted; both culminating in episodes in which the characters basically relive Tolkien's own Great Wave dream and report of their experiences in Númenor/Atlantis, adding some depth to it by bringing forth some details about Atlantean history.

*The Lost Road* follows a father and son who dream themselves back in time and carry the thread of their folk memory. A collective memory is passed down the bloodlines. Quite indicatively the two main characters are named Oswin, Anglo-Saxon for "God-friend," and Alboin, the Lombardic and modern form of Anglo-Saxon Ælfwine, meaning "Elf-friend." Alboin's full name is Alboin Errol, Errol (Eriol) meaning "One who dreams alone."

The title, *The Lost Road*, points to what is referred to in the book and in other places as the "Straight Road to the Ancient West," which is no longer possible after the Flood of Atlantis, when the world is bent. By this Tolkien means that human consciousness is radically changed after the end of Atlantis and that it is no longer possible to sail west to Atlantis or further west to the primeval paradisiacal lands of Erissea and Valinor.

In Númenor we find another father-son pair, this time Elendil and Herendil. Through the contrast of Elven and human time, time is treated like space, like a road back in time. But it is clear Tolkien had at least considered other time travel possibilities. In drafts to *The Lost Road*, the symptomatic character Dolbear comments at the early stages about a way to travel back in time: "Then try reincarnation, or perhaps transcarnation without loss of memory."[126] And because Tolkien was of two minds and was treading treacherous grounds in terms of Catholic doctrine he found a way out in "hereditary memory."

---

[125] Flieger, *Green Suns and Faërie*, 100–101
[126] Tolkien, *The Lost Road and Other Writings*, 213.

Arriving to the pivotal time of the Great Wave dream in *The Lost Road*, Tolkien writes:

> And there is that ominous picture: the great temple on the mountain, smoking like a volcano. And that awful vision of the chasm in the seas, a whole land slipping sideways, mountains rolling over; dark ships fleeing into the dark. I want to tell someone about it, and get some kind of sense into it.[127]

Note that this reaction is typical of people having spiritual experiences: they are confused and want to make sense of it. That we are having to do with spiritual experiences, and that Tolkien had first-hand experience of them, transpires from the fact that in the narrative, when the Númenor adventure is over, Audoin is shutting the door while Alboin still sits in his chair.

In *The Notion Club Papers* the individuals experiencing a previous life are transported into the full sensory perception of the times; they recall old names and are immersed in another life experience. Lowdham and Jeremy relive their emotions fully, remember facts alien to their present culture, mention words in an unknown language. Apart from the already mentioned phenomenon of xenoglossy, recent findings of spontaneous previous-life memories corroborate the identifications of the person with emotions of another time, another place. A child who will remember an event from a previous life will sound older than his age and refer to concepts beyond the grasp of his age. The attention of the child is totally turned inward, and he or she may say things that have little relationship with present conditions, such as "I have a wife and two sons" or "My house is much bigger than this one." The child is completely immersed in the reality of what he recounts. Such is the case of a child who had memories of drowning in a swimming pool. Asked about what she was wearing, while immersed in the recall, she simply looked at her body and indicated a swimming suit.[128]

---

[127] Tolkien, *The Lost Road and Other Writings*, 52.
[128] Bowman, *Children's Past Lives*, 213.

From the many confirmations about the nature of spontaneous previous-life memories we can surmise that Tolkien observed and related very accurately what was his own experience. One may wonder whether there was more than one such experience beyond his Great Wave dream. Another observation could support this hypothesis. Various personal experiences that have been extensively covered in modern literature emphasize how spontaneous previous-life recollections tend to occur in a moment of loosening of consciousness, such as the onset of a serious illness. Tolkien had one such protracted instance through trench fever in the recovery from his war experience.

An experience of previous-life recollections through illness has been narrated first-hand by Betty Riley, in a book called *A Veil Too Thin: Reincarnation Out of Control*. The chief interest in Betty Riley's account lies in the modality of awakening of these memories. The first time they occurred, Betty was forty and recovering from illness. Although the antecedents are not stated in an unequivocal fashion, mention of a flu appears before the first recall episodes, and mention of being "very ill" before another series of dreams close in time to the first ones.[129]

It was the encounter with an unusual patient that propelled doctor-turned-author Arthur Guirdham toward the adventure through space, time, and consciousness that he portrays in three successive books.[130] The story began in 1944, with the first encounter between a patient, Ms. Smith, and Dr. Guirdham. At age eleven Ms. Smith had been saved from an attack of peritonitis. During her illness she had dreams in which she would call out loudly to someone named Roger. In a delirious state she talked about having another baby, and when the Catholic priest approached her with the Last Sacrament, she screamed in terror. During her illness she kept notebooks in which she recorded experiences one would surmise that she otherwise would have at least partly forgotten. From all of these scraps of information the doctor was able to connect her memories with the records of individuals and events that had been kept by the Catholic Inquisition. We know that many of Tolkien's visions of the episodes that provided the inspirations for *The*

129 Riley, *A Veil Too Thin*, 81–82 and 86.
130 Guirdham, *The Cathars and Reincarnation*, *We Are One Another*, and *The Lake and the Castle*.

*Silmarillion* occurred during his long bouts of trench fever. Could these be recollections, not of previous lives, but of legends known in previous lives?

In the projected *The Notion Club Papers*, when Ramer asks Lowdham where the name *Númenor* comes from, he replies, "'Oh, I don't know', opening his eyes and looking round with a rather dazed expression."[131] Later on he says: "It comes to me, now and again. Just on the edge of things, you know. Eludes the grasp."[132] This too could allude to biographical elements in Tolkien's life.

To conclude, the threads we have followed pertaining to what resembles memories of previous lives are highly consistent with what we now know from spontaneous recorded experiences. It seems Tolkien had a thorough insider's view about the phenomena. However, experience and doctrine stood at odds in Tolkien's breast. A last witness of it is an unsent letter to a fellow Catholic, in which Tolkien says he wants to at least have the freedom to explore reincarnation [in relation to Elves] in the creative process:

> Reincarnation may be bad theology . . . as applied to Humanity. . . . But I do not see how even in the Primary World any theologian or philosopher, unless very much better informed about the relation of spirit and body than I believe anyone to be, could deny the possibility of reincarnation as a mode of existence prescribed for certain kinds of rational incarnate creatures.[133]

Significantly, the draft was not sent. And the paradox remained unsolved in Tolkien's life.

## Some Other Spiritual Experiences

Tolkien's spiritual experiences were not confined to the receiving of fragments of old languages, fragments of one previous life, or visions. We know of at least two experiences of which he wrote, both related to his

---

[131] Tolkien, *The Lost Road and Other Writings*, 194.
[132] Tolkien, *The Lost Road and Other Writings*, 232.
[133] Carpenter, *Letters of J. R. R. Tolkien*, 95–96.

most pressing spiritual questions. The first happened, not surprisingly, while preparing to receive Communion:

> [Your reference to the care of your guardian angel] also reminded me of a sudden vision . . . I perceived not long ago when spending half an hour in St Gregory's before the Blessed Sacrament. . . . I perceived or thought of the Light of God and in it suspended one small mote (or millions of motes to only one of which was my small mind directed) glittering white because of the individual ray from the Light which both held and lit it. . . . And the ray was the Guardian angel of the mote: not a thing interposed between God and the creature, but God's attention itself, personalized. And I do not mean "personified," by a mere figure of speech according to tendencies of human language, but a real (finite) person. . . . It has occurred to me that . . . this is a finite parallel to the Infinite. As the love of the Father and Son (who are infinite and equal) is a Person, so the love and attention of the Light to the Mote is a person (that is both with us and in Heaven): finite but divine.

Immediately after he wrote to Christopher Tolkien, "I have with me now a definite awareness of you poised and shining in the Light—though your face (as all our faces) is turned from it."[134] At the time of the experience Tolkien was writing his essay "On Fairy Stories," which includes an important section about the Resurrection of Christ as "eucatastrophe."

Reflecting on this very same topic, Tolkien writes in a letter about another experience he had while riding a bicycle. He says that this appeared to him as one of the "sudden clarities which sometimes come in dreams (even anaesthetic-produced ones)." He finds the revelations to be true as a matter of fact, without remembering

---

[134] Carpenter, *Letters of J. R. R. Tolkien*, 99.

any argument that had led to this, though the sensation was the same as having been convinced by *reason* (if without reasoning). And I have since thought that one of the reasons why one can't recapture the wonderful argument or secret when one wakes up is simply because there was not one: but there was (often maybe) a direct appreciation by the mind (sc. reason) but without the chain of argument we know in our time-serial life.[135]

We have come to know the deeper Tolkien, the one of which Tolkien himself would only speak in veiled terms, or only to his most trusted friends. We will look now at the Tolkien who lived in some dimension of the world of Faery itself. Fantasy or the epic romance was for Tolkien an escape to higher dimensions of reality, escaping in order to return more fully to the reality of the senses. And in many ways he has given us traces of what his experiences in Faery looked like. This found a culmination in his *Smith of Wootton Major*, which points in part to the later Tolkien reflecting over his life.

# LIVING IN FAERY

Tolkien was at times deeply skeptical about the psychology of his times, and for good reasons. Many of his experiences felt completely real and could not be explained as some undigested psychic remnant of life experience. Flieger concludes that in relating to dreams Tolkien was "more psychic than psychological, and more medieval than either [Jung and Freud]."[136] And that he saw forces at play which, at least in many instances, are stronger than the dreamer's unconscious.

## Exploring Faery

Let us return to the drafts *The Notion Club Papers*, from which we will draw extensively. The first chapters build up towards adopting "dream" as the tool for time travel. Dream can occur both in "Other Time" and

---

[135] Carpenter, *Letters of J. R. R. Tolkien*, 101.
[136] Flieger, *Interrupted Music*, 176.

"Other Space." And by "dream" Tolkien is really referring to the most vivid dreams, and mostly to visions that occur in day consciousness. He compares those dream experiences to those of the writer who is a good visualizer, able to simultaneously see his immediate surroundings and the story that enters his field of consciousness. About these the character Ramer comments:

> You are really seeing both scenes, because you can recollect details later. Details of the waking scene not attended to, because you were *abstracted*, there's no doubt of that. I should as certainly add: details of the inner scene, blurred because you were to some extent *distracted*.[137]

By "abstracted" Tolkien means that we are taken away from the pressing world reality and immersed deeply into another one. And as for visualizing, Ramer also adds something that could apply to Tolkien: that what he visualizes is independent of the will or the planning mind. The scene "comes before the mind's eye, as we say, in a way that is very similar to opening closed eyes—on a complete waking view."[138] On such occasions the mind is split between two places of attention. As for the content of the images, it is almost impossible to alter them.

Although the mind can be in more than one place at one time, it chiefly goes where it directs its attention more keenly. Nevertheless, Ramer goes on to say that when he looks at something specific that he wrote, he can bring back to memory the environment in which it appeared to his mind's eye, such as the desk with the papers that were on it, even though this aspect of reality was secondary to the mind's focus at the moment of visual inspiration.

In ways that are relevant to his differences with psychoanalysis, the literary Tolkien differentiates the degrees of depth of dreams: "In some dreams there's no distraction at all, some are confused by distractions, some *are* just distractions."[139] Then to the question of whether one could

---

[137] Tolkien, *The Lost Road and Other Writings*, 176.
[138] Tolkien, *The Lost Road and Other Writings*, 177.
[139] Tolkien, *The Lost Road and Other Writings*, 186.

revisit his dreams, Tolkien has Ramer explaining that the mind could hardly go back at will to the same places or times as a spectator; when that happens the difference lies in the spectator being a later form of the individual, who is now anchored in a different time reality.

Where Tolkien gets supremely fascinating is in his whole understanding of mind and its spiritual activity. "Minds can be lazy on their own account. Even for the energetic ones sleep is largely a rest. But of course, for a mind rest is not oblivion, which is impossible for it." And then he characterizes what a mind that has acquired great focus on particular interests can achieve.

> If it has by nature, or has acquired, some dominant interest—like history, or languages, or mathematics—it may at times work away at such things, while the old body is recuperating. . . . I fancy that all waking art draws a good deal on this sort of activity. Those scenes that come up complete and fixed that I spoke of before, for instance; though some of them, I believe, are visions of real places.[140]

One could surmise here is Tolkien reflecting on Tolkien: "waking art . . . scenes that come up complete . . . visions of real places."

And Ramer points further than the dreams to a true spiritual realm: "But out of some place beyond the region of dreams, now and again there comes a blessedness, and it soaks through all the levels, and illumines all the scenes through which the mind passes out back into waking, and so it flows out into this life."[141] It's very interesting to hear about the nature of communication in such visions: "You don't talk, or don't need to: you get the meaning of minds (if you meet any) more directly."[142] Tolkien shows us that he understand the nature of the realm of Imagination—to which we will return in Chapter 6—that beings make us hear and see them

---

[140] Tolkien, *The Lost Road and Other Writings*, 189.

[141] Tolkien, *The Lost Road and Other Writings*, 195.

[142] Tolkien, *The Lost Road and Other Writings*, 200.

in some appropriate form, by producing a direct impression on the mind. The clothing of this naked impression in terms intelligible to your incarnate mind is, I imagine, often left to you, the receiver. Though no doubt they can cause you to hear words and to see shapes of their own choosing, if they will.[143]

Ramer explains how he trained himself to acquire a more vivid recollection, referring to examples of visual and nonvisual impressions by strengthening the "will to remember" and widening the field of remembrance. What the fictional Ramer offers us in the pages of a book can be completed by Christopher Tolkien's recollections about his father: "My father once described to me his dream of 'pure Weight,' but I do not remember when that was; probably before this time."[144] A similar experience is conveyed by Ramer, together with the examples of dreams about Speed or Fire (Elemental Fire, "a mode or condition of physical being") and Endlessness (or Length, applied to Time). The latter is expanded upon thus: "Time; unendurable length to mortal flesh. In that kind of dream you can know about the feeling of aeons of constricted waiting."[145] And in that realm Ramer expresses experiencing what it is not to have free will. All of this serves Ramer to conclude, "The waking mind is not confined to the memories of the body; it can use that as a platform to survey the surroundings from." All of the above seems to be connected with Tolkien's life experience. The reader may remember that in his early drawings Tolkien worked on similar abstract themes, witness his *Before* and *Afterwards*, *Wickedness* or *Thought*, *Undertenishness* and *Grownupishness* paintings.

From the above experiences Ramer says he turned to "dream-inspection," turning to big dreams like serial or repeating dreams, such dreams that transcend the waking mind, to the point of looking like pages taken out of a book. This is repeated differently: "My significant fragments were actually often pages out of stories, made up in quieter

---

[143] Tolkien, *The Lost Road and Other Writings*, 202.
[144] Tolkien, *The Lost Road and Other Writings*, 215.
[145] Tolkien, *The Lost Road and Other Writings*, 182.

dream-levels, and by some chance remembered. Occasionally they were bits of long visions of things not invented."[146]

If Tolkien draws the above from personal experience, much becomes understandable about the writing of *The Silmarillion*, in which Tolkien first received some imaginations, then others that connected with the previous ones; but the writing proceeded in random order, and much of it in reverse order. His first work took the form of the "Lay of Earendel." (Chapter XXIV of *The Silmarillion*) This was followed by "The Fall of Gondolin" (chapter XXIII).[147] The story links with that of Earendel because Earendel (later Eärendil) is the main hero who escapes from Gondolin. In 1917, lying in a hospital in Hull, Tolkien wrote the tale that grew into "The Children of Hurin" (Chapter XXI).[148] Later in time he started composing what eventually became the story of Beren and Lúthien/Tinúviel. (Chapter XIX).[149] As we can see the writing of *The Silmarillion*'s early chapters went in reverse order, simply because this was the order of Tolkien's inner experiences. And many of the visions were vividly captured in Tolkien's paintings.

Ramer talks about the experience of "falling wide asleep" (awake in the dream experience), which refers to what today could be called lucid dreams. He asserts that he can remember all the dreams that were part of certain sequences. "At least, I remember that I could remember them while I was still 'there,' better than I can 'here' remember a long sequence of events in waking life." The memory remained after waking up and did not disappear subsequently, though it was subdued over time. Over time Ramer acquires a long series of very vivid dreams that he can remember, dreams that are "wide and long and deep." Tolkien must be speaking candidly through Ramer of his mind and personal experience in the safe place of a book that he is not under pressure to publish.[150]

In his further explorations Ramer talks about "minds" visiting us in dreams, and warns that some of them could be malicious, and likewise that some dreams awaken a fear that goes well beyond the dream

---

[146] Tolkien, *The Lost Road and Other Writings*, 189.
[147] Carpenter, *Tolkien: A Biography*, 92.
[148] Carpenter, *Tolkien: A Biography*, 96.
[149] Carpenter, *Tolkien: A Biography*, 97.
[150] Tolkien, *Sauron Defeated*, 184.

situation. In the footnotes Tolkien distinguishes between *perceiving* as visiting real scenes and *apparitions* in which one is visited by "another mind." Then he further distinguishes *reading*, which is like the activity of going over records of someone else's experiences, or perceiving second hand. And finally he adds *lying*: "There's lying in the universe, some very clever lying. I mean some very potent fiction is specially composed to be inspected by others and to deceive, to pass as record; but it is made to the malefit [a word invented by Tolkien for the opposite of benefit] of Men."[151] This indicates that Tolkien not only dug deeply into the content of his dreams; he also carefully sifted through them. One cannot help but be awestruck by the depth of Tolkien's intent in studying the mind that can apprehend the spirit, and the depth of his personal experiences.

## About Entry into the Realm of Faery

*Smith of Wootton Major* is one of Tolkien's last works. In the story we can sense the grief at the loss of access to the enchanted realm, but it's a grief colored with acceptance. Smith is like Frodo: the one who visits Faery and then returns to normal daily occupations and passes on the staff to the new generation. He can return to his life inspired by what he has known and witnessed and bestow blessings upon his fellow human being.

Flieger sees in *Smith of Wootton Major* the writing through which Tolkien reflects on his own adventures in Faery as well as his later exile from it.[152] Tolkien wrote an unpublished commentary on the story in which he said "A time comes for writers and artists, when invention and vision cease and they can only reflect on what they have seen and learned," adding further that "that is not the whole point of the tale. Which includes sacrifice, and the handing on, with trust and without

---

[151] Tolkien, *The Lost Road and Other Writings*, 196.

[152] Tolkien wrote in effect, "a time comes for writers and artists, when invention and vision cease and they can only reflect in what they have seen and learned," (adding further that "that is not the whole point of the tale. Which includes sacrifice, and the handing on, with trust and without keeping a hand on things, of power and vision to the next generation"). From an unpublished essay quoted in Flieger, *Interrupted Music*, 236.

keeping a hand on things, of power and vision to the next generation."[153] What is of added interest is that the author (in the story, Smith) is led into the other world of Faery by one who knows its ways: Prentice, who is also Alf and the king of Faery. He is the one who can enter at will and knows its ways in and out. Alf was brought in by "first Cook," of whom mention is given only at the beginning of the story. At the end of the story Alf tells Smith that the first Cook is his own grandfather, and a great "traveler between worlds."

In *Smith of Wootton Major*, more than everywhere else, Tolkien had come to a new view of Faery as a two-way-street, at least to some extent; a reality that influences our sense world, as much as a place towards which we can travel. In the unpublished essay Tolkien asserts that the story illustrates Faery's relationship to Wootton as much as Wootton's relationship to Faery.

Faery is seen as a world that is essential to the health and well-being of our own world. However, it is also perilous.[154] In the unpublished essay, Tolkien distils his views about Faery thus:

> Faery represents at its weakest a breaking out (at least in mind) from the iron ring of the familiar, still more from the adamantine ring of belief that is known, possessed, controlled, and so (ultimately) all that is worth being considered—a constant awareness of the world beyond these rings. More strongly it represents love. . . . This Faery is as necessary for the health and complete functioning of the Human as sunlight for physical life.[155]

One can surmise that he felt this was also the case for Tolkien's health and "functioning."

---

[153] Unpublished fol. 36r. in Flieger, *Green Suns and Faërie*, 236.

[154] In *The Lost Road* Alboin is given the possibility to go back to his dream experiences. He hears about the conditions for going back thus: "The roads and the halts are prescribed. That you cannot return at your wish, but only (if at all) as it may be ordained. For you shall not be as one reading a book of looking in a mirror, but as one walking in living peril" (48–49).

[155] Flieger, *Green Suns and Faërie*, 247.

In his unpublished essay Tolkien wanted to present "the spatial and temporal relationship of Wootton and Faery."[156] He hypothesized that Faery and our world occupy time and space differently or are present in them in different ways; that Smith's short evening absence from our world accounts for much more time spent in Faery, and a week away from home would account for the equivalent of months and years in Faery.[157]

Finally, in relation to the communication between the two worlds, Tolkien offers that

> the Elven Folk, the chief and ruling inhabitants of Faery, have an ultimate kinship with Men and have permanent love for them in general. . . They do from time to time assist them, avert evil from them and have relationships with them, especially through certain men and women whom they find suitable.[158]

Let's review what has been brought forward so far. We have looked at Tolkien's inner experiences, especially from his letters and two of his unfinished and unpublished books. Tolkien had such a thorough relationship with language that it blossomed in many directions. It led him to the creation of fictitious languages of literary and artistic value, as well as towards the study of ancient Northern European languages. This led to a complete immersion in the reality of language and the word itself, which led Simonne d'Ardenne asking him, "You broke the veil, didn't you, and passed through?" I have called this faculty of Tolkien "living in the word."

Tolkien had some spiritual experiences, chief among which was his memory of Atlantis, which has all the hallmarks of a previous-life experience, as they have become more commonly known in recent decades. And other experiences led him to place value on what emerged from visions and dreams, though only those dreams that could be called big dreams or visions, which most of us could simply yearn for or count

[156] Flieger, *Green Suns and Faërie*, 248.
[157] Flieger, *Green Suns and Faërie*, 249.
[158] Flieger, *Green Suns and Faërie*, 252.

on less than the fingers of one hand in a lifetime. I have called this experience "living in the dream."

Different from the above, though related to them, is the source of much of Tolkien's writings, of his artistic inspiration. Images flooded his inner vision, and he strove to bring clarity to what seemed to come from other times and places. His unfinished *The Silmarillion* is an example of the power of these images, and his never-ending effort to imbue with meaning and clarity what first often came as a given. I have called this faculty "living in Faery."

Tolkien was himself an "Elf-friend," one of the agents whom Faery found suitable—much to his own surprise and in spite of the limitations he would have been the first one to acknowledge. In *The Lord of the Rings* such agents are characters like Gandalf and Aragorn, but also the much more humble, Tolkien-like Frodo. It seems Tolkien had much first-hand knowledge of what he was talking about.

# PART II

# THE LORD OF THE RINGS

# CHAPTER 4

# INTRODUCTION TO
# *THE LORD OF THE RINGS*

---

> I have drained the rich cup and satisfied a long thirst.
> Once it really gets under weigh the steady upward slope of
> grandeur and terror (not unrelieved by green dells, without
> which it would indeed be intolerable) is almost unequalled
> in the whole range of narrative art known to me.
> —C. S. Lewis

Because the success of Tolkien's work lies in the very many "clever" layers in the plot interweaving a multitude of themes, his work can be seen from many different angles, and this requires approaching in steps. The first step will consist in looking at how the work came about, the various stages of its development; then we should look at the first most general connection between the parts of the book. Many gems of the books lie embedded in the interlace motif we have touched on in Chapter 1. Pointing to some of the interconnections between the various parts of the trilogy in this introduction will allow us to more easily acquire an eagle-eye's view of the whole before approaching the details in the next chapters. We will also explore what Tolkien himself said about *The Lord of the Rings* in relation to the rest of his work. In the next chapters we will enter more deeply into the substance of the book and the depth of the images it builds.

When we look at Tolkien's themes we can see some objective/ archetypal truths known in spiritual traditions the world over, which explains the book's hold over the modern mind. Tolkien approached these truths simply with an inner, deeply artistic knowing, not from any esoteric insight. In fact his Catholicism was a safeguard against any of these interests—witness his hesitation in admitting the possibility of reincarnation, even to himself. His is nevertheless a higher understanding of mythology and of the forces at work in prehistory and history rising from within his soul, as we will see in the next chapters.

## THE WRITING OF *THE LORD OF THE RINGS*

It took twelve years to write *The Lord of the Rings*, 1937 to 1949. And the book was only published five years after its completion due to many revisions and the need for appendices that explained what was contained in embryo in *The Silmarillion*, which was only published posthumously.

The book itself began as a request from the publisher for a sequel to *The Hobbit*. Tolkien at first found it hard to give Bilbo further adventures after he had retired for a happy life in *The Hobbit*. And he struggled to find a way to connect to some of the themes of the book. Finally, he opted for the Ring as the link. In his notes appear these lines: "The Ring: whence its origin? Necromancer? Not very dangerous, when used for good purpose. But it exacts its penalty. You must either lose it or *yourself*."[159]

An important connection between the two works is found in the figure of the Necromancer, of which Tolkien comments:

> I had no conscious notion of what the Necromancer stood for (except ever-recurrent evil) in *The Hobbit*, nor of his connection with the Ring. But if you wanted to go from the end of *The Hobbit* I think the ring would be your inevitable choice as the link. If then you wanted a large tale, the Ring would at once acquire a capital letter; and the Dark Lord would immediately appear. As he did unasked, on the hearth at Bag End as soon as I came to that point. So the essential Quest started at once.[160]

---

[159] Carpenter, *Tolkien: A Biography*, 187.
[160] Carpenter, *Letters of J. R. R. Tolkien*, 216.

This was the beginning of the twelve-year journey of an epic book written by a busy Oxford don and father of four. It took that long partly because Tolkien could not get to the book as much as he wanted. But it also took twelve years for the inner maturation needed to overcome what proved to be important blockages in artistic inspiration. Tolkien's understanding of the subject matter itself needed to grow, as is revealed by many of his letters. Humphrey Carpenter himself, having sifted all of Tolkien's letters and documents and interviewed the man, doesn't see any of the blockages as "ascribable to any specific external cause."[161]

We will review now the genesis of the book, with an eye to the artistic process, particularly the flashes of inspiration and the phases of blockage. Most of the comments come from Tolkien's letters; a few exceptions are Carpenter's notes from the biography.

Tolkien announced the completion of chapter 1, "A Long Expected Party," to Furth, Allen, and Unwin on December 19, 1937. In February 1938 he commented to Stanley Unwin, "I find it too easy to write opening chapters—and for the moment the story is not unfolding."[162]

Only a month later Tolkien had written three chapters, and already he experienced a surprise along the creative path: the arrival of the sinister Black Riders. Carpenter calls this "the first of several unpremeditated turns that the story was to take."[163] The future *The Lord of the Rings* was intended as a sequel to *The Hobbit*. But Tolkien was much keener on linking it to *The Silmarillion* and therefore on publishing the two books together. He felt that Bilbo had been dragged into the mythology of *The Silmarillion* much against Tolkien's will.

By August 1938 he announced that he had resumed working on the "sequel" and had now reached chapter 8 and that the book "progresses towards quite unforeseen goals. I must say I think it is a good deal better in places and some ways than the predecessor."[164] The next surprise in the narrative was the appearance of Strider in the inn at Bree.[165] In relation to the same event Tolkien also wrote very significantly: "Most

[161] Carpenter, *Tolkien: A Biography*, 194.
[162] Carpenter, *Letters of J. R. R. Tolkien*, 29.
[163] Carpenter, *Letters of J. R. R. Tolkien*, 187.
[164] Carpenter, *Letters of J. R. R. Tolkien, Letters of J. R. R. Tolkien*, 40.
[165] Carpenter, *Letters of J. R. R. Tolkien*, 188.

disquieting of all, Saruman had never been revealed to me, and I was as mystified as Frodo at Gandalf's failure to appear on September 22."[166] At the time he still didn't know why the Ring would be so central to the story. Then he hit upon the ideas of the "Ruling Ring" and its disappearance.[167] Although the general idea of the book was present in Tolkien's mind soon after writing chapter 2, the various drafts he wrote "were seldom of much use: the story unfolded itself as it were."[168]

By August 1938 Tolkien had realized that the story would not address the originally targeted audience, that it would not be a typical children's story. Two months later he took advantage of a doctor-recommended break to reach chapter 11, and he felt newly inspired. He repeated that the story was seemingly unrolling out of itself, but becoming even more terrifying than *The Hobbit*, therefore not really a children's theme. And very tellingly he added, "The darkness of the present days [signs leading to World War II] has had some effect on it. Though it is not an 'allegory.'"[169]

By February 1939, he essentially restated the above and playfully blamed the turn the story was taking on the readers who wanted to know more about the Necromancer. He also realized that the writing would be more laborious than *The Hobbit*, and that the story would acquire greater depth and meaning. At the time he optimistically believed he could finish it by June 1939.[170] However, by late 1940 Tolkien experienced almost a year blockage at the time when the fellowship discovered Balin's tomb in Moria.[171]

---

[166] Carpenter, *Letters of J. R. R. Tolkien*, 217.

[167] Carpenter, *Letters of J. R. R. Tolkien*, 188.

[168] Carpenter, *Letters of J. R. R. Tolkien*, 258.

[169] Carpenter, *Letters of J. R. R. Tolkien*, 40–41. How present reality and tale mix up is indicated in this comment in the foreword of *The Lord of the Rings*: "The crucial chapter, 'The Shadow of the Past,' is one of the oldest parts of the tale. It was written long before the foreshadow of 1939 had yet become a threat of inevitable disaster, and from that point the story would have developed along essentially the same lines, if that disaster had been averted." (Tolkien, *The Fellowship of the Ring*, xiv).

[170] Carpenter, *Letters of J. R. R. Tolkien*, 42.

[171] Carpenter, *Tolkien: A Biography*, 194.

By December 1942 Tolkien announced again that the sequel was nearing completion, and he was hoping to finish it by early 1943. He had reached chapter 31, "Flotsam and Jetsam," and had another six chapters sketched out. Tolkien explained he was "longest held up—by exterior circumstances as well as interior ones—at the point now represented by the last words of Book III," which refers to the chapter "The Palantír." Interestingly he added, "I knew nothing of the *Palantiri*, though the moment the Orthanc-stone was cast from the window, I recognized it and knew the meaning of the 'rhyme of lore' that had been running in my mind: *seven stars and seven stones and one white tree*. These rhymes and names will crop up; but they not always explain themselves."[172] This is another instance, as in the two lines about Earendel in the *Crist*, in which Tolkien is first inspired by some sentence and then finds meaning in it, and is able to write a story about it.

In another letter Tolkien returned to the same place, explaining that "[The Voice of Saruman] was growing out of hand, and revealing endless new vistas—and I wanted to finish it, but the world was threatening. And I was *dead stuck*, somewhere about Ch. 10 [The Voice of Saruman] in Book III." He added that most of the fragments ahead of it proved wrong, especially those in relation to Mordor.[173]

By early 1944 Carpenter points out that the book had lain untouched for many months. Tolkien probably resumed it in April.[174] Interestingly, he wrote the drafts of *The Notion Club Papers* between October 1944 and the summer of 1946, after he had finished Book IV (see the Book Overview section below for more on the book numbering). He presented it to his publisher as an improvement of his *The Lost Road*.[175] He had interrupted his work because of needing to correct the chronology of Frodo's and Sam's travels on one hand, and of the other two Hobbits on the other, respectively east and west of the great river Anduin.

---

[172] Carpenter, *Letters of J. R. R. Tolkien*, 217.
[173] Carpenter, *Letters of J. R. R. Tolkien*, 321.
[174] Carpenter, *Letters of J. R. R. Tolkien*, 196, 199.
[175] Flieger, *A Question of Time*, 119.

It is curious to note how, soon after Tolkien gave it up, an important element of his Númenor/Atlantis attempt of *The Notion Club Papers* entered *The Lord of the Rings* via literary inspiration. We hear in effect that

> a new character has come on the scene (I am sure I did not invent him, I did not even want him, though I like him, but there he came walking into the woods of Ithilien): Faramir, the brother of Boromir—and he is holding up the "catastrophe" by a lot of stuff about the history of Gondor and Rohan . . . but if he goes on much more a lot of him will have to be removed to the appendices.[176]

It is through Faramir that echoes of the Númenorean history and Flood are introduced in the narrative of *The Lord of the Rings*. Elsewhere Tolkien points out that of all his characters he felt the greatest kinship to Faramir. Thus, Tolkien managed to include his Great Wave dream—and the Atlantean history associated with it—as part and parcel of *The Lord of the Rings* and thus had less of a need for *The Notion Club Papers* as a separate project. In *The Lord of the Rings* different characters make reference here and there to the history of Númenor/Atlantis, including the great catastrophe of its demise. At the end of the Third Age, Sam connects the present events with the memories of the destruction of Númenor.

In the same vein as the Faramir surprise, concerning the development of the book in May 1944 it is fascinating to note Tolkien's surprise that "Gollum continues to develop into a most intriguing character."[177] This is an example of another artistic inspiration that grew and grew. Soon after however, the muse ceased to inspire. Tolkien wrote, "I am absolutely dry of any inspiration for the Ring and am back where I was in the Spring, with all the inertia to overcome again."[178]

In a letter of November 29, 1944, Tolkien announced he had sent the last two chapters and gotten to the end of Book IV and puzzled, "I

---

[176] Flieger, *A Question of Time*, 79.
[177] Flieger, *A Question of Time*, 81.
[178] Flieger, *A Question of Time*, 91.

have got the hero into such a fix that not even an author will be able to extricate him without labour or difficulty."[179] Always in connection to "The Hobbit sequel," Tolkien admits to Stanley Unwin in another letter that his effort to bring the book to a close failed.[180] Even by summer of 1946 Carpenter assesses that "he had scarcely touched it since the late spring of 1944."[181] And in July 1946 Tolkien stated to the publisher that he had made a great effort to finish the "Hobbit sequel" but failed, and ironically added "I shall now have to study my own work in order to get back to it."[182]

In April 1948 Tolkien mentioned that he was experiencing the "difficulty of writing the last chapters."[183] It was only by October of that year that in a letter to Hugh Brogan he announced the narrative had reached its ending.[184] All things told, revisions, appendices, and commentaries would still keep Tolkien and the publisher occupied until 1954.

## BOOK OVERVIEW AND POINTERS

In the following summary of the books, we will point here and there to the interlace motifs of parallels and repetitions, or echoes and anticipations that appear within one of the six original books and between books. For this we will partly refer to the excellent work of Richard C. West and Randel Helms concerning the structure of *The Lord of the Rings*.[185] In addition—based on Randel Helms' work—we will point to the proverbs through which often in the books one or the other of Tolkien's characters epitomizes the lessons learned.

---

[179] Flieger, *A Question of Time*, 103.

[180] Carpenter, *Letters of J. R. R. Tolkien*, 114.

[181] Carpenter, *Tolkien: A Biography*, 201.

[182] Carpenter, *Letters of J. R. R. Tolkien*, 118.

[183] Carpenter, *Letters of J. R. R. Tolkien*, 129.

[184] Carpenter, *Letters of J. R. R. Tolkien*, 131.

[185] See West, "The Interlace Structure of *The Lord of the Rings*" and Helms, *Tolkien's World*, chapter 5: "Tolkien's World: The Structure and Aesthetics of *The Lord of the Rings*."

Tolkien would have liked to publish the whole of his work in one single volume because he perceived it as an indissoluble unity, though this was clearly impossible in modern publishing practice. It is not the modern division in three books that is important in *The Lord of the Rings*, but Tolkien's original division in six books, the equivalent of parts. The original book titles were: Book I: The First Journey; Book II: The Journey of the Nine Companions; Book III: The Treason of Isengard; Book IV: The Journey of the Ring-Bearers; Book V: The War of the Ring; Book VI: The End of the Third Age. Books I and II were published as *The Fellowship of the Ring*; Books III and IV form *The Two Towers*, and V and VI are *The Return of the King*.

## Book I: The First Journey

To understand the trilogy we need to refer to the being called Sauron who was the original owner of the Ring, which through magic powers binds the three rings of the Elves, nine rings of Men, and seven rings of the Dwarves. Sauron desires to repossess it in order to enslave to his will all living beings in Middle-earth.

In *The Hobbit* Bilbo Baggins, a Hobbit, accidentally finds the coveted Ring in a dark cave. While he is trying to escape from the one called Gollum, who initially owned the Ring and then lost it, Bilbo discovers that the Ring has the power to render him invisible. He retains the Ring after the end of his adventures in *The Hobbit*, but does not become aware of the origin of the Ring nor of its greater powers.

At the beginning of Book I of *The Fellowship of the Ring* Bilbo is holding a very large party for his 111th birthday at his home in the Shire. The wizard Gandalf the Grey has become aware of the powers of the Ring and wants Bilbo to pass it on to Frodo, knowing that the infamous Ring can cause much havoc. He manages to overcome Bilbo's resistance, and indicates to Frodo that the Ring must be removed from the Shire, where it will attract the attention of Sauron and his nine Ringwraiths who have taken the form of fearful Black Riders.

Frodo leaves the Shire after being joined in his quest by three Hobbit friends—Sam, Merry, and Pippin. They soon find themselves pursued by the Ringwraiths. They are at first providentially rescued by a party of Elves, led by Gildor, who have wandered far off their beaten tracks and who promise to invite further help as the Hobbits move along. Once out of the Shire the Hobbits have to face the dangers of the Old Forest and are ensnared by Old Man Willow who swallows up Merry and Pippin, while Frodo and Sam can only withstand his power for little longer. They are rescued by the enigmatic Tom Bombadil, the oldest being of Middle-earth, who has power over this strange land. Out of the forest the companions spend some time in the house of Tom Bombadil and his companion, Goldberry. Here they receive a first level of instruction and are sent on their way to the Barrow-downs. In this second realm of Tom Bombadil they are made captive in a barrow by a Wight, a sort of evil ghost. Once again it is Bombadil who rescues them.

The Hobbits arrive at the first town out of the Shire, Bree, where Men mingle with Hobbits. The four are still quite naïve and unaware of the dangers that lurk over them. First Pippin, telling stories of Bilbo, and then Frodo, unable to resist the pull to wear the Ring, call attention to themselves. They would be easy prey for the Black Riders were it not for the providential presence and help of the one called Strider, a Ranger. Strider, later known as Aragorn, is a heir to the kings of Westernesse (Númenor), who have ruled over the kingdoms of Arnor to the north and Gondor to the south. As a Ranger, Aragorn roams Middle-earth to protect its inhabitants from the emissaries of Sauron and Saruman.

Aragorn, who has witnessed the Ring accident, advises the Hobbits to change rooms at the inn in Bree, and in so doing saves their lives from the Ringwraiths. Providentially the innkeeper enters in their trust and delivers them a letter from Gandalf advising them to take refuge in Rivendell, an Elf enclave. The company sets off early the next day in the direction of Weathertop hill. Five of the Ringwraiths have found their tracks and attack them in the night. The other four have been distracted in the pursuit of Gandalf, who was delayed in his arrival after having been made captive by Saruman. The part of the events relating to Gandalf, however, will only be revealed later. Frodo, who has worn the Ring during the attack, is wounded by a magic weapon crafted by a servant of Sauron, and is now in critical condition. He needs Strider's healing skills and the aid of his companions to carry him along the way to Rivendell.

Near their destination the Hobbits are met by the Elf-lord Glorfindel, who has been seeking them. At the critical moment of entering the safe haven, Frodo, riding Glorfindel's horse, is pursued by the now full company of the nine Ringwraiths. He crosses the Ford of Bruinen pursued by the Black Riders. Here the Elf-magic of Elrond, Lord of Rivendell, comes to the rescue of the company by causing the swelling waters of the river to engulf the riders.

By the end of Book I Frodo and his friends have been saved many times by providential helpers. But Frodo has been steeled and has developed the courage needed of a quest-bearer, fulfilling Gildor's prophetic words to him, "Courage is found in unlikely places." Gandalf reinstates this idea later: "Fortune or fate have helped you, . . . not to mention courage." And Elrond will tell him, "There is nothing that you can do, other than to resist, with hope or without it," announcing the trials of Book II.

## Book II: The Journey of the Nine Companions

Like Book I, Book II begins with festivities, this time in Rivendell in honor of the arrival of the Hobbits and the others who want to join the quest. Frodo has time to recover, and his healing is furthered by Elrond's skills. A council is held in which more information comes to light about the Ring and decisions are taken about how to rid Middle-earth of it. Frodo accepts the responsibility of taking the Ring to the Cracks of Doom, part of the Orodruin mountain, deep into Sauron's stronghold of Mordor, and throw the Ring into the melting lava of the volcano. The Ring would thus return whence it was first forged. The discussions at the council form a parallel to chapter 2 of Book I: The Shadow of the Past. They continue the instructions about the lore of the Ring.

Frodo heard from Gandalf in Book I that he was meant for the task of the Ring. Now Elrond announces that "this task is appointed for Frodo." In chapter 3 of Book I the three Hobbits are chosen. Now in Book II, chapter 3, the other companions are added to the Hobbits: Gandalf the wizard, Aragorn the Númenorean (Westernesse) heir, Legolas the Elf, Gimli the Dwarf, and the human Boromir. All the people of Middle-earth are thus represented.

The company travels south with the aim of crossing the Misty Mountains. It first attempts to do so through the pass of Caradhras, where they are repelled by an unseasonal snow blizzard. The only way left is through the much more dangerous old Dwarf Mines of Moria. The company is attacked and saved by Gandalf's confrontation with the Balrog demon. At the last moment the beast drags the wizard down into the chasm of Khazad-dûm. In the events of Moria, Frodo is attacked by an Orc chieftain, receives a blow on the right side, and is saved by the *mithril* (an alloy both harder and lighter than tempered steel) mail shirt that Bilbo gifted him. A little later an arrow hits Frodo and springs back on the *mithril* shirt. Aragorn helps his healing through his knowledge of herbs. The survivors hold Gandalf for dead. But this is only the end of Gandalf the Grey. Note in passing that Caradhras echoes the ordeal of the Old Man Willow; the ordeals of Moria those of the Barrow Wight in Book I.

The company now finds its way into another, even more powerful Elven stronghold of Lórien, the forest of the Galadhrim Elves. The nine are received by Lady Galadriel, who will play a great role in the rest of the quest. She submits Frodo and Sam to the test of her mirror, which will give them images of past and future that they will only be able to integrate when the time of their need comes. She also offers presents to each, every one of which will play an important role in the quest: chief among these the phial with the light that had been originally part of the Silmarils; *lembas*, the waybread of the Elves; and finely woven cloaks that will disguise and conceal the members of the fellowship. Galadriel knows about the power of the Ring, and has to overcome the temptation to wield it for her own benefit in the meeting with Frodo, who would willingly give it to her.

Galadriel offers the company special Elven boats to take them down the Great River, Anduin, deep into enemy territory. At this point some of the company become aware of being followed by Gollum, determined to repossess the Ring he once owned. Arriving at the Falls of Rauros the company is partly split on whether to proceed east towards Mordor, or head west to Gondor to lend help to the besieged city of Minas Tirith. Frodo, in great distress, makes his way to the top of the mountain to the seat of Amon Hen from where he can survey the lands all around.

He once again slips on the Ring and manages to save himself at the last moment from the roaming Eye of Sauron who senses the presence of the Ring. This is a parallel episode to the wearing of the Ring at Weathertop.

Boromir of Gondor has succumbed to the pull of the Ring, naively believing he can use it for the good of his own city, Minas Tirith, and its realm of Gondor. He confronts Frodo who has just become aware of the strength of the Ring, and who now knows that he alone can carry it to Mordor. Frodo averts the threat of Boromir and determines to set out alone for Mordor without putting anybody else in peril. He uses the Ring once more to leave the scene unseen. Fortunately for him and for the quest, the devoted Sam manages to catch up with him before he embarks down the river. The two search for a way to reach Mordor.

Frodo has been stripped of his fears and complacencies in Book I. He is now also stripped of all external help in Book II, especially considering that he believes Gandalf dead. He is now assuming the final responsibility for the fate of the Ring in accordance to Elrond's edict at the council.

## Book III: The Treason of Isengard

The book chronicles the adventures of the Hobbits' minor pair. Frodo and Sam left the fellowship just before part of it is overrun by a large party of Orcs. Merry and Pippin at first resist the onslaught of the Orcs, thanks in great part to Boromir's valiant defense, who dies in the attempt. They are then captured by a party of Orcs, entrusted with the order of bringing them back alive to Saruman, who knows about the Ring and covets it. The Orcs are proceeding at great speed, pursued by the rest of the fellowship—Aragorn, Legolas, and Gimli—through the plains of Rohan. As they are getting closer to the Orc party, the three meet with the Rohirrim of Rohan, led by Éomer.

Merry and Pippin are the object of conflicting interests on the part of the Orcs. A band of them—the Uruk-hai, subject to Saruman—attempt to kidnap them. Merry and Pippin manage to escape before the Rohirrim encircle and destroy the Orcs. They find refuge in the forest of Fangorn and after some wandering meet with its guardian spirit, the Ent Treebeard, (also known as Fangorn) who takes them under his wing and introduces them to an Entmoot (Ent assembly). Having listened to the Hobbits, the anger of Treebeard is roused against Saruman, who has been cruel to the beings of the forest. He manages to stir the fellow Ents and convince them to engage in war against the wizard.

Aragorn, Legolas, and Gimli attempt to find the Hobbits but are first waylaid by the disguised Saruman, who lets their horses loose. Soon after the pursuers meet with a figure of great power, all dressed in white. They do not immediately recognize Gandalf, reborn as Gandalf the White after his ordeals with the Balrog, which have led him through death itself. Helped by the Ents Merry and Pippin rejoin Aragorn, Legolas, Gimli, and Gandalf. The fellowship with the Rohirrim of Éomer go to Edoras, the golden hall of king Théoden. In a dramatic confrontation with the wicked counselor Gríma, called Wormtongue, Gandalf shows his new powers and unmasks the counselor as a spy of Saruman. This helps bring healing to the king, who had lost all will under the spell of Saruman. It brings him close again to Éomer, whom Wormtongue had estranged from the king. In Edoras Merry feels impelled to declare fealty to king Théoden.

Théoden has been roused just in time to rally his forces to stand against the onslaught of the Orcs and allies of Saruman at the fortress of Helm's Deep. The Rohirrim manage to stand against the formidable forces of Saruman thanks in great part to Théoden and Aragorn, to the return of Gandalf bringing fresh new forces, and to the unexpected help of the Huorns—beings similar to the Ents—who destroy all the Orcs that try to escape.

Gandalf now leads the fellowship and the Rohirrim in pursuit of Saruman's stronghold of Isengard. They are surprised to find the fortress already laid waste by the fury of the roused Ents. Saruman, now joined by Wormtongue, is entrenched in the impregnable tower of Orthanc. Gandalf feels impelled, though with little hope, to reach the best in Saruman's soul and remind him that they once were allies. He fails in the attempt but gains a precious object, the *palantír*, which Wormtongue hurls down from the tower in hope of killing Gandalf. The *palantír* is one of seven seeing-stones that the kings and rulers of old used to see at a distance and connect with each other.

The curious Pippin cannot refrain himself from looking into the *palantír* when the others are sleeping. He narrowly escapes the influence of Sauron, but in the act prevents Gandalf from unmasking himself and allows the wizard insight into how Sauron and Saruman operated and communicated.

Book III chronicles two victories: the first at Helm's Deep, the second at Isengard. Both of these follow upon, and are aided by, Saruman's attempted capture of the Hobbits. Two proverbs seem to sum up the adventures of the two Hobbits: Gandalf's "Often does hatred hurt itself" and Théoden's "Oft evil will shall evil mar." Gandalf offers the example of how the Hobbits could not have reached Fangorn and roused the Ents, were it not for the plans of Saruman and the unwitting help of the Orcs. In addition to the two victories, there are two awakenings: Merry and Pippin help to awaken Treebeard; Gandalf awakens Théoden. Further wisdom is shared by Éomer who, saved by Gimli whom he first opposed, utters "Oft the unbidden guest proves the best company." Gimli, the unbidden Dwarf, saves Éomer; the unexpected Huorns are critical in the victory at Helm's Deep; Wormtongue wanting to kill Gandalf delivers the *palantír* to him.

## Book IV: The Journey of the Ring-Bearers

Book IV is concerned with the Hobbit major pair. Frodo and Sam, separated from the rest of the fellowship, now need to do the impossible: find their way into the enemy's stronghold in Mordor. For a while they are lost in the mountains of Emyn Muil. Frodo reasons, "It's my doom to go to that Shadow yonder, [marshes] so that a way will be found. But will good or evil show it to me?'"[186]

Frodo and Sam are aware of being followed by Gollum. They manage to capture him and Frodo realizes that he is their only salvation. The two form a precarious alliance with Gollum, who knows his way through the marshes and into Mordor, though it is clear that it is lust for the Ring that guides him. Through his keen sight Gollum can help the company travel under the cover of night, and help Frodo overcome

---

[186] *The Two Towers*, 590.

the spell of the ghosts of the slain warriors haunting the waters of the Dead Marshes.

The group reaches the Black Gate that bar entrance to Mordor, and realize that massive forces will prevent their entrance into Sauron's realm. On the way to the gate the three have seen a Nazgûl, one of the reborn Ringwraiths now carried on large, winged Fell Beasts that spread terror under them. The two Hobbits decide to trust once more Gollum, who is aware of a little-known and little-guarded access to Mordor from the south.

On the way to the secret path to Mordor the party is intercepted in Ithilien by the men of Gondor under the leadership of Faramir, Boromir's brother. This is a providential move, saving the party from armies coming from the south. Faramir is at first suspicious of the Hobbits, wondering what part they played in his brother's death. He finally understands that Boromir was unable to resist the spell of the Ring that brought him to his death. He decides to support the Hobbits. As for Gollum, whom the men discover only later, he narrowly escapes death through Faramir's men, and is rescued by the pleading Frodo who knows he still needs Gollum's help.

The apparent detour of the Gondorian captivity plays a key role in informing Gandalf, through Faramir, that Frodo and Sam are alive and marching to their goal. Gollum takes the Hobbits up the mountain path that leads to the fortress of Cirith Ungol. He secretly intends to have Frodo killed by the giant evil spider Shelob, who guards access to the pass and the fortress. Sam and Frodo resist the spider partly through the help of Galadriel's phial. Sam causes the spider great harm, but Frodo is paralyzed by the spider's sting. Sam mistakenly believes him dead, while he's only asleep under the effect of the spider's poison. While Sam, debating on what to do, escapes from the onrushing Orcs, Frodo is captured and brought to the tower of Cirith Ungol. Sam has retained the Ring and now uses its power to follow the Orcs, realizing through them that Frodo is alive. Frodo is now more alone than ever.

In Book III Merry and Pippin manage to travel through Rohan at top speed thanks to the Orcs. In Book IV Frodo and Sam arrive close to Mordor thanks to Gollum's help. As the two lost their way in the Old Forest so now they are lost in the Emyn Muil. And as they were haunted in the Barrow-downs, now they are haunted in the Dead Marshes. The four Hobbits manage what seems impossible thanks to the help of enemy forces. In Books III and IV both pairs of Hobbits encounter enemies in "forbidden territories": Merry and Pippin in Fangorn; Sam and Frodo in Ithilien. They meet two key figures: Treebeard in Fangorn; Faramir in Ithilien. Each pair of Hobbits works at the destruction of one tower; Merry and Pippin the tower of Orthanc, Sam and Frodo that of Barad-dûr, the fortress of Sauron. A key proverb is uttered by Frodo to Gollum: "You must help us, if you can. One good turn deserves another."

## Book V: The War of the Ring

Just like Book III, this book is concerned once more with the Hobbit minor pair. In Edoras Merry declares fealty to Théoden. Pippin and Gandalf ride towards Minas Tirith. Gandalf hopes to be able to arouse Gondor's steward Denethor, but he is clearly unsuccessful, partly because Denethor has become delusional. Pippin, in a gesture parallel to Merry, offers his services to Denethor in great part as a sign of gratitude for his son Boromir, who saved his life.

Sauron is launching his attack and preceding it with the cover of his own created darkness that plunges the land and its people into discouragement and despair. Meanwhile Aragorn, pressed to come to the help of Minas Tirith, realizes he has only one way to get there in time—through the dreaded underground Paths of the Dead that none have taken before him. With him go Legolas and Gimli. The company following him is tested by the dead, but Aragorn shows true leadership and enlists them to his own help, fulfilling an age-old prophecy. Accompanied by the dead he emerges south of Minas Tirith because he knows he has to address another pressing situation first.

In the besieged city the proud Denethor sends his son Faramir to hold an impossible position in the nearby city of Osgiliath. Faramir complies but soon has to retreat to Minas Tirith, and there take refuge badly wounded by a poisoned arrow of a Nazgûl.

Just when Minas Tirith is about to be overwhelmed by the armies of Mordor, the Riders of Rohan come to the city's rescue. Théoden is challenged by the Lord of the Nazgûl, the Witch-King of Angmar also called the Black Captain, and is wounded to death. The disguised

Éowyn, who has been riding disguised as a man, challenges the Black Captain and is wounded by him. So is Merry, who summons all his courage to come to her defense; in so doing they manage to defeat the Nazgûl. Meanwhile Aragorn, with his army of the dead, has defeated the Corsairs of Umbar, who threatened the city from the south. He arrives just in time to offer critical help to Minas Tirith before the enemy forces can regroup.

Denethor in his delusion decides to seek death for himself and his son by laying Faramir on a pyre. He is prevented from doing so by Pippin, who calls on Gandalf's help. Denethor goes to his death, but Faramir is rescued. Aragorn comes under cover in the town and offers his skills in healing for the good of Éowyn, Faramir, and Merry. People recognize in him the one that the prophecy foretold as both a king and a healer, and future king of Gondor.

Gandalf knows that no victory, however significant, will stop Sauron until the Ring is destroyed. He plans a great wager. To distract Sauron from what Frodo and Sam are attempting, he leads a force of six thousand to take by storm the Black Gate, something clearly impossible. In so doing he wants Sauron to believe that one of the company is in possession of the Ring and is blinded by its power. At the gate Sauron's lieutenant wants to destroy Gandalf's hope and undermine the whole effort by showing them Sam's sword, a grey cloak, an Elven brooch, and the *mithril* mail shirt worn by Frodo, leading him to believe that the two have died. Though stricken, Gandalf stands his ground and challenges Sauron's great armies.

It is interesting to note that in Book V Merry becomes Théoden's knight, and Pippin the knight of Denethor. They each find an affinity with the ruler they want to serve. Merry saves Théoden's daughter; Pippin saves Denethor's son from his father. Éowyn will end up marrying Faramir and strengthening the bonds between Gondor and Rohan. Gandalf sums the lessons with a fitting expression "Generous deed should not be checked by cold counsel." Merry was not even supposed to take part in the battle. Pippin followed his best instincts in saving Faramir, foregoing his pledge of allegiance to Denethor.

## Book VI: The End of the Third Age

The last book is concerned with the Hobbit major pair, just like Book
IV, though the two pairs of Hobbits will converge at the end. In Mordor
Sam sets out to free Frodo from the Cirith Ungol fortress. He is aided
in this by dissensions among two ranks of competing Orcs, who have
fought and decimated each other. Sam rescues a weary Frodo, and
together they set into the heart of Mordor, under the disguise of Orc
vestments. They have little water and the last provisions of Elven
waybread, but hardly enough for the journey ahead. And they have to
go first north, then east, and finally south because the plain below them
is filled with Orc armies. The Ring on Frodo's neck is a burden that
grows heavier by the hour.

The two Hobbits struggle to reach Mount Orodruin because they
have to take detours. They are captured by Orcs, who believe them
to be deserters, and driven in a forced march. After they manage to
escape, they start the most grueling part of the ordeal, in scorching heat,
without the shelter of shade, and with little water. Frodo grows weaker
and weaker under the spell of the Ring, and Sam resorts to carrying
him. When at last the Hobbits reach Mount Doom, Frodo cannot
overcome the pull of the Ring and bring himself to throwing it into the
molten lava of the Cracks of Doom. At this point Gollum reappears and
fights Frodo for possession of the Ring. He manages to wrest it from
Frodo by biting off his finger with it, but in the exultation that follows,
Gollum falls back into the lava pit taking the Ring to its undoing.

At the Black Gate the fate of the battle is tilted against the Captains
of the West until the Ring falls at the Cracks of Doom. At the precise
moment of the Ring's undoing, the panicked forces of Mordor are
overtaken. Gandalf, losing no time, calls on the help of Gwaihir, Lord
of Eagles, to rescue Frodo and Sam from the erupting volcano that
threatens to engulf them.

Finally Sauron's darkness is dispelled and the Captains of the West
return to Minas Tirith. Aragorn is now made king of Gondor and
marries the Elf Arwen. Faramir marries Éowyn. The Hobbits return
to the Shire, where they find their homes ravaged by intruders who
have taken power over the Hobbits. Just as Sam and Frodo played a key
role in Mordor's realm, so now Merry and Pippin play the leading role

in the "scouring of the Shire." Saruman, who had taken the lead of the occupation of the Shire, is spared by Frodo, but Wormtongue, unable to contain Saruman's daily humiliations, stabs and kills him.

The Hobbits return home as heroes and start rebuilding the Shire. Frodo occasionally suffers from his wounds, and no longer feels at home in the Shire. He has been offered by Arwen the possibility to sail from the Grey Havens, and he does so in the company of Bilbo, Gandalf, and the Elven Ring-bearers, Elrond and Galadriel. They make their way together towards the Undying Lands. If a proverb would sum up the experience, it is the same as in Book V: "Where will wants not, a way opens."

## GENERAL THEMES

Similarly to the great epics of the Middle Ages, *The Lord of the Rings* adopted the interlace structure of narration. Similarly to these, as long as it is, the epic is nevertheless only one fragment that is better understood in relation to something larger. Tolkien indicated that *The Lord of the Rings* and *The Silmarillion* were intimately interconnected, and he wanted us to understand the second in time in relation to the first one.[187] This is why he naively would have loved to publish them both at once. And this is why in *The Lord of the Rings* Tolkien added the appendices that refer to what is elaborated in *The Silmarillion*.

Christopher Tolkien indicates that *The Silmarillion* had become "the vehicle and depository of [Tolkien's] profoundest reflections."[188] And for cause: Tolkien worked on it from about 1916 to 1973, the year of his death. *The Silmarillion* is a book written in many voices and addressing different stages of consciousness. Verlyn Flieger sees *The Silmarillion* as "something which begins as 'a definite spiritual reality,' becomes divided into 'pure human thinking' and 'physical light,' and ultimately splinters, both as percept and as word, into myriad fragments."[189] *The Silmarillion* is the story of the Fall through the fragmentation of light, language, and

---

[187] Tolkien, *The Silmarillion*, xii.
[188] Tolkien, *The Silmarillion*, viii.
[189] Flieger, *Splintered Light*, 67.

people. *The Lord of the Rings* will announce the redemption through the smallest of Middle-earth's people, the Hobbits.

There is a major difference between what lives in *The Silmarillion* and what comes to life in *The Lord of the Rings*. Much time has elapsed between one and the other. *The Lord of the Rings* follows in time after what Tolkien describes in the closing chapters of *The Silmarillion* with the chronicle of Akallabêth, relating to the downfall of Númenor/Atlantis. In his aborted *The Notion Club Papers* Tolkien, speaking through his characters, indicates Númenor/Atlantis as the dividing line between myth and history. This change is indicated in the concept of a transition from a flat to a round world. The Lost Road itself is the "Straight Road West" that it is no longer possible to tread after the end of Númenor/Atlantis.

With *The Lord of the Rings* we are entering into historical consciousness. In talking about *The Lord of the Rings* Tolkien's biographer Humphrey Carpenter says:

> He explains it all in great detail, talking about his book not as a work of fiction but as a chronicle of actual events; he seems to see himself not as an author who has made a slight error that must now be corrected or explained away, but as a historian who must cast light on an obscurity in a historical document.[190]

The above is expressed by Tolkien himself thus:

> [*The Lord of the Rings*] was written slowly and with great care for detail, and finally emerged as a Frameless Picture: a searchlight, as it were, on a brief period in History, and on a small part of our Middle-Earth, surrounded by the glimmer of limitless extensions in time and space. Very well: that may explain to some extent why it "feels" like history; why it was accepted for

[190] Carpenter, *Tolkien: A Biography*, 4.

publication; and why it has proved readable for a large number of very different kinds of people.[191]

There is more that is of interest to our study in this quote and what follows, and we will return to it in our conclusions.

In a long letter that Tolkien wrote to Waldman he expresses, "As the high Legends of the beginning are supposed to look at things through Elvish minds, so the middle tale of the Hobbit takes a virtually human point of view—and the last tale [*The Lord of the Rings*] blends them. *The Lord of the Rings* blends thus human and elvish perspectives."[192] Let us then look at these two perspectives.

Elves and men present two different aspects of the human race; they allow us to explore the problem of death from two different perspectives. Human beings are doomed to leave the world; Elves not to leave it. In Elves we have more properly deathlessness than immortality. Men introduce in Middle-earth the polarity of free will/fate because Men alone can act beyond the creational design of the music of Ilúvatar, the creator God, as it is portrayed in *The Silmarillion*. Men can alter external events, whereas Elves seem at most able to alter some attitudes towards themselves, other beings, or God, but not outer events.

And Hobbits? They are a splinter people of the human beings. "The hobbits are, of course, really meant to be a branch of the specifically *human* race (not Elves or Dwarves)."[193] They live closer to earth; they are more immersed and more in touch with it. In the Hobbit Frodo, Tolkien exemplifies the highest degree of fragmentation and splintering of all the races devised by his mythology. And the invention of the Hobbit character carries with it much of the West Midland and of Tolkien's soul: they like gardens and trees; they are fond of mushrooms and good plain food (not French style, which Tolkien abhorred). They have a very simple sense of humor; they like going to bed late and waking up late, and smoking a pipe. Unlike Tolkien, however, Hobbits have little imagination and great courage under trial.

---

[191] Carpenter, *Letters of J. R. R. Tolkien*, 413.

[192] J. R. R. Tolkien, undated letter of late 1951 to Milton Waldman in *The Silmarillion*, xv.

[193] Carpenter, *Letters of J. R. R. Tolkien*, 158.

*The Lord of the Rings* was written as a work of art but also as a scientific report, bringing together the two aspects of the Word that Tolkien cherished, and the two aspects of his personality, the writer and the researcher. In the explanations appearing in the book Tolkien moves from the story itself to its various alleged versions; to the historical artifact of the Red Book; to the book itself with editorial prologue and appendices. Tolkien devised and mentioned in the book an oral tradition that gave way to ancient manuscripts, and finally found its way into a modern book. To the form of the tradition Tolkien had to add a mechanism of communication: a line of historical bards, minstrels, storytellers, scribes, and redactors in order to finally reach print. All of this had to start from a believable oral tradition.[194]

Flieger summarizes the levels from which Tolkien would like us to look at *The Lord of the Rings* thus: as the story itself; as one version of that story embodying references to other versions; as a historical artifact—the Red Book; and as modern edition of that book complete with scholarly commentaries of the prologue and the appendices.[195]

The scholar is never too far from the artist when we look at Tolkien, the Tolkien that dealt with "Lit" and the Tolkien that dealt with "Lang," in the Oxford slang. Thus it may seem puzzling to hear the following statements from Tolkien, though they are completely in keeping with the individuality we have tried to uncover. Explaining what the book was to him, Tolkien says "It [*The Lord of the Rings*] is to me, anyway, largely an essay in 'linguistic-asthetic,' as I sometimes say to people who ask me 'what is it all about?'"[196] To another enquirer asking the same question Tolkien went further: "And I said it was an effort to create a situation in which a common greeting would be *elen síla lúmen*

---

[194] In *The Lord of the Rings* Tolkien refers to the Red Book of Westmarch. In "Note on the Shire Records" we are told that "This account of the Third Age is drawn mainly from the Red Book of Westmarch" and further that this was in origin "Bilbo's private diary, which he took with him to Rivendell." And his work is described as "work of great skill and learning in which, between 1403 and 1418 he had used all the sources available to him in Rivendell, both living and written." Of the Red Book of Westmarch we are told that only various copies of the original have survived. (From *The Fellowship of the Ring*, 14)

[195] Flieger, *Interrupted Music*, 80.

[196] Carpenter, *Letters of J. R. R. Tolkien*, 220.

*omentielmo* [A star shines on the hour of our meeting], and that the phrase long antedated the book."[197]

Before we turn to the themes of the book, let us have a general idea of Tolkien's intention in his own words. When pressed hard about the whole book Tolkien said:

> I do not think that even Power or Domination is the real centre of my story. . . . The real theme for me is about something more permanent and difficult: Death and Immortality: the mystery of the love of the world in the hearts of a race "doomed" to leave and seemingly lose it; the anguish in the hearts of a race "doomed" to not leave it, until its evil-aroused story is complete.[198]

Adding specifics, Tolkien emphasizes that Death is not the enemy, that it is the work of the Enemy to make it appear so, and that immortality should not be confused with the limitless, serial longevity sought by the Númenoreans.[199] "Longevity or counterfeit 'immortality' (true immortality is beyond Eä) is the chief bait of Sauron—it leads the small to a Gollum, and the great to a Ringwraith."[200]

We have thus far looked at the genesis of *The Lord of the Rings*. It was one that required a process of openness and discovery on the part of its author. It also rested on Tolkien's ability to grow into the archetypal quality of myth and its correlation in human biography. This was partly a growth that had been "given" to him through life's trials leading to his experiences during World War I, comprising both the abyss of trench war and the heights of the first artistic inspirations that formed the germs of *The Silmarillion*. It is my impression that it further grew through humanity's trials of World War II, which Tolkien followed with keen interest. He inwardly battled with an innate pessimism, that art lifted up and transformed into a scatological vision of the future.

---

[197] Carpenter, *Letters of J. R. R. Tolkien*, 264–65.
[198] Carpenter, *Letters of J. R. R. Tolkien*, 246.
[199] Carpenter, *Letters of J. R. R. Tolkien*, 267.
[200] Carpenter, *Letters of J. R. R. Tolkien*, 286.

As some authors have pointed out—especially Richard C. West—*The Lord of the Rings* presents ingeniously interrelated themes, parallels and contrasts within some of the six original books, or between two given books. Another constant is the contrast between the Hobbit major pair, Frodo and Sam, and the minor pair, Merry and Pippin.

In line with Tolkien's use of the interlace structure of the story is a worldview that echoes the traditional view of the ages of humankind that is known through myths and legends, an outlook that survived in Western consciousness until the Middle Ages. Tolkien renews and refreshes this cyclical outlook concerning the workings of history.

Finally, as we know from some of Tolkien's letters, the various characters of his trilogy—e.g. Elves and Men—allow the narrative to explore in imagination themes such as mortality, deathlessness, and immortality. The theme of the eternal confrontation of good and evil, seen through the lens of ages of humankind, acquires a higher significance. It emerges through the ebbs and flows of each cycle, through the movements of evolution, stagnation, decline, and decadence, leading to pivotal turning points of prehistory or history. A turning point in one cycle mirrors and echoes a turning point in another.

The above are only very general guidelines and themes. The charm of Tolkien's narrative is built on the richness of countless literary imaginations. We will now turn our gaze to these and try to uncover patterns, and larger archetypes.

# CHAPTER 5

# THE ARCHETYPAL HUMAN BEING

---

But of course, *The Lord of the Rings* is a deeply spiritual book.
Everything has a deeper meaning, a mysterious denseness of
significance that often has its background in mythological
events outside the story itself; these are hinted at but
frequently not explained, even over the course of the story.
—Pia Skogemann

Myths, legends, fairy tales, Homer's *Odyssey*, Shakespeare's plays—all speak to the human mind and heart across continents and centuries because they tap into something deeper than the intellect. They convey in artistic fashion universal truths that cannot be conveyed through the intellect alone, or at least not through the ordinary intellect. In Jungian terms they speak of universal archetypes that live in our souls, regardless of our culture of origin, lifestyle, or political or religious choices. *The Lord of the Rings* need not invoke God, Christ, spirit, or religion, though many have perceptively realized that all of these are somehow tangibly present. Tolkien's rich personality was inspired from these living archetypes and succeeded in a remarkable degree to convey them as living imaginations.

This chapter will explore basic premises of the archetypal world to which Tolkien's imaginations point. All the elements of the trilogy's narrative are tightly interrelated and interwoven. All the characters have depth and stature and, at first sight, seem to act fully on their own. On second look, here as in the structure of the book itself, all the elements of the narrative support each other, and so do the various individuals, their character, and their deeds. Together they offer us a picture of what it means to be fully human.

## ARCHETYPES IN *THE LORD OF THE RINGS*

How far did Tolkien succeed in bringing archetypes to life? How accurate was he? Are these questions that no one could answer other than he who can see these archetypes directly? We can at least come close to it. Our approach will be to look at the book as closely as possible through the phenomena—Tolkien's imaginations down to their minutest details—to detect what they convey of a larger reality through the lenses of Jungian psychology and through the living concepts of Rudolf Steiner's spiritual science. This will be successful if it does not dissect and diminish the power of Tolkien's imaginations, but rather points to something still larger that has the power to further inspire us. It is in fact a common perception that there is no way to exhaust the power of an artistic imagination, be it a myth or Tolkien's work, because it can still be viewed under further lenses. Thus, this is still only a beginning. To all of you, Tolkien readers and fans, I hope this will give an incentive to read *The Lord of the Rings* again, and encourage you to live with new questions, and eventually give rise to new answers.

The parallels between Carl Jung and Tolkien are quite striking, as Pia Skogemann points out. Both of them were at home in the world of the archetypes. In a sense they held a kind of consciousness that is mostly absent in modern humanity. They looked back to the past to warn us about dangers lying ahead for modern human beings. This is how Jung expressed it: "Does [man] know that he is on the point of losing the life-preserving myth of the inner man which Christianity has treasured for him? Does he realize what lies in store if this catastrophe ever befall him?"[201] Tolkien said about myths that they "will also reflect a splintered fragment of the true light, the eternal truth that is with God. Indeed only by myth-making, only by becoming a 'sub-creator'

---

[201] Skogemann, *Where the Shadows Lie*, 4.

and inventing stories, can Man ascribe to the state of perfection that he knew before the Fall."[202] And he lamented to his son Christopher that "even if people have ever heard the legends (which is getting rarer) they have no inkling of their portent."[203]

There is a lawfulness in looking at Tolkien through Jung's eyes because there is more than one direct parallel in the way the two of them worked. Describing escapism to his son Christopher, Tolkien writes: "I took to 'Escapism; or really transforming experience into another form and symbol with Morgoth and Orcs and the Eldar (representing beauty and grace and artefact) and so on . . . I still draw on the conceptions then hammered out."[204] Through this Tolkien wanted to express that much of his work lay in returning to imaginations that emerged in his psyche in the years of his youth—particularly what took the shape of *The Silmarillion*—and penetrate them with ever-deeper awareness and the wisdom of old age. No wonder that he endlessly chiseled and remolded versions upon versions of his early imaginations, and that being a perfectionist at heart, he could never rest content at what felt, no matter the effort involved, as good as an approximation. Jung too drew from the inspiration he received early in life for the rest of his life's work. In his own words:

> The years when I was pursuing my inner images were the most important in my life—in them everything essential was decided. It all began then; the later details are only supplements and clarifications of the material that burst forth from the unconscious, and at first swamped me. It was the *prima materia* for a lifetime's work.[205]

And it is about the realm of the archetypes that Tolkien can say:

---

[202] Carpenter, *Tolkien: A Biography*, 147.

[203] Carpenter, *Letters of J. R. R. Tolkien*, 88.

[204] Carpenter, *Letters of J. R. R. Tolkien*, 85.

[205] C. G. Jung, *Memories, Dreams, Reflections*, quoted in Skogemann, *Where the Shadows Lie*, 3.

In that realm [of fairy-story] a man may, perhaps, count himself fortunate to have wandered, but its very richness and strangeness tie the tongue of the traveler who would report them. And while he is there it is dangerous for him to ask too many questions, lest the gates should be shut and the keys be lost.[206]

Tolkien was keenly aware of communicating through art something that went beyond his personality and that biographers and psychologists could not dig out of his unconscious or the external threads of his life. I agree with Pia Skogemann that Tolkien penetrated the horrors of war to the archetypal level. What today is called "post-traumatic stress disorder" is elevated in Frodo's experience to the archetypal level of the intrusion of evil in all layers of the consciousness.

And what does Rudolf Steiner's spiritual science add to this? The step from Jungian interpretation to spiritual scientific enquiry lies in seeing that archetypes are more than fields of soul and spiritual activity that break out of the collective unconscious and are embodied in symbols. They are realities of a higher order, and all reality indicates "beingness," i. e., the presence of beings of a higher order of reality: spiritual beings at work in the universe and in the human soul and spirit.

# THE THREE AND THE ONE: THE PATHS OF GANDALF, ARAGORN, AND FRODO

The charm of *The Lord of the Rings* lies in bringing together various orders of reality: from the legendary, more divine than human Aragorn, who lives in the dimension of myth; to the ordinary human being like Frodo who accomplishes extraordinary feats. From the quest of restoring a kingdom of old in a new form to the anti-quest of a Hobbit whose goal is to get rid of a dangerous weapon of power while trying to remain alive. And in between these two figures, or beyond them, lies the dimension of magic dear to science fiction and fantasy fans that nobody embodies better than Gandalf.

---

[206] Tolkien, "On Fairy-Stories," in *Monsters and the Critics*, 109.

Gandalf, Aragorn, and Frodo express the greatest differences possible and yet work as one towards the same goal. Let us look at the each one of them, and then at how they work together.

## The Path of Gandalf

Gandalf has already been alive for some two thousand years at the time of Bilbo's birthday party. The wizards (Istari), according to Tolkien, came out of Valinor. They are Maiar beings, or lesser Valar beings. Although we are told there were five of them, we only know the name of three: Saruman the White, Gandalf the Grey, and Radagast the Brown. "They came therefore in the shape of Men, though they were never young and aged only slowly, and they had many powers of mind and hand. They revealed their true name to few."[207]

Gandalf's name carries the *Alf* of Elves. *Gand* is associated with wizardry or sorcery. So the whole would make him *wizard elf.* Tolkien also tells us that his true name is *Olorin*, though he does not offer us a precise meaning. Among Men, *Olorin* is known as "the elf of the wand."[208] In short, Gandalf is in this middle sphere between Ilúvatar, the supreme deity, and his emissaries the Valars above him; Elves and Men below him.

One of the first tests that will meet Gandalf is announced by his long-ranging awareness. As in many other places, he is able to sense the future: "There are many powers in the world, for good or for evil. Some are greater than I am. Against some I have not yet been measured. But my time is coming. The Morgul-lord and his Black Riders have come forth."[209] And a real test is indeed not far from coming.

At the Council of Rivendell, just before the fellowship forms, Elrond calls Gandalf to speak, "for it is the place of honour, and in all this matter he has been the chief."[210] The great Elrond subordinates himself to Gandalf, and so does Aragorn later. At the Council Gandalf points out that when Sauron was sent out of Dol Guldur, the time coincided with the finding of the Ring. And Gandalf comments that

---

[207] Tolkien, *The Return of the King*, Appendix B, 1059.
[208] Flieger, "Missing Person," in *Green Suns and Faërie*, 226–27.
[209] Tolkien, *The Fellowship of the Ring*, 214.
[210] Tolkien, *The Fellowship of the Ring*, 243.

this could hardly be a coincidence. However, Gandalf falls in with Saruman's reassurance that the Ring would never be found in Middle Earth. Nevertheless, for safe measure he decides to inquire more deeply into the history of the Ring and finds documents in Gondor. In one of these he finds mention of the inscription it carries.

Soon after, through the detour of a meeting with fellow wizard Radagast the Brown, Gandalf learns that the nine Ringwraiths are moving westward towards the Shire, and have taken the form of black riders. Radagast directs Gandalf to Saruman, but not before Gandalf asks him to alert the animals and birds that are allied to him. This means informing Gwaihir the Windlord as well. Upon coming to Isengard, Gandalf realizes he is afraid. Saruman seems not to respond to the title "White," but prefers "Saruman the Wise, Saruman Ring-Maker, Saruman of Many Colours." His robes, which had seemed white, were in reality woven of all colors. Gandalf challenges him by saying that he preferred them white, and what follows is a dialogue central to the book:

> "White!" he sneered. "It serves as a beginning. White cloth may be dyed. The white page can be overwritten; and the white light can be broken." "In which case it is no longer white," said I [Gandalf]. "And he that breaks a thing to find out what it is has left the path of wisdom."[211]

Saruman turns down Gandalf's advice and announces that a new age is coming in which people like him must have dominion over the world of Men. He explains that a new power is rising that Men and Elves will not be able to oppose. Showing scorn for Men, whom he sees as hindering the work of wisdom, he pressures Gandalf to yield to the coming power of Sauron in the illusion that it can be controlled for the higher purpose of "Knowledge, Rule, Order." Saruman further presses Gandalf to reveal where the Ring lies, to get hold of it. When Saruman tellingly refers to it as "the precious thing," Gandalf has no choice but to oppose the fellow wizard, thus becoming his prisoner. Gandalf is confined to the pinnacle of the Orthanc tower, with little hope of

---

[211] Tolkien, *The Fellowship of the Ring*, 252.

escape, there passing bitter days. He is rescued after a time by Gwaihir, lord of the Eagles. This test is the prelude to a stronger ordeal against an even stronger opponent who stands in the way of the fellowship.

Gandalf plays a role even without meeting the fellowship. Soon after his release from Orthanc he goes to the Shire, then to Bree, where the Black Riders were directed. When he knows that Frodo has left with Strider, to whom he is relieved to relinquish leadership, Gandalf gallops to Weathertop, reaching it two days after leaving Bree. The Black Riders try to attack him, but he protects himself with fire. In so doing he has drawn behind him four Black Riders, and diverts them from attacking Frodo and Aragorn.

In Rivendell Elrond announces the forming of the fellowship, and declares: "With you and your faithful servant, Gandalf will go; for this shall be his great task, and maybe the end of his labours."[212] Gandalf is truly the head of the party, Aragorn a close second; but to Frodo falls the central task of the quest. Interestingly, and in an uncharacteristically boastful way, Gandalf says, "Someone said that intelligence shall be needed in the party. He was right. I think I shall come with you."[213] But he leaves this suggestion open to Elrond's advice.

In the mines of Moria, Gandalf walks in front of the group, and, silent and determined, Aragorn in the rear. It is always Gandalf who has the last word, while Aragorn shows his complete trust in him, even in the most trying moments:

> "Do not be afraid!" said Aragorn. . . . "I have been with
> him on many a journey, if never on one so dark. . . .
> He will not go astray—if there is any path to find. He
> has led us here against our fears, but he will lead us out
> again, at whatever cost to himself."[214]

Before leaving the mines of Moria, Gandalf indicates they have to go across a bridge. When they get to the bridge they see that it is narrow and dangerous, without curb or rail. Below is a wide chasm.

---

[212] Tolkien, *The Fellowship of the Ring*, 268.
[213] Tolkien, *The Fellowship of the Ring*, 266.
[214] Tolkien, *The Fellowship of the Ring*, 303.

Pursued by a frightful creature, a Balrog, the company can only cross in single file. To protect the fellowship, Gandalf takes a stand against the Balrog. Gandalf and the Balrog are both Maiar spirits; they are equal, but the Balrog served the defiant spirit Melkor already in olden times. In defiance of the Balrog Gandalf proclaims his allegiance to another power: "I am a servant of the Sacred Fire, wielder of the flame of Anor."[215] Anor is a name for the Sun deity. The Balrog nevertheless leaps unto the bridge. Gandalf's staff is torn from him. The bridge breaks and the Balrog falls downwards, dragging the wizard along. Aragorn takes command of the fleeing fellowship.

Only much later can Gandalf explain in part what was the nature of his initiation. After being dragged down by the Balrog, Gandalf fell for a long time. First he was wrapped in fire, then they both fell in the deep and dark water. "Long I fell, and he fell with me. His fire was about me. I was burned. Then we plunged into the deep water and all was dark. Cold it was as the tide of death: almost it froze my heart."[216]

The magician came to the bottom, "beyond light and knowledge," still with the Balrog at his heels. The two fought in the entrails of the earth, "where time is not counted." At last the Balrog fled into dark tunnels, and in utter despair Gandalf realized that following his enemy was his only hope. The Balrog carried him back to the heart of Khazad-dûm to the "Endless Stair." After ascending the seemingly endless spiral he found himself at last in Durin's Tower, in a high, narrow, and inaccessible place, far from the world.

The Balrog burst into flame again. The mountain looked crowned with storm and thunder roared, lightning flared. Gandalf managed to hurl his enemy against the mountain, where he ran to his ruin. He concludes, "The darkness took me, and I strayed out of thought and time, and I wandered far on roads that I will not tell." The rest is better retold verbatim:

> Naked I was sent back—for a brief time, until my task is done. And naked I lay upon the mountain-top. . . . I was alone, forgotten, without escape upon the hard

[215] Tolkien, *The Fellowship of the Ring*, 344.
[216] Tolkien, *The Two Towers*, 490.

horn of the world. There I lay staring upward, while
the stars wheeled over, and each day was as long as a
life-age of the earth. Faint to my ears came the gathered
rumours of all lands: the springing and the dying, the
song and the weeping, and the slow everlasting groan
of overburdened stone.[217]

It is once more Gwaihir, Lord of Eagles, who bears him to Lórien
in the presence of Galadriel for healing.

Pia Skogemann indicates that Gandalf is initiated first through the
sphere of the elements in the entrails of the earth: fire and heat, water
and cold, earth, stone; and finally through an ascent into the air that
involves the same elements anew: fire in the lightning, water in the ice
and rain, earth in the rock. He meets this initiation through the Balrog,
another Maya being, like himself.

As Skogemann indicates, that Gandalf is sent back into the world
naked means that he has been able to greatly transform his physical
body. This is why Gwaihir calls him "light as a swan's feather." But he
still needs healing, and that is why Galadriel calls him to Lórien. Later
Gandalf can say that no weapon can hurt him because his physical
body is like none other. In battle he needs no helm nor mail to protect
himself, and his white robes and snowy long hair make him look as
radiant as the sun.

When the party with everyone except Frodo and Sam meet with
Gandalf again, the wizard is so transformed that even his companions
fail to recognize him at first, and he reacts with some surprise to his
own name. At first the companions confuse him with Saruman, then
Legolas is the first to shout *Mithrandir*, Gandalf's Elven name. They
notice that "his hair was white as snow in the sunshine; and gleaming
white was his robe; the eyes under his deep brows were bright, piercing
as the rays of the *sun*; power was in his hand."[218] (emphasis added)
Indeed Gandalf proves in his appearance that he is the servant of
the sacred flame of Anor, the flame of the Sun. He indicates to the

---

[217] Tolkien, *The Two Towers*, 491.
[218] Tolkien, *The Two Towers*, 484.

107

companions that none of their weapons can hurt him at present. This is because he has gone through some degree of death and resurrection.

To the party Gandalf now announces the coming of the great storm. In what becomes a theme through the book, he proclaims:

> "Yes, I am white now," said Gandalf. "Indeed I am Saruman, one might almost say, Saruman as he should have been. . . . I have passed through fire and deep water, since we parted. I have forgotten much that I thought I knew, and learned again much that I had forgotten. I can see many things far off, but many things that are close I cannot see."[219]

Then he offers an understanding of the Enemy and how he can be defeated. Sauron lives in angst that someone else would be availing himself of the Ring in his stead, seeking to overthrow him. What he could not possibly fathom is that someone would simply want to destroy the Ring. And the fellowship has this advantage over him—that their plans defy his understanding.

Now armed with new power, Gandalf enters the Hall of Edoras as if by storm, defeating Grima/Wormtongue who has subjected Théoden's mind to Saruman's influence. After openly defying Grima, Gandalf raises his staff, and thunder rolls and the hall turns dark. Théoden is reawakened after a long spell under the subjugation of his counselor, and is ready to lead his army in battle.

In Minas Tirith Gandalf assumes leadership of the city after Denethor relinquishes it, prey to his growing madness. In Gandalf's presence Men recover courage. But as soon as he passes, they lose it. Now the attackers come with renewed strength, and spurred by the Black Captain, the gate at the entrance of Gondor breaks. Behind the gate stands Gandalf, ready to challenge him. The Captain says, "Old fool! . . . Old fool! This is my hour. Do you not know Death when you see it? Die now and curse in vain!"[220] Gandalf does not move. At that moment a cock crows, welcoming the dawn that breaks through

---

[219] Ibid
[220] Tolkien, *The Two Towers*, 811.

Sauron's darkness. And in answer come the sounds of the horns of the riders of Rohan.

After victory is achieved in Gondor, because Sauron's attention is completely drawn towards the assembled company, Gandalf wants him to keep doing so. All of his energy is devoted to the service of the seemingly humble Hobbit Frodo. Gandalf wants to induce Sauron to empty Mordor of his forces, and offers his forces as a bait, goading him to believe he can capture the Ring hidden among them. Thus Gandalf asks his allies to walk into a trap with little other than hope, knowing that they could perish. Gandalf's stance could summarize the nature of the transition to the new age. In his own words, it is "better [to risk death without warranties] than perish nonetheless—as we surely shall, if we sit here—and know as we die that no new age will come." And he sums up: "We come now to the very brink, where hope and despair are akin. To waver is to fall."[221] Once this mad wager is over, Gandalf's task for the aeon is completed.

In order to ensure Frodo's mission, Gandalf sacrifices himself in the ordeal against the Balrog, which leads him to an underworld journey, a death and resurrection. He knows at that moment what could be in store for him, and he does not shrink from it. This is what leads him to the transformation from Gandalf the Grey to Gandalf the White. Among the three main characters of the trilogy, he is the only one able to oversee all the threads of the odyssey. In a Jungian sense Gandalf represents the positive archetypal spirit that shows that "living nature, of course, is not opposed to the spirit but is a part of it."[222]

To Denethor Gandalf says, "But all worthy things are now in peril as the world now stands, those are my care. And for my part, I shall not wholly fail of my task, though Gondor should perish, if anything passes through this night that can still grow fair and flower again in days to come."[223] Gandalf wrestles to rescue what can be carried into the future. He works out of an intuition of the future, as is made clear in his approach to Saruman; even a black magician can hear the words of the spirit, and these can mature at some later point in his soul.

---

[221] Tolkien, *The Two Towers*, 862.

[222] Skogemann, *Where the Shadows Lie*, 129.

[223] Tolkien, *The Two Towers*, 741–42.

As exalted as Gandalf can be, he is still subjected to the laws of Middle-earth. He is already afraid upon meeting Saruman in Orthanc, and only the more so with the Balrog. Likewise, when Faramir remembers his first encounter with Frodo and Sam and recounts it to Gandalf, Pippin notices that Gandalf's hands tremble and realizes that the wizard himself is shaken and afraid. The same happens at the Black Gate, when Gandalf parleys with the Mouth of Sauron, who brings him a bundle containing Sam's sword, a grey cloak, an Elven brooch, and the *mithril*-mail coat worn by Frodo. Those near Gandalf see the anguish in his face but, even when all seems lost, Gandalf can summon some hidden reserve of true spiritual strength.

Gandalf is the image of the self in the realm of the spirit. He is the one whose consciousness spans all realms of earth, the one who can speak to everyone their own language. He is the one who calls to higher awareness and therefore is seen as a bringer of doom by those who are unprepared to take the next evolutionary step. When people meet higher aspects of the spirit, they react in the measure of their development, as in the case of Saruman or Denethor. If they are torn in themselves, they feel shame, and this turns to anger or aversion. Théoden is ready for change, and his healing is almost immediate; Denethor has only loathing towards Gandalf and sinks deeper into his madness.

In Gandalf the divine aspect stands in the foreground; he is first and foremost a Maia. His body is secondary; after his initiation, for all intended purposes, he has known and overcome death and cannot be defeated in the body.

## The Path of Aragorn

Aragorn has the overtones of the chosen one, the larger-than-life hero. His is a path of those destined for greatness, a path carved by continuous adversity, something of a character of legend. This begins at his very birth.

Aragorn's father, Arathorn son of Arador, wants to marry Gilraen the Fair. Her father, Dírhael, is opposed to it, partly due to a great age difference, but also because he intuits the tragic fate of Arathorn. This in fact comes to pass after the two marry, when Arathorn is killed by Orcs only two years after the birth of Aragorn. The newborn is taken to live with his mother in Rivendell. He is first called Estel (Hope), and his true name and lineage are kept hidden at the wish of Elrond, who doesn't want Sauron to discover the whereabouts of the heir of Isildur, the one who had wrested the Ring from Sauron's finger. At age twenty-five Estel accomplished great, unspecified deeds in the company of Elrond's sons. Elrond, recognizing his nobility and stature, decides to reveal to him his true origin, and to give him the family heirlooms, among which is Narsil, the broken sword of Elendil and his son, Isildur.[224]

Aragorn first sees Arwen, grand-daughter of Galadriel, while she is walking in the woods in Rivendell. In memory of the legends of his forebears, he calls her "Tinúviel." Aragorn realizes she is the daughter of Elrond who has just returned from Lórien, and has not been in Rivendell for a long time. Arwen, an Elf, has much longer earth experience than he does. Elrond, ill disposed towards their marriage, foretells Aragorn the difficult path that awaits them both. He warns Aragorn that she is too far above him. Elrond feels that Aragorn is asking too much in separating Arwen from him and from all the other Elves. In Lórien, however, Aragorn has the favor of Galadriel. It is she who allowed him to first meet Arwen.

At age forty-nine Aragorn, returning from his missions and wanderings, comes to Lórien and spends "a season" with Arwen and, on a Midsummer eve, they dedicate their lives to each other. Elrond, informed of their choice, places as a condition for his assent that Aragorn regain his crown before being united to Arwen. Thus Aragorn sets out from Rivendell, while Arwen remains. Because of her choice, Arwen relinquishes Elven deathlessness and becomes a mortal woman.

In the following years Aragorn is taken under Gandalf's wing to serve a kind of apprenticeship. These are long years of wanderings as a Ranger, protecting Middle-earth from Sauron's emissaries. Up to this point Aragorn has been raised by Elrond; Gandalf has acted as his spiritual father and Galadriel as his spiritual mother. The fate of the three holders of the Elven rings is bound to his. First of all, Aragorn's formative years are shaped by the encounters with these three high

---

[224] Tolkien, *The Return of the King*, 1032–33.

Elves; second, the success of Aragorn's mission spells the end of their presence in Middle-earth.

In *The Fellowship of the Ring* we first meet Aragorn at the inn of Bree. Frodo first notices what he calls "a strange-looking weather-beaten man." The stranger introduces himself to Frodo as Strider. In fact both future members of the fellowship meet under disguise names: Mr. Underhill and Strider. From the beginning we see that Strider knows about the Ring and has the power to submit the Hobbits to his will if he so wishes, but he can resist the temptation of the Ring. And two paradoxical parts of Strider come to the fore from the beginning. The first is his grim, worn-out external appearance due to years and years of wandering. On the other hand Aragorn/Strider periodically alters his appearance; his nobility shines through him. And this happens for the first time in front of the Hobbits at the inn at Bree. "He stood up, and seemed suddenly to grow taller. In his eyes gleamed a light, keen and commanding."[225] The Hobbits witnessing the scene do not dare move.

In the absence of Gandalf at Bree, Aragorn leads Frodo on the next stages of his quest. Gandalf, informed of the fact later on, feels Aragorn is the best suited to fill the role that he was unable to play due to his delay under Saruman's captivity. The fellowship without Gandalf arrives at Rivendell. At the Council, Elrond produces the sword of Aragorn's forbear Isildur, which was long broken and has now been reforged. And he introduces officially Aragorn as son of Arathorn and descendent of Isildur, and chief of the Dúnedain [Rangers] of the North. Aragorn explains that the Rangers have protected the North by hunting down adversaries and preserving the peace. However, they are looked upon and treated with contempt from most of Middle-earth's inhabitants, and they have to accept it in order to protect Middle-earth from dangers they cannot yet reveal. Aragorn now receives the reforged Narsil, to which he gives the name of Anduril, or "Flame of the West." Leaving Rivendell, Gandalf leads the nine members of the fellowship with Aragorn as close second. And Aragorn takes the lead at the apparent death of Gandalf in the mines of Moria, bringing them to the refuge of Lórien.

---

[225] Tolkien, *The Fellowship of the Ring*, 168.

Before leaving Lórien, Galadriel asks Aragorn whether he wants a gift. He answers: "only through darkness shall I come to it [Arwen]."[226] Through this answer he seems to foresee the kind of test that awaits him. Galadriel gives him a sheath for his sword, and a silver brooch in the likeness of an eagle with outspread wings, with a green stone set on it, and reminds him of his kingly names: Elessar, the Elfstone of the house of Elendil. When he takes the stone, Aragorn stands once more as if transfigured.

The group descends the Anduin River while Aragorn still mulls about the best course to take. When fate intervenes and forces his hand, the fellowship is disbanded. Aragorn, heavily affected, reflects "Alas . . . Now the Company is all in ruin. It is I that have failed. Vain was Gandalf's trust in me."[227] Here the future king, as in many other places, subordinates himself to the wise wizard. He feels that his own task is best furthered by submitting himself to Gandalf.

At the foot of Tol Brandir the fellowship is broken. The Hobbits take different paths. The major pair—Frodo and Sam—ride down the river searching for a way to enter Mordor's realm. Merry and Pippin— the minor pair—are abducted by a party of Orcs who intend to bring them to Saruman's stronghold in Isengard. Aragorn, Legolas, and Gimli are in hot pursuit of the Orcs that have kidnapped the younger Hobbits. When wondering about what course to take, Aragorn can put his ear to the ground and feel the earth's vibrations. He can detect that the enemies lie afar, but that Rohan's horses are getting closer to his party. He can also sense finer influences at work in Rohan—as he did before arriving in Moria: "There is something strange at work in this land. I distrust the silence. I distrust even the pale Moon. . . . There is some will that lends speed to our foes and sets an unseen barrier before us: a weariness that is in the heart more than in the limb."[228]

When Éomer and the riders of Rohan meet the three friends, Aragorn reveals his deeper being to Éomer and displays Anduril. Once more the companions are amazed at Aragorn's change in stature. Later

---

[226] Ibid, 391.

[227] Tolkien, *The Two Towers*, 404.

[228] Tolkien, *The Two Towers*, 417.

Aragorn shines at the battle of Helm's Deep. He infuses his troops with great courage in a seemingly desperate resistance.

After the battle at Helm's Deep and the destruction of Isengard, Gandalf entrusts the Orthanc seeing stone (*palantír*) to Aragorn, for it comes from the treasure of Elendil and it had been set in Orthanc by the kings of Gondor; therefore it belongs to Aragorn by right. And he counsels Aragorn not to use it yet.

Aragorn, however, makes use of the seeing stone and reveals his ordeals in looking into the *palantír* to Legolas, adding that it took more strength to do this than to stand at the battle of Helm's Deep. In so doing Sauron was able to behold Aragorn, his arch-enemy, and Aragorn in defiance has shown him the reforged blade of Anduril. This no doubt pushes Sauron to major haste, which will play against him. In looking into the *palantír* Aragorn also detects the peril that is coming from the south—the Corsairs of Umbar, who threaten the ruin of Minas Tirith. It is this information that speeds him on to take the Paths of the Dead that will allow him to overcome the Corsairs.

Aragorn intuits more and more the kind of trial that is coming: "It is dark before me. I must go down also to Minas Tirith, but I do not yet see the road. An hour, long prepared, approaches."[229] Much later Aragorn is told about the Paths of the Dead by the Ranger Elrohir, who speaks for his father Elrond: "The days are short. If thou art in haste, remember the Paths of the Dead." And immediately after another Ranger, Halbarad, conveys a message from Arwen: "The days now are short. Either our hope cometh, or all hopes end."[230]

The task that Aragorn has to face is holding the dead to their ancient promise. The oath they broke was to fight against Sauron; and at Erech stands the Stone brought from Númenor by Elendil. The Kings of the Mountain (now the dead) had sworn allegiance to Isildur upon the Stone, but had recanted and worshipped the Dark Lord. Isildur had laid a curse upon them never to find rest until they would fulfill their oath. The people of the mountains hid themselves and had no dealings with other people, and then faded out of existence.

---

[229] Tolkien, *The Return of the King*, 756.
[230] Tolkien, *The Return of the King*, 758.

Aragorn shows great strength of soul in entering the Dark Door, and the Rangers and the others follow him even though in great fear into the entrails of the mountain. Upon entering the darkness Aragorn summons the Dead to the Stone of Erech. He is met with utter silence, and a darkness and cold in which the torches go out and cannot be rekindled. In the darkness the company of the dead grows more and more terrible to endure during four days of travel. It falls upon Aragorn to contain their impetus, and to subdue them to his will.

Shortly after emerging from the caves, the company reaches the Stone of Erech. Aragorn tells the dead that they will be going to Pelargir upon Anduin and promises them that after they help him against the Corsairs, he will fulfill his promise and set them free. The next day the darkness does not lift due to Sauron's doings, and, providentially protected by the enemy's darkness, the company marches south followed by the dead. At Pelargir the company confronts the fifty-ship fleet of the Haradrim of Umbar. Though they are a small force against the Corsairs, they have the dead on their side, and these instill great fear on their foes, who are thus vanquished. True to his word, Aragorn releases the dead from their oath.

Aragorn's last important deed is once more one of healing. Remember that earlier on he saved Frodo at least for the time that it took to reach Rivendell. In Minas Tirith, after the enemy forces have been provisionally repelled, Gandalf comes to the rescue of the wounded Faramir, Eowyn, and Merry, but feels he cannot cure this new illness caused by the Black Shadow that has been inflicted by the Nazgûl. Those afflicted fall into a deepening dream state and then progressively lose consciousness, turn cold, and die.

Gandalf hears the providential words of the old nurse Ioreth, "The hands of the king are the hands of a healer," and realizes that such a king has returned. Aragorn does not want to claim his kingship yet, so he comes to the city in disguise. He willingly relinquishes command for the time being to Gandalf.

Aragorn asks his assistants in the houses of healing to fetch a special plant and to prepare it in an infusion. Faramir suffers from weariness, from grief imparted from his father's behavior, the wound itself, and the Black Breath of the Nazgûl. Aragorn is in contact with the soul of the young man; he is calling him back from remote regions. Those who witness hear him ever more faintly, as if he were traveling farther and farther away from earth in search of one who is lost. To the awakening Faramir, who recognizes with love the future king, Aragorn says, "Walk no more in the shadows, but awake!"

Then Aragorn tends to Éowyn. Aragorn has perceived upon their first meeting her unhappiness, like that of "a white flower. . . shapely as a lily, and yet as if wrought by elf-wrights out of steel. Or was it, maybe a frost had turned its sap to ice. . . . Her malady begins far back before this day."[231] And Gandalf completes the picture of her trial, of being tied to her father in spite of her valor, and seeing him decay while being unable to affect change. Aragorn recognizes the pain of the love Éowyn has for him, which cannot be returned. When he initially perceived this, he was afraid for her fate. Now Aragorn realizes that he can heal her body but cannot predict in what state of mind she will awake, and if she awakens to despair, more healing will be needed. Aragorn calls her back from the shadows: "Awake, Éowyn, Lady of Rohan! . . . The Shadow is gone and all darkness is washed away clean!" And Éowyn replies "To health? . . . It may be so. . . . But to hope? I do not know."[232]

Soon after, Aragorn turns to Merry. The future king is more optimistic about him, realizing the strong spirit that lives in the Hobbit. He predicts that although he will not forget his grief, this will strengthen him and generate new wisdom. In fact Merry awakens with desire for a meal and a pipe. In the three examples just mentioned, we see how keenly Aragorn follows the paths of the soul, and how clearly he recognizes the nature of each one's trials.

As a sovereign Aragorn comes to establish a new era of peace. Verlyn Flieger sees in Aragorn an image of the sacred king of old. This kind of king is known in Greek, Germanic/Norse, and Celtic mythology.[233] Among other things, the sacred king is the warrant of the land's fertility, which depends on his manliness and vitality. Skogemann calls Aragorn a "cultural hero." She contrasts Gandalf's vertical path to what is essentially a horizontal path in Aragorn. Gandalf is caught

[231] Tolkien, *Return of the King*, 848.
[232] Tolkien, *Return of the King*, 850.
[233] Flieger, *Green Suns and Faërie*, 149.

in Saruman's Orthanc tower and rescued by Gwaihir, Lord of the Eagles. Later on he descends to the depths with the Balrog and ascends Durin's Tower. Gandalf's path is that of the heights and depths of the spirit. Aragorn knows the path of the human soul. He can fathom and understand each individual's path of soul, and help heal physical and psychological wounds. He wrests the souls of the dead from their submission to Sauron, who has bound them through the years in which they served him in Middle-earth. They recognize in him the one who has power over death of the soul. And this is the same in the case of Faramir, Éowyn, and Merry. The text of the story emphasizes quite clearly that Aragorn can follow them into the other world—or underworld—and call upon their souls to find their way back to earth, away from the pull of the Black Shadow. He works with human beings from one side to the other of existence.

Gandalf meets with a being who is his peer, the Balrog, a spiritual being. And ultimately he fights Sauron, another peer, in every possible way. Aragorn is a knight who protects his fellow Middle-earth inhabitants through his sword, his awareness and alertness. He is deeply related to the needs of his people, but also to the earth itself with whom he is intimately connected, and he places himself completely at the service of Gandalf.

Aragorn takes command when the latter is made captive by Saruman or by the Balrog. But he is ever mindful of following Gandalf's inspiration. This is his beacon and his compass. In the mines of Moria, Aragorn reminds the company of how much trust he has in the wizard. He exhorts them to follow him with confidence.

Aragorn, like Gandalf, naturally resists the temptation of the Ring, which he first demonstrates to Frodo at Bree. He can resist it because he is motivated by love. He also wins over his people through the love he puts in their healing, and they reciprocate with a natural gesture of love.

Aragorn doubts that he can be the rightful leader for the beginning of a new age. Gandalf helps him dissipate those doubts. At his crowning the new king acquires a mythical stature: "Wisdom sat upon his brow, and strength and healing were in his hands, and a light was about him."[234]

---

[234] Tolkien, *The Return of the King*, 947.

If Gandalf represents the spirit and the self, then Aragorn is quintessentially the representative of the human soul. Gandalf is a Maiar, essentially a divine being in a human body. Aragorn is Half-Elven (a Man with some Elf in his genealogy), and a heir of Númenorean descent, a descendant of those people who had access to the realm of Valinor through the Elves. He is most fit to play the role of messenger between the world of spirit and the physical world. We will turn now to the one who is most human of all, or most Hobbit: Frodo.

## The Path of Frodo

Names were very important to Tolkien, and this is why, after playing unsatisfyingly with the choice of Bingo, he opted for Frodo. The name *Frodo* is found in Germanic mythology, for example in the version Frodi in the Prose *Edda*, which was very familiar to Tolkien. Flieger sees in him the counterpart of the Norse fertility god Freyr. The word *froor*, from which it is derived, stands for "fruitful: or "wise."[235]

Tolkien says little about Frodo's childhood except that his father, Drogo Baggins, married Primula Brandybuck, Bilbo's first cousin on the mother's side. The couple was drowned while boating on the Brandywine. Frodo is a pure Hobbit; but through his Took strain he carries an inclination towards adventure. At the time of the story Bilbo is 111 and Frodo 33, which in Hobbit terms corresponds to the coming of age. Frodo Baggins was Bilbo's favorite nephew, and they had the same birthday, September 22.

When first presenting Frodo with the Ring Gandalf leaves the decision of taking it up with him and out of the Shire to Frodo, and he adds "But *I will always help you*. . . . I will help you bear this burden, as long as it is yours to bear" (emphasis added),[236] And Gandalf remains true to his word to the end of the odyssey. It is also Gandalf that tells Frodo: "Bilbo was *meant* to find the Ring, and not by its maker. In which case you were also meant to have it. And that may be an encouraging thought."[237] In his larger view of things, Gandalf knows that he has to

---

[235] Flieger, *Green Suns and Faërie*, 230.
[236] Tolkien, *The Fellowship of the* Ring, 60.
[237] Tolkien, *The Fellowship of the* Ring, 54–55.

encourage Frodo to take up his task but that Frodo will only be able to do it if Gandalf lends him his continued help.

Frodo feels very small and inadequate for the task, but he has great love for Bilbo and longs to meet him again. This is what first gives him courage. Interestingly, before he leaves the Shire, he has a dream that announces the theme of the sea—not just any sea but the Western Sea: "sound of the Sea far-off . . . strange salt smell in the air . . . a tall white tower."[238] He wants to go climb the tower but is prevented from doing so.

As Randel Helms points out, Book I of the six original books (parts) presents us with Frodo's preliminary, one could say preparatory, experiences. In each of these he seems to fall short, but he also receives precious help and tempers his spirit. Each of these brings about a danger for the Ring-bearer. And in each one of these Frodo is saved by an external agent—a force or individual. In the first two he musters courage and presence of mind, so that in the later ones he acts out of his strength of heart and will. By the end of these trials Frodo gathers the courage to accept the task of bearing the Ring.[239]

Before leaving the Shire a Ringwraith smells the presence of Frodo, who is about to succumb to the temptation of wearing the Ring. Frodo is saved by the unlikely presence of Elves, which cause the Ringwraith to flee.

In traversing the Old Forest, Merry invites his friends to take a nap. Frodo tries to resist and urges the others to do so. As the two younger Hobbits, Merry and Pippin, fall asleep, Frodo himself finally cannot resist the urge. Sam remains awake because he does not trust the tree. Frodo, Merry, and Pippin are saved partly by Sam, but mostly by Tom Bombadil.

Tom Bombadil has not heard Frodo's cry for help; his arrival is purely providential. In the adventure Frodo discovers the elemental malice of nature that exists independently of Sauron, that there are both good and evil things in nature. He also sees that the Ring doesn't make Tom invisible—and that Tom has no interest in the Ring, nor can he understand its power.

---

[238] Tolkien, *The Fellowship of the* Ring, 106.

[239] Helms, "Tolkien's World," chapter 5.

The test that follows is the encounter with the Barrow-wight. Here too the companions involuntarily fall asleep and lose sight of each other. Frodo's consciousness is challenged by a song, a "cold murmur," "far away and immeasurably dreary." He hears strings of words, "grim, hard, cold words, heartless and miserable." He resists the urge of putting on the Ring and remembers that "there is a seed of courage hidden (often deeply, it is true) in the heart of the fattest and most timid hobbit, waiting for some desperate danger to make it grow."[240] The words of Gildor seem to echo in his soul. And Frodo discovers that he can be both angry and afraid. He awakens courage upon seeing his companions made captive. He strikes at the spectral hand of the Wight and summons the presence of Bombadil, who has previously promised his help.

From the domain of Tom Bombadil onward we face an escalation and alternation of highs and lows. After Bree, the challenge at Weathertop; after the oasis of Rivendell, Caradhras mountain and the even more formidable mines of Moria, with the accompanying loss of Gandalf's guidance. After the otherworldly haven of Lórien and the encounter with Galadriel come first the labyrinth of Emyn Muil, then the Dead Marshes, leading to the no-man's-land ahead of the Black Gate and Mordor itself, with the pause of the forbidden pool of Ithilien providentially inserted in between. To every new heaven-sent shelter with its regenerative power follows the challenge/opportunity to work and meet the power of the enemy with some newly acquired strength.

It is interesting to follow Frodo's trials at the hand of the Ring. At the Prancing Pony, following Pippin's dangerous disclosures, Frodo decides to step in and rescue the day, but he has been served drinks and forgets himself. At a point in the song he leaps in the air, and to his surprise unconsciously slips the Ring on and disappears, immediately crawling toward the corner of the room where Strider is. It seems that the Ring has a power stronger than Frodo at this point, and that it simply wants to reveal itself. It is Strider who rescues the beleaguered company of Hobbits.

At Weathertop Frodo realizes fully his homelessness and the perils of the quest. He now regrets having left the Shire. At night the Black Riders attack the company, and Frodo is engulfed in terror. Under the

---

[240] Tolkien, *The Fellowship of the* Ring, 137.

spell of the Ring he longs to surrender, knowing full well that it will offer him neither solace nor relief. After he puts on the Ring his vision is altered, and he can see under the figures' mantles into their cold and hateful eyes. Frodo responds to the attack shouting, "O Elbereth! Gilthoniel!" and is impacted by a poisoned sting of a sword in his left shoulder. Fortunately, the wraith recoils upon hearing the name Elbereth and upon seeing Aragorn rescuing Frodo by holding flaming wood brands. Frodo has made the mistake of wearing the Ring, but he is rescued by new courage and by Aragorn.

At the Ford of Bruinen Frodo can resist the urge of slipping on the Ring and defies the wraiths. But it is mostly through Gandalf and Glorfindel's help that he can find rescue. When Glorfindel enjoins Frodo to ride forward, Frodo is held by a "strange reluctance," the power that the wraiths hold over him. Frodo is helped by the speed of Glorfindel's horse. However, the nine Riders are behind him. And now they renew their commands to take hold of his will. Once more Frodo invokes Elbereth and Lúthien the Fair. Nevertheless, as he sees them approaching, Frodo's will is as if paralyzed. The Riders are led into the water by a "shining figure of white light" (Glorfindel) and by people holding flames. Through Elven magic the swelling waters of the river engulf them.

By the end of Book I Frodo has put on the Ring twice, and has been seriously wounded. He has been overpowered and fallen unconscious or asleep while meeting with Old Man Willow, the Barrow-wight, and the Ring-wraiths, and soon after crossing the Ford of Bruinen. Book I ends with Frodo becoming unconscious, and Book II starts with his awakening in the House of Elrond.

In Rivendell Frodo is cured by an important Elf figure, Elrond, the one who wears the Ring of Air, Vilya, and who preserves great knowledge about the affairs of Middle-earth. Elrond tends Frodo for four days and removes the splinter of the blade that would otherwise have found its way into Frodo's body and placed him under the spell of Sauron, who could thus inflict pain on him until he would release the Ring to his power. Gandalf notices the changes after Frodo's healing: "There was a faint change, just a hint of transparency about him, and especially about the left hand that lay outside upon the coverlet." And he predicts, "He may become like a glass filled with clear light for eyes to see that can."[241]

In Rivendell's Fire Hall Frodo listens to the music and poems, and he is held in a spell even though he does not fully understand. He feels transported beyond himself; the environment transforms itself in front of his eyes, and he beholds visions of distant places. He feels like he is living in a dream. He reveals the above to Bilbo, who recognizes it is a challenge to stay awake in Rivendell until one gets used to it.

At the council Gandalf declares the "folly" of throwing the Ring into the fire. While all eyes are turned on him and all voices silent, Frodo accepts the challenge, though feeling a pull to stay in Rivendell with Bilbo. "At last with an effort he spoke, and wondered to hear his own words, as if some other will was using his small voice. 'I will take the Ring,' he said, 'though I do not know the way.'"[242]

In the caves of Moria Frodo experiences uneasy feelings, leading to dread. Though he has been healed in Rivendell, he carries as a result of wearing the Ring a keener sense awareness and ability to sense and see in the dark, and forebodings of evil events. Thus, together with Aragorn, he can sense the presence of Gollum following them. In Moria Frodo is attacked by a huge Orc chieftain, and receives a blow on the right side. He is saved by the *mithril* shirt mail that Bilbo gifted him in Rivendell. Frodo, bruised and in pain, finds breathing painful. Only a little later, outside of the mines, an arrow hits Frodo and once more springs back on the *mithril* coat. Aragorn's healing skills help Frodo recover. Notice in passing that physical wounds that befall Frodo are a pattern that is unknown to Gandalf and Aragorn.

In Lórien Galadriel beckons to Frodo and Sam to look into her mirror. Among other things Frodo sees a figure clothed like Gandalf but in white, holding a white staff; however, he cannot see his face, and he has doubts of whether it is Gandalf or Saruman, a theme that appears a number of times later in the narrative. Frodo once again has a vision of the Sea; this time he sees a great storm and a ship riding out of the West.

Suddenly the mirror goes dark. From the darkness arises Sauron's Eye, rimmed with fire, growing and filling nearly all Mordor. The

---

[241] Tolkien, *The Fellowship of the Ring*, 217.
[242] Tolkien, *The Fellowship of the Ring*, 264.

eye roves around and seeks, and Frodo feels the Ring on his neck growing heavier. Then the vision fades, leaving Frodo shaking all over. Galadriel indicates that she knows what he saw last, because that is also very present in her mind. In the act of perceiving the strength of Sauron, Frodo has also perceived that Galadriel wears the Ring of Water, Nenya, while Sam is unable to see it.

Galadriel offers gifts to all the members of the fellowship. To Frodo she gives the small phial in which "is caught the light of Eärendil's star. . . . It will shine brighter when night is about you. May it be a light to you in dark places, when all other lights go out."[243] But this is not the only gift. Upon leaving, Frodo hears Galadriel sing in an Elvish tongue. Though he cannot understand it, he will carry the memory of what he heard and interpret it later. Among other things is said, "Maybe you shall find Valimar [the city at the center of Valinor, land of the Valar]. . . . Varda is the name of the Lady whom the Elves in these lands of exile name Elbereth."[244] Elbereth is the one whom Frodo has already invoked at Weathertop, and whom he will invoke later.

Before the fellowship disbands, Frodo fights against Boromir, who tries to induce him to give him the Ring. Trying to determine his course of action, Frodo flees and arrives at the top of Tol Brandir. He sits on the high seat of Amon Hen. He hears no sounds, but is offered a vast visual panorama in every direction around him. He apprehends the magnitude of the power Sauron has put in motion. In looking towards Mount Doom, he feels hopeless and senses the presence of the Eye coming from the Dark Tower, as if searching for him and getting ever closer. Frodo throws himself off the seat and covers his head with the Elven hood.

> He heard himself crying out: *Never, never!* Or was it: *Verily I come, I come to you?* He could not tell. Then as a flash from some other point of power there came to his mind another thought: *Take it off! Take it off! Fool, take it off! Take off the Ring!*[245]

---

[243] Tolkien, *The Fellowship of the Ring*, 367.

[244] Tolkien, *The Fellowship of the Ring*, 369.

[245] Tolkien, *The Fellowship of the Ring*, 392.

Frodo experiences the two powers battling in himself, until he can return to himself, and takes off the Ring just in time. One could sense that the redeeming power in Frodo is the one that resonates with Gandalf, the only character to use the expression "You fool" in *The Lord of the Rings*. Frodo, greatly weary, feels his heart lighter and his will stronger. He affirms his resolve to leave alone, which would happen except for Sam's determination.

While still in the Emyn Muil the two experience a wild wind roaring, and with it a high, shrill cry similar to what they had heard while fleeing Hobbiton. It provokes horror and despair. It comes from the new, now winged versions of the Black Riders—the Nazgûl. Frodo slips and falls forward, losing sight of what's ahead of him: all seems black around him. When Sam sends him down the Elven rope, gift from Lórien, Frodo can see again all around him: "The darkness seemed to lift from Frodo's eyes, or else his sight was returning."[246] Later Frodo, reviewing the episode, realizes that he lost his sight because of lightning or, more likely, something much worse.

While looking for a way out of the mountains, Sam and Frodo capture Gollum, and Frodo is now in the same position Bilbo was in *The Hobbit*. He could kill the repugnant creature, but has pity on him instead. He realizes that in Gollum lies their way to Mordor. So he wants to commit Gollum to them with a binding promise. Gollum swears over the "Precious [Ring] to be very good." Before accepting the promise, Frodo makes him notice that this is a dangerous pledge because the Ring will exact its due from him no matter what. But Gollum is committed not to have Sauron get hold of the Ring.

Sam notices the effect of such a promise. Gollum is affected from this moment for a while, both speaking directly to the Hobbits rather than to his precious, and seeming overeager to please. Here begins a central motif for the rest of the story. The relationship between Frodo and Gollum determines the growth of Frodo and the outcome of the quest.

In the Dead Marshes Gollum plays a critical role in offering cover to Sam and Frodo by hiding them in the day and guiding them at night. Frodo starts lagging behind under the burden of the Ring. As

[246] Tolkien, *The Two Towers*, 594.

they travel on, the darkness thickens, the air grows more oppressive. They start to see dimly shining smoke and flames flickering. These are the light forms emanating from corpses. Gollum, who has previously experienced them, asks them not to look at them. Frodo cannot resist their call and is as if one returning from a dream, when Sam pulls him back. Frodo describes what he saw: "grim faces and evil, and noble faces and sad. Many faces proud and fair . . . I know not who they are; but I thought I saw there Men and Elves, and Orcs beside them."[247] Gollum speaks of a great battle of ages long gone, about which he had heard before acquiring the Ring.

The Ring grows more and more burdensome for Frodo. It drags him down towards the earth. But he is even more troubled by Sauron's Eye, by which he feels scrutinized and pursued. It is such a real experience that he can tell with certainty from which direction it comes.

Coming out of the Dead Marshes, Frodo and Sam are progressing towards the heart of the Black Shadow. The landscape turns bleaker and bleaker. Frodo's consciousness is deeply altered. He "saw strange phantoms, dark riding shapes, and faces out of the past. He lost count of time, hovering between sleep and waking, until forgetfulness came over him."[248] Gollum keeps following them and is even more afraid than either of the hobbits. Only the compulsion of the Ring moves him forward. When Gollum foolishly reclaims the Ring, Frodo warns him of the danger that awaits him in a way that predicts Gollum's end, and is worth quoting at length:

> You swore a promise by what you call the Precious. Remember that! It will hold you to it; but *it will seek a way to twist it to your undoing.* Already you are being twisted. You revealed yourself to me just now, foolishly. *Give* [*the Ring*] *back to Sméagol* you said. Do not say that again! Do not let that thought grow in you! You will never get it back. But the desire of it may betray you to a bitter end. . . . In the last need, Sméagol, I should put on the Precious; and the Precious mastered you long ago. *If*

---

247  Tolkien, *The Two Towers*, 614.
248  Tolkien, *The Two Towers*, 618.

> I, wearing it, were to command you, you would obey, even if
> it were to leap from a precipice or to cast yourself into the fire.
> And such would be my command.[249] (emphasis added)

Gollum is terrified by this speech. The end of the story will bear out Frodo's foreboding.

Here Tolkien indicates in a veiled manner that Frodo is not as alone as he feels; while this is going on Gandalf is dealing with Saruman. When the *palantír* is thrown down the Orthanc tower in an attempt at Gandalf's life, Tolkien indicates that Gandalf's thought turned to Frodo

> in hope and pity. Maybe Frodo felt it, . . . even though
> he believed that Gandalf was gone, gone for ever into
> the shadow in Moria far away. He sat upon the ground
> for a long while, silent, his head bowed, striving to recall
> all that Gandalf had said to him. But for this choice he
> could recall no counsel. . . . Perhaps [Gandalf] could
> not say.[250]

It seems that Gandalf is present spiritually; he always accompanies Frodo and Aragorn. He comes into Frodo's mind as if it were out of the latter's own initiative, but could it be that it is Gandalf who is trying to make contact? Tolkien leads us to believe it. Like Aragorn, Frodo too seems to often ask himself, "What would Gandalf do?"

Making his way into the darkness of the East, Frodo's senses and mind are clouded. This is what pulls Frodo, as if under a hypnotic pull towards the bridge of Minas Morgul. Called by the force of the Ring, he ventures towards the bridge and feels impelled to run toward the gate of the city and its tower. When Sam pulls him back, he feels that the Ring is resisting his initiative. As Frodo looks away from the city, he is as if blinded. Simultaneously a company of horse riders with a Black Rider converge on the bridge that the three just left behind. The leader is the same that wounded Frodo at Weathertop. And Frodo feels the old wound throbbing with pain and a chill cold seizing his heart. He

---

249 Tolkien, *The Two Towers*, 626.
250 Tolkien, *The Two Towers*, 630.

feels called to slip on the Ring; instead he has the strength to reach for Galadriel's phial. At that moment the Ring-wraith loses the mental connection with Frodo and stops searching around.

The respite of Ithilien with Faramir's men of arms seems a necessary step in regenerating the ailing Hobbits. They connect to one who will be an important figure in the events to come—Faramir—and through the latter, news will reach Gandalf of the two Hobbits and their progress towards the heart of darkness.

What follows in the antechambers of Gondor is an intensification of the no-man's-land. Out of Shelob's Lair "came a stench . . . as if filth unnameable were piled and hoarded in the dark within." It was even darker than what they had experienced in Moria, and

> here the air was still, stagnant, heavy, and sound fell
> dead. They walked in a black vapour of veritable darkness
> itself that, as it was breathed, brought blindness not only
> to the eyes but to the mind, so that even the memory of
> colours and of forms and of light faded out of thought.
> Night always had been, and always would be, and night
> was all.

For Frodo, "time and distance soon passed out of his reckoning."[251] Smell seems to be the only and pervading sense that torments them. And it perverts all perception of time so that the two are unable to tell hours from weeks. The blotting out of memory goes a step further than before. It is now almost total.

Frodo uses Galadriel's phial at the inspiration of Sam, and hope returns to him, as if Eärendil were bringing the light of the Silmaril from the heavens. But soon after, Shelob overpowers Frodo, and Sam sees that he has been stung in the neck and that his hands and feet are cold. Thus arrives another wound. And this is like a true initiation death, in many ways parallel to Gandalf's initiation in Moria, especially considering that the sting is followed by captivity under the Orcs. In his

---

[251] Tolkien, *The Two Towers*, 701.

Letters Tolkien indicates, "Frodo's face goes livid and convinces Sam that he's dead, just when Sam gives up hope."[252]

When Sam comes to free him in the Orcs' tower, Frodo doesn't know if he is still in a dream. And what was barely more than a day feels to him like weeks. Frodo has been questioned and threatened by the Orcs and has pain on the back of his neck, above the left shoulder. During the time before Sam's arrival, he strives to remember the scenery of the Shire but can no longer do so; another step in the loss of memory that continues what happened in Shelob's Lair. In addition he is devastated at the idea of having lost everything that he carried, believing the quest has failed. He doesn't know that Sam has rescued the Ring, the sword Sting, and the Phial.

Now Frodo asks for the Ring to be returned to him, and Sam finds himself reluctant. The two act under the influence of the Ring's power. Frodo sees Sam under the guise of an Orc threatening him. Finally, he realizes the deceit and the power of the Ring, and apologizes. He restates to Sam that the Ring is his "doom," and his alone. This is a repetition of the experience in which Bilbo requests to see the Ring from Frodo, but this time Frodo recognizes his own shadow and the power of the Ring more objectively.

In flight from the tower, Frodo feels the presence of a Nazgûl overhead, but this time he does not experience the usual dread and terror. And Sam notices that something new is emerging, that the wind has changed, and intuits Sauron is not having things according to his plans. The narrator adds: "It was the morning of the fifteenth of March, and over the Vale of Anduin the Sun was rising above the eastern shadow, and the south-west wind was blowing. Théoden lay dying on the Pelennor Fields."[253] This is the time in which the Lord of the Ringwraiths has been defeated.

Sam is heartened by the turn of events and wants to give hope to Frodo, though Frodo does not respond as Sam expects. The Ring is becoming more and more burdensome and Frodo begins to see it in his mind "all the time, like a great wheel of fire." Frodo's next sleep is heavy with dreams about fire, but does nevertheless restore his

[252] Carpenter, *Letters of J. R. R. Tolkien*, 101.
[253] Tolkien, *The Return of the* King, 898.

strength. At this time the whole attention of the Eye is turned towards what it perceives as the threat of the Captains of the West, led by the "usurper king" with the terrible sword. Gandalf is carrying on his plan of distracting Sauron from the real threat to his power.

Sam and Frodo realize that they now must make their way into the open, and that only luck can save them from being discovered. Four days have passed since their flight from the tower, and the weight of the Ring becomes hardly bearable for Frodo. Sam keenly observes that Frodo's left hand comes up as if he were protecting himself from a blow, or protecting his sight from an intruding Eye. His right hand gropes towards his breast as it to reach for the Ring and then retreats. What sustains the two is the Elven waybread—the *lembas*—which, as their sole sustenance, seems to acquire stronger power, feeding their will beyond the measure of their personal means. Sam offers to carry the Ring to relieve Frodo, but he answers: "You can't help me in that way again. I'm almost in its power now. I could not give it up, and if you tried to take it I should go mad."[254]

Frodo has now lost all memory of his life on Middle-earth. He still knows what has happened, but cannot call to mind any sense impression. To Sam he says, "I am naked in the dark, Sam, and *there is no veil between me and the wheel of fire.* I begin to see it even in my waking eyes, and all else fades" (emphasis added).[255] A new night passes; Frodo's physical strength ebbs, and he starts to stagger and fall upon his knees. Sam resolves to carry him, finding to his surprise that he is not daunted by the added burden. Sam also helps Frodo resist the irresistible urge to wear the Ring.

While Sam is defending himself from Gollum, Frodo arrives at the brink of the chasm, clutching at the Ring. Sam now sees the following scene as if from a heightened perception. First he pierces through to Gollum's true being: a poor defeated Hobbit devastated by the alien power of the Ring, no longer a match for Frodo. Frodo casts aside Gollum and declares that Gollum's time is coming to an end, and that he will no longer be able to betray or slay him. Once more Frodo is

---

[254] Tolkien, *The Return of the* King, 916.
[255] Tolkien, *The Return of the* King, 916.

predicting Gollum's end, as he had done when Gollum had promised to guide them out of Emyn Muil over the "Precious."

What comes next is seen by Sam in a vision. Gollum appears as a completely ruined being, yet possessed of insatiable rage and lust, and

> before it stood stern, untouchable now by pity, a *figure robed in white*, but *at its breast it held a wheel of fire. Out of the fire there spoke a commanding voice.* 'Begone and trouble me no more! If you touch me ever again, *you shall be cast into the Fire of Doom.*[256] (emphasis added)

This is the third time that Frodo predicts Gollum's ending. Note that the figure in white, reminiscent of Gandalf, indicates that Frodo is undergoing an initiation to some degree parallel to that of the wizard in the caves of Moria.

After a while Sam sees Frodo approaching the fiery abyss. He tries to use Galadriel's phial, but it throws no light into this darkness. In the heart of darkness not even Galadriel can offer the Hobbits solace. Here only Sauron's power can be felt. All spiritual powers have to withdraw if Frodo is to accomplish his most challenging deed. Frodo cannot do it out of himself, but he has now complete dominion over Gollum, as he has foretold various times before.

Frodo is standing next to the brink of the chasm, his will as if paralyzed, unable to let go of the Ring, which he decides to wear. Gollum is now fighting with the invisible Frodo on the brink of the chasm. In a mad frenzy he bites off Frodo's finger together with the Ring. Gollum holds the Ring like a trophy, which "shone now as if verily it was *wrought of living fire*" (emphasis added).[257] Gollum in his unconsciousness falls over the abyss with the Ring, wailing "Precious" for the last time.

Frodo and Sam come to their senses and see the surrounding devastation caused by the loss of the Ring to the fire. Frodo remembers with gratitude Gandalf's prediction that even Gollum may play an important role in the destruction of the Ring, making it easier to forgive

---

[256] Tolkien, *The Return of the* King, 922.
[257] Tolkien, *The Return of the* King, 925.

him. As Gandalf has been present at the very beginning of Frodo's quest, so now he appears to rescue him from death's clutches thanks to the help of Gwaihir, Lord of Eagles.

After her wedding to Aragorn, Queen Arwen offers two presents to Frodo. The first is the possibility for Frodo to go to the Grey Havens to seek healing and regeneration, since she herself has forfeited this privilege. Moreover, she offers him a "white gem like a star hanging on a silver chain," adding, "When the memory of the fear and the darkness troubles you, this will bring you aid."[258] Passing through Rivendell on the way back from Gondor, Sam expresses that here is found something of everything: of the Shire, of Lórien, and Gondor. Frodo comments "except the Sea," and he later repeats this to himself. Frodo's longing for the Sea and the true West of Valinor, which guided him from the early days of his quest, is now becoming all-absorbing.

When passing the Fords of Bruinen Frodo seems loath to wade the stream; he is unable to see in front of him and is silent throughout the day. It is October 6, the anniversary of his wound at Weathertop. Gandalf tells him that some wounds cannot be fully cured, and Frodo predicts that he will not find complete solace in the Shire: "There is no real going back. Though I may come to the Shire, it will not seem the same; for I shall not be the same. I am wounded with knife, sting, and tooth, and a long burden. Where shall I find rest?"[259] However, thanks to Arwen's gift, the pain is no longer present the next day.

Back in the Shire Frodo is the one of the four who has the greatest understanding of human nature; he knows how individuals like the Hobbit Lotho think they can take advantage of a situation by becoming the oppressors of their people, and in reality become prisoners of other powers themselves. And to Pippin, who talks about fighting, Frodo recommends moderation and asks to avoid Hobbit bloodshed, and to spare Hobbit traitors. Behind the façade of the ruffians who tyrannize the Shire, the Hobbits find Saruman at work. Saruman is intent on causing chagrin to the four Hobbits in vengeance for his humiliation at Isengard. The younger Hobbits want justice meted out to Saruman on the spot. Frodo orders otherwise; he lets him go freely, and tells them

---

[258] Tolkien, *The Return of the* King, 952–53.

[259] Tolkien, *The Return of the* King, 967.

that he has lost all powers save his voice. Saruman tries to kill Frodo, who is protected once more by the *mithril*-coat and escapes harm. Frodo orders Sam not to kill him even so. Saruman looks at Frodo with wonder, respect, and hatred. "You are wise and cruel. You have robbed my revenge of sweetness, and now I must go hence in bitterness, in debt to your mercy."[260] Frodo has become like Gandalf in his understanding of human nature; Saruman has not changed and cannot tolerate having feelings of gratitude towards another human being.

On more than one occasion, on anniversary dates of fateful events, Frodo seems pale, far away, and in pain. He clutches at Arwen's white gem, which brings him solace, and he knows that his wounds will never fully heal, though the gem allows him to recover promptly. Frodo no longer feels at home in the Shire; and very few have recognition for what he has done.

Frodo finally goes to the Grey Havens with Bilbo, Gandalf, Galadriel, and Elrond. All of them have been ring-bearers, and this is now the end of the Third Age and of the rings of power. Frodo's longing for the Western Sea is at last fulfilled. Frodo now lives as a reality his passage into the West that had appeared as a vision in the house of Tom Bombadil. "And then it seemed to him that as in his dream in the house of Bombadil, the grey rain-curtain turned all to silver glass and was rolled back, and he beheld white shores and beyond them a far green country under a swift sunrise."[261]

## Gandalf, Aragorn, and Frodo

The quest is not primarily the affair of Frodo, nor of Gandalf, nor of Aragorn. It is the joint deed of the three. Gandalf, Aragorn, and Frodo act as a higher unity. Let us look first at Gandalf and Frodo, then at the three. When Frodo sets out for the quest, he is accomplishing something that Gandalf himself knows to be beyond his means. The Ring is too formidable a temptation even for him. In fact, we know what it does to Saruman, his equal. But Gandalf offers to be responsible for the whole mission at Frodo's side. And Tolkien shows it in subtle ways. When Gandalf is delayed by the captivity in Orthanc, this is

260 Tolkien, *The Return of the* King, 996.
261 Tolkien, *The Return of the* King, 1007.

communicated to Frodo via a significant dream in the house of Tom Bombadil. He sees the figure of a man with white hair atop a tall tower, then the eagle that bears him away. That dream was important, as we find out later on in Rivendell.

In a more conscious way the role of Gandalf is also announced in Frodo's future within the mirror of Galadriel. There he sees a figure clothed like Gandalf but in white and holding a white staff, though he cannot see his face and he has doubts of whether it is Gandalf or Saruman.

Aragorn and Frodo subordinate themselves to Gandalf's guidance willingly and without hesitations. When Frodo and Strider meet at the inn at Bree, Barleyman Butterbur delivers to Frodo Gandalf's letter in which he recommends to accept the help of "a Man, lean, dark, tall, by some called Strider." And then he adds that his true name is Aragorn. When Gandalf vanishes at the chasm of Khazad Dûm, Aragorn reluctantly assumes leadership. Later on Aragorn and Frodo assume their own responsibilities, but in some part of their mind they are always consulting with Gandalf, wanting to know what the wizard would do in their shoes. And Gandalf seems to be present spiritually.

When Frodo is left alone with Sam in the most important part of the task, Gandalf is still present through the judgments he has offered Frodo, and in the life of his dreams and subconscious. Gandalf on the other hand maintains awareness of Frodo and Sam and makes it his task to accompany them spiritually and strategically.

The interconnectedness and complementary roles of the three are recognized by Aragorn in the ceremony of his crowning. He first recognizes the leading role of Gandalf once more, and honor Frodo's feat. "I would have the Ring-bearer bring the crown to me, and let Mithrandir [Gandalf] set it upon my head, if he will; for he has been the mover of all that has been accomplished and this is his victory."[262]

Frodo is the humblest of the three heroes. He is also the lowliest in line of descent; the pure Hobbit. He seems to have been cast into adventure in spite of himself. The only other one to volunteer has been Bilbo, but he has been turned down.

---

[262] Tolkien, *The Return of the King*, 946.

Frodo is initiated by Old Man Willow, by the Barrow-wight, then by the Ringwraith and by Shelob, who brings him close to death; and finally at the chasm in Mount Orodruin; in short he is initiated by all the representatives and shades of evil present in the world. And he faces constantly a new kind of monster at his side, something unlike the dragons of the Middle Ages: Gollum, himself a fallen Hobbit, an outcast among his race. His greed and selfishness are portrayed in his behavior and in his outer appearance.

Frodo is tested in the body. He alone of the three heroes is wounded repeatedly. He has to tread the harshest of physical conditions, the scorched earth of Mordor. Gandalf is tested, but his physical body is transformed and actually placed beyond hurt. Aragorn is always present in battle; indeed he has fought all his life. Yet he seems immune to hurt; he is worn and beaten but never wounded. Frodo has to face the harrowing trials of heat, darkness, stench, hunger, thirst, and fire. He is the furthest removed from the perfection of an Aragorn or a Gandalf and actually closest to the aspect of the physical body and the psyche's double or shadow, embodied in Gollum/Sméagol.

When we look at the three main characters of *The Lord of the Rings* we find a whole representation of the human being as we know it from spiritual science. Gandalf is more than human. He is in fact a divine being taking on human semblance; he is a Maiar, one of the minor deities who serve the Valar, emissaries of the one God, Ilúvatar. Gandalf is an apt representative of that which is the human spirit in the human being: the individuality, or ego, whose fullness lies beyond the confines of the body and the confines of life on earth. Gandalf shows this in his ability to encompass in knowledge all of the relevant factors in the life of Middle-earth and in the confrontation with Sauron. With Shadowfax—another image of the spirit—he is the one able to practically fly from one place to the other.

Aragorn brings in his inheritance both the mortal, human element, and the Elven deathlessness that conveys him a long life. He also carries the wisdom of the lords of Númenor, the inheritance of times past, and the right to rule. He is a king, almost a conduit between the higher wisdom of the spirit and the affairs of earth. He is the one who knows intimately both the things of the spirit and the things of earth.

He displays a far-from-usual connection with and understanding of the earth as a living organism. He also knows the human soul, even more than Gandalf; he shows it in his ability to heal and to follow the soul between this world and the next one. In this realm Gandalf recognizes he has to delegate to the future king. In Aragorn we find a representative of the human soul: that which links the human spirit, the ego, with the body, the divine with the earthly.

And finally it is in Frodo that we find the representative of the last component of the human being: the physical body endowed with life. Frodo is the humblest of the three by birth. Only a strain of Took brings the taste for adventure to the Hobbit. Frodo is the closest to the limitations of the body in as much as in a certain measure he fails to accomplish his task. He is the one who is wounded over and over again, the one who is most often reminded of the physical limitations.

## Of Spirit, Soul, and Body

Let us look now at what can be understood from the perspective of spiritual science in relation to body, soul, and spirit. This will build some foundation for exploring other archetypal dimensions of Tolkien's masterwork.

The physical structure of the body is what human beings have in common with minerals. But, whereas the forces that allow the mineral to come into being are inherently present in the substances that form it—e. g., silicon and oxygen in the case of quartz—the forces of all living beings are at work in the reproductive cells of the parent form, whether we have to do with plants, animals, or human beings. Steiner introduces here the central notion of "formative life forces" thus: "The species is therefore what determines how the substances are put together. Just as mineral forces express themselves in crystals, the formative life force expresses itself in the species, or forms, of plant and animal life."[263]

We can perceive the mineral forces through our senses; not so the life forces. We would need to develop new organs of perceptions to behold the spiritual form taken by the life forces. To the carrier of the formative forces in each living organism, and in the human being,

---

[263] Steiner, *Theosophy*, 33.

Steiner gives the name of "ether body" or "life body." It is important to underline that "the ether body is not merely a result of the physical body's substances and forces, but a real, independent entity that calls these same substances and forces to life."[264] The life body is what preserves the form and animates the physical body through life. Although the substances that fill the physical body are constantly renewed, its form is preserved. It is the ether body that holds the form constant regardless of the flow of substances. At death, when the ether body withdraws, the physical body is finally subjected to purely physical forces.

The form of the body is held and preserved by the life body. In the realm of the body reign the laws of inheritance: "Every life body is a repetition of its immediate ancestor, and because this is so, the form the life body assumes is never arbitrary, but is the one that it has inherited. The forces that have made my human form possible came from my ancestors."[265] The human bodily form can only be inherited through sexual reproduction. It is passed down the generations through the laws of heredity.

Physical bodies vary only slightly, and ether bodies still show great similarities; greater differences are present at the level of soul and spirit. The soul is only present in the life between birth and death. On one hand the physical body confines the soul to physical existence; on the other the spirit allows the soul to find itself at home in growing dimensions of the spiritual world. The bodily nature sets limits on the soul; the spirit releases it. In life on earth the degree of the soul's development will determine to what extent it can receive the impressions of the physical world and to what extent it can develop an individualized expression of the spirit. Summarizing the above and expanding on it, Steiner concludes:

> The soul plays a mediator's role, in a sense, and its task
> is accomplished in playing this role satisfactorily. The
> body forms impressions for the soul, which reshapes
> them into sensations, stores them in the memory as
> mental images, and passes them on to the spirit to be

---

[264] Steiner, *Theosophy*, 35.

[265] Steiner, *Theosophy*, 70.

made lasting. The soul is what actually makes us belong to this earthly life. Through the body, we belong to the physical human genus; we are members of the genus. With our spirit, we live in a higher world. The soul binds the two worlds together for a while.[266]

By *spirit* let us designate what lives beyond the laws of the physical, that which lies beyond growth and decay. The spirit of the human being has its seat in the self or "I." Through the I a person expresses the whole experience of being in body and soul. Body and soul are the vehicles through which the I finds its expression in the world. This means that we have our true being in the I and that the soul and physical body serve as its vehicles, which we learn to devote over time to the I. It is remarkable that "I" is the name that one can only apply to oneself: "The soul can only designate itself as 'I' from within through itself."[267] As the I lives in the body and the soul, so the spirit, whose laws lie beyond the physical, lives in the I.

The I receives on one hand what comes to it through the senses and on the other hand what comes to it through the spirit. The spirit is alive and active through the I; it uses the I as its vehicle. By aspiring to the truth and uniting our personal impulses with it, the I achieves immortality. By this Steiner means that "the spiritual world, with its spirit substances and spirit forces, builds up a spiritual body in which the 'I' is able to live and perceive spiritual realities by means of intuitions."[268] Intuitions in the spirit stand as a counterpart to perceptions in the physical world.

The human spirit also assumes a form, or gestalt, though this must be thought of in spiritual terms. Contrary to the human bodily form that is passed down the generations, the human spiritual forms are strictly individual, completely unique for each individual. Human beings have biographies, and these, contrary to animals, have a beginning when we start seeing something beyond genus or species. In fact every human being is so different from another in what constitutes his or

---

[266] Steiner, *Theosophy*, 83.
[267] Steiner, *Theosophy*, 49.
[268] Steiner, *Theosophy*, 53.

her biography and individuality, that each person can be considered its own species: "The point is that a human biography corresponds to the description of an animal species rather than to the biography of an individual animal."[269] In other words, there is as much difference between two human beings as there is between two animal species. This indicates that the spiritual form cannot have descended through inheritance. Every individual can only have acquired this form through itself. Since my ancestors' biographies cannot explain mine, and since I have unique capacities and challenges, I must have worked at these and acquired them before my birth. Expanding upon these realizations, we arrive through thinking alone to the idea of repeated earthly lives.

> The human physical form is a repetition or re-embodiment, over and over again, of what is inherent in the human genus and species. Similarly, a spiritual individual must be a re-embodiment or reincarnation of one and the same spiritual being, for as a spiritual being, each person is his or her own species.[270]

The human spirit carries the fruits—abilities and consequences of actions—of one life into another life.

Steiner concludes:

> The body is subject to the laws of *heredity*; the soul is subject to self-created destiny or, to use an ancient term, to *karma*; and the spirit is subject to the laws of *reincarnation* or repeated earthly lives. The interrelationship of body, soul and spirit can also be expressed as follows: The spirit is immortal; birth and death govern our bodily existence in accordance with the laws of the physical world; and the life of the soul, which is subject to destiny, mediates between body and spirit during the course of an earthly life.[271]

---

[269] Steiner, *Theosophy*, 73.
[270] Steiner, *Theosophy*, 75–76.
[271] Steiner, *Theosophy*, 89.

Returning to our three characters, we can thus see how these archetypes, or truths of a higher order, are encapsulated in Gandalf, Aragorn, and Frodo. Aragorn and Frodo subordinate themselves to Gandalf, who seems to hover over much of the story, even when he is not physically present. Aragorn and Frodo ask themselves what Gandalf would do in a given situation, or remember his words in order to address given situations. When Gandalf is engulfed by the mines of Moria, it is Aragorn who takes the lead. At Bree the letter of Gandalf had already legitimized his authority.

Of the three characters Gandalf is the most exalted: Aragorn and Frodo have been his pupils, Aragorn already for many years and Frodo much more recently. Through his initiations at the hands of the Balrog, Gandalf has attained a state of being in which his body has been spiritualized to the extent that he can walk through battle as if oblivious to physical danger. It is Gandalf alone who can gather in his thinking all the complex threads through which the fate of Middle-earth stands in balance.

Aragorn, as a soul figure, is the one who mediates between the living and the dead, and between Gandalf and Frodo. He is of mixed human and Elven descent. He carries the memory of Númenor, when rulers had converse with Elves, who transmitted the knowledge of the Valar. He is placed in between the two worlds. And this is continued later on through his marriage to Arwen, who has relinquished her Elven heritage.

Frodo stands as s stark contrast to the two. He is battered and wounded, besieged by his shadow Gollum. He ploughs his way through the harshest, deadest of all physical surroundings. He confronts the Enemy in the starkest of mineral environments, in which life has no longer a place. He has barely the strength to accomplish his task, and he cannot throw the Ring in the fire out of his own will. He stands bereft of energy and will at the end of his trials to the point of needing regeneration through his departure from the Grey Havens. Of all the Hobbits he is the one who exemplifies most the strengths and limitations of the physical body.

*The Lord of the Rings* brings to life archetypal reality in vivid images in the figures of Gandalf, Aragorn, and Frodo. Gandalf. As we will see later, Gandalf, Aragorn, and Frodo's trials represent different aspect of initiations, even different kinds of initiations into the spirit: Gandalf in the wide spiritual world, Aragorn in the elemental world of the soul, Frodo in the extreme mineral world of the body. To this we will return in the next chapter. But first we will look more closely at what can be met closer to earth, in the characters of the Hobbits. Here too Tolkien brings to life another important archetype, one that is related to the traditional four elements of earth, water, air, and fire and that was known in antiquity.

## THE FOUR AND THE ONE: THE PATHS OF THE FOUR HOBBITS

The four Hobbits have been divided by some into a major pair—Sam and Frodo—and a minor pair—Merry and Pippin. We will look at them in that order. Although they are four Hobbits, in a higher sense they too form a unity, much as Gandalf, Aragorn, and Frodo do. We could say that we have a threefold unity at a higher level, ranging from the divine (Gandalf) to the human (Hobbit) and a purely human unity with the four Hobbits. This fourfoldness illustrates another important spiritual dimension of the human condition.

Concerning the Hobbits, Tolkien states that they are very ancient people, closer to Men than Elves and Dwarves are. Not unlike Men and Elves, we find a natural threefolding of Hobbit races:

- Harfoots: smaller and shorter; they prefer highlands and hillsides. They have much interchange with Dwarves, and are the most representative type and the most numerous of Hobbits. They preserved the habit of living in tunnels and holes.
- Stoors: broader and heavier in build with larger feet and hands, who like the flat lands and riversides, and are less shy of Men. Among them is Sméagol/Gollum.
- The Fallohides, fairer of skin and hair, taller and slimmer, who love trees and woodlands. They are the least numerous and cultivate relationships with the Elves, hence their greater skill

in language, song, and handicrafts. They tend to be bolder and more adventurous than the others, and tend to become leaders or chieftains; among them are the Tooks and the Masters of Buckland.[272]

At the beginning of the story Frodo is fifty, Sam thirty-five, Merry thirty-two, and Pippin twenty-eight. Since Tolkien places the hobbits' coming of age at thirty-three, the major pair is, at least nominally, more mature than the other. Frodo has Took/Fallohide ancestry on the mother side, hence a closer connection to the Elves and a more adventuresome make up. Merry is a Brandybuck, one of those who are used to sail the rivers, presumably a Stoor. But he also has Tookish blood through his mother and his father's grandmother, Mirabella Took. He is first cousins with Pippin (Peregrin), himself a Took, in fact a great-great-grandson of the famed Old Took. Through his father Pippin is a second-cousin, once-removed, of Frodo. Sam is the most quintessentially pure Hobbit.

It is interesting to note that the major pair moves in the direction of Mordor and will face a parched landscape of scorched earth and fire; Merry and Pippin will practically fly through the plains of Rohan before finding themselves in the soothing, humid forest landscape of Fangorn and back to Rohan and Gondor. We will look first at the major pair, and first of all to the seemingly simplest of them all, Sam.

## The Major Pair

We have already looked at length at Frodo, so we will only return to him briefly after considering Sam. In the appendices of *The Lord of the Rings*, Tolkien says the "true" or Westron form of Sam's name is Banazîr Galbasi. As with "Samwise," *Banazîr* indicates "halfwise" or "simple." And at first this is what Sam appears to be: the very naive son of a gardener. But Sam teaches himself to read and write, learns from Bilbo, and eavesdrops on Frodo. Already early on he shows a great thirst for knowledge. He also carries a constant childlike enthusiasm and naivete, a surprising optimism, and a rock-solid common sense. Sam bears in himself the paradoxical contrast of one with a true thirst for knowledge

---

[272] Tolkien, *The Fellowship of the* Ring, 2–3.

but also the desire to hold on to the familiar. It is only over time that he can overcome this reticence and love for comfort. But most of all he bears in himself a fierce and complete devotion to Frodo, an uncanny capacity to walk in his shoes, to understand and anticipate his way of thinking and his needs.

The first signs of Sam's maturation appear in his encounters with the Elves, most particularly at the very beginning with Gildor and later with Galadriel. After seeing the Elves' party of Gildor, he understands that he is looking at another paradigm, for which his usual frame of reference does not apply. "They seem a bit above my likes and dislikes . . . so old and young, and so gay and sad, as it were."[273] Here he first intuits the need to tackle paradox and encompass polarities. He completes the above by saying that he himself feels different. And this comes with the resolve: "I have something to do before the end, and it lies ahead, not in the Shire. I must see it through."

Speaking of Lórien after the fact, Sam says, "I feel as if I were inside a song,"[274] or that being there is "like being at home and on holiday at the same time."[275] In Lórien itself Sam shows his ambivalence about its "magic." On the surface he sees nothing of what he would like to recognize as magic, but rather what seems to offer the appearance of stagnation. But part of him also intuits that Lórien's magic may be of a different nature from what he surmises. When he expresses to Frodo his wish to see Galadriel one last time, she immediately appears to him, indicating that she could show Sam some Elven magic. Looking in Galadriel's mirror, Sam sees himself in the future: fast asleep under a great, dark cliff; climbing an endless winding stair, looking urgently for something he doesn't know. Remembering, shortly after, his experience with Galadriel, Sam says: "I felt as if I hadn't got nothing on, and I didn't like it. She seemed to be looking inside me and asking me what I would do if she gave me the chance of flying back home to the Shire."[276] Sam's common sense and grounding in the everyday matter-of-fact still partly holds him back, but his love for Frodo will move him further.

[273] Tolkien, *The Fellowship of the Ring*, 96.
[274] Tolkien, *The Fellowship of the Ring*, 342.
[275] Tolkien, *The Fellowship of the Ring*, 351.
[276] Tolkien, *The Fellowship of the Ring*, 348.

Isn't it appropriate in this regard for Galadriel to offer Sam something as earthy as a box containing soil from Lórien, which will act like magic when placed in Sam's garden? This is another demonstration of that ordinary magic that Sam does not fully apprehend yet.

As the fellowship progresses in enemy territory, Sam knows that Frodo is simply terrified, though he knows what he has to do. As Frodo comes to one of his major turning points after the experience of the seat of Amon Hen, it is Sam once more who can best fathom the mind of the one he calls his master. He first reads correctly that Frodo has decided to proceed to his "doom" alone; then valiantly overcomes his dread of water to come to his rescue. Frodo can intuit how good it will be to have Sam at his side.

As Sam steels himself to his task and moves closer to Mordor, his understanding grows, particularly in relation to Galadriel. He now comments about her: "But perhaps you could call her perilous, because she's so strong in herself. You could dash yourself to pieces on her, like a ship on a rock; or drownd [*sic*] yourself, like a hobbit in a river. But neither rock nor river would be to blame."[277]

When Shelob starts making her presence felt, the memory of Lórien and Galadriel returns to Sam, and with it the memory of her phial, and he asks Frodo to take it out since it is *"a light when all other lights go out."* Later Sam sees that Frodo has been stung in the neck, and his hands and feet are cold. But Shelob, wounded in the belly by Sam's dagger, retreats to her lair. Sam returns to his master, but doesn't know what do with him and thinks he is beyond hope. Sam then realizes that he has just gone through what was announced to him in Galadriel's mirror. Significantly, Sam repeats something that he has said before: "I have something to do before the end. I must see it through, sir, if you understand."[278] With his newly acquired maturity, Galadriel will ever be present in Sam's footsteps, and thus at Frodo's side as well.

Sam even contemplates going alone to the Cracks of Doom, taking strength from the fact that neither Bilbo nor Frodo ever seemed to be the ones meant to tackle such a daunting task. Sam is now having a

---

[277]  Tolkien, *The Two* Towers, 665.

[278]  Tolkien, *The Two Towers*, 714.

"mini Frodo experience." He slips on the Ring for the first time in order to follow the Orcs. His inner world changes.

> All things about him now were dark but vague; while he himself was there in a grey hazy world, alone, like a small black solid rock, and the Ring, weighing down his left hand, was like an orb of hot gold. He did not feel invisible at all, but horribly and uniquely visible; and he knew that somewhere an Eye was searching for him.[279]

The Ring gives him a fortunate understanding of the language of the Orcs, but not courage.

Sam, who now carries the sword Sting and the Phial of Galadriel, is truly passing through his dark night of the soul: "He was in a land of darkness where *all days seemed forgotten*, and where *all who entered were forgotten too*" (emphasis added).[280] And he feels utterly alone. In the midst of these trials, Sam feels roused to come to the rescue of Frodo because of the power that love for Frodo has in his soul. And he fully perceives for the first time what it means to have crossed into Mordor. Removing the Ring, he sees the harsh landscape in front of him, and for the first time he perceives Orodruin, the Mountain of Fire.

Sam is now resolute in entering through the gate of the tower of Cirith Ungol. While aware of the growing power of the Ring, even though he has already removed it, he is tempted by it. He sees that he can only abandon the Ring or claim it and challenge Sauron. Wild fantasies assail him; he sees himself as Samwise the Strong, Hero of the Age, or the one who brings Mordor back to life, transforming it into a garden full of flowers and trees. What preserves his sanity is his love for his master and his earthy common sense. And he realizes that he cannot use the Ring, even though it seems to be the thing that gives him the most power. He comes now under the walls of the tower. Sam is accompanied by the silent presence of Galadriel through her phial as he passes the gate to the tower, overcoming the power of the Silent Watchers.

---

[279] Tolkien, *The Two Towers*, 717.
[280] Tolkien, *The Two Towers*, 877.

At this hour it is Sam who renders hope to Frodo who, devastated at having lost everything that he carried, believes the quest has ended. He doesn't know that Sam has rescued the Ring, Sting, and the phial. From this moment on it is Sam who can sustain, nurture, and imbue with hope Frodo, who has entered another stage of inner darkness. Sam, whose inner strength is growing, now calls to Galadriel: "If only the Lady could see or hear us, I'd say to her: 'Your Ladyship, all we want is light and water: just clean water and plain daylight.'"[281] And in quick succession he realizes that somehow the wind is turning on Sauron. Then he rejoices to see the light of a star. Shortly after he also finds water, exclaiming "If I ever see the Lady again, I will tell her! Light and now water!"[282] And all of this he offers to Frodo to revive his dwindling hope.

Having to descend into the plains of Gorgoroth, Frodo expresses openly that Sam is the only hope he has left and asks him to lead him. It is now clear that Frodo could not have carried the Ring alone to Mount Doom and held any hope along the way. He needed Sam all along. With Mount Doom in sight Sam realizes that they will have no way to return from Mount Doom alive. With iron determination he resolves: "So that was the job I felt I had to do when I started . . . to help Mr. Frodo to the last step and then die with him? Well, if that is the job then I must do it."[283] Even what amounts to losing the last hope of staying alive brings in Sam new resolve. His will hardens in resolve, and he finds new hope and energies he never surmised possible.

The weight of the Ring becomes hardly bearable for Frodo. Sam notices the inner battle that rages in Frodo's soul and is his sole support in helping him resist the pull of the Ring. After escaping the Orc company. the consciousness of the two is altered. Sam cannot tell if he is awake or dreaming: "[Sam] saw lights like gloating eyes, and dark creeping shapes, and he heard noises as of wild beasts or the dreadful cries of tortured things; and he would start up to find the world all dark

---

[281] Tolkien, *The Two Towers*, 897.
[282] Tolkien, *The Two Towers*, 899.
[283] Tolkien, *The Two Towers*, 913.

and only empty blackness all about him."[284] Sam, who has been a Ring-bearer, continues in effect to experience some of Frodo's inner world.

When the worst part of the challenge arrives on the slopes of Mount Doom, Sam is in complete pain and so parched that he cannot swallow food. His inner struggle intensifies. And it is difficult to breathe in the air full of fumes. He only knows vaguely what Frodo intends to do with the Ring, but knows they need to find the Cracks of Doom. Here Sam is having an inner dialogue, recognizing his own shadow, and keeping at bay his disbelief and sense of hopelessness. The best of him finally takes the upper hand: "I'll get there, if I have to leave everything but my bones behind. . . . And I'll carry Mr. Frodo up myself, if it breaks my back and heart. So stop arguing."[285] Resolve and strength are the qualities that Sam displays and intensifies at every turn of the quest.

Steeled to an iron will Sam now has to accompany Frodo through the greatest part of the test. And here it is interesting to note that the narrative focuses completely on Sam. Time for him acquires another dimension: "The night seemed endless and timeless, minute after minute falling dead and adding up to passing hour, bringing no change. Sam began to wonder if a second darkness had begun and no day would ever appear."[286] Then Sam notices that Frodo's physical strength is ebbing, and he resolves to carry him, finding that he is not daunted by the weight or the added burden of the Ring.

The transformed Sam now sees the reappearing Gollum under a new light. Having worn the Ring he can detect the effect it has had on Gollum and be moved to compassion. And this is when in vision Sam is able to see the figures of Frodo and Sam under their true light. And again in vision he beholds the cataclysmic effect of the Ring being thrown into the fire and realizes this is the beginning of a new aeon. It is Sam once more who takes care of Frodo's earthly needs, who carries him to safety before the eagles arrive. In the middle of desolation and destruction, he is able to experience complete peace.

Coming back home to the Shire, it is Sam who can restore nature thanks to the earth of Lórien, Galadriel's gift. And he plants the seed

[284] Tolkien, *The Two Towers*, 915.
[285] Tolkien, *The Two Towers*, 918.
[286] Tolkien, *The Two Towers*, 919.

of the *mallorn*, to replace the tree under which Bilbo had celebrated his last birthday in the Shire before the beginning of the quest.

Sam the gardener is the one who knows how to tend to all of Frodo's primary needs, down to feeding him and carrying him. His is the consummate example of selfless earthly love. His common sense has all the trademarks of one with his feet firmly on the ground. It is no wonder that he can see the danger that Gollum poses to Frodo and witness the dialogue in which Gollum indicates he is going to betray Frodo. And it is Sam who renews the Shire's nature from its devastation, thanks to his deep concern for the earth that Galadriel recognizes in him when she offers him the gift of Lórien's earth.

Frodo is to Sam like fire is to earth. It is Frodo who sets the spark and initiates, and Sam who supports and sustains; Frodo who can see the larger picture in the carrying of the Ring, and Sam who can help carry it to fruition. Frodo is so determined that he is willing to go the way alone at the very early stages of the quest. He hears the call of the higher self and carries the task that requires the highest degree of determination, courage, and trust in the help of the spirit.

Another aspect of Frodo is revealed most of all at Mount Doom, though it is announced before. When Frodo looks into the mirror of Galadriel, he sees that "the Eye was rimmed with fire, but was itself glazed, yellow as a cat's, watchful and intent, and the black slit of its pupil opened on a pit, a window into nothing." At this point the Ring and the Eye become as one in the vision, as Pia Skogemann intuits. On the flanks of Mount Orodruin Frodo experiences them as one: "I am naked in the dark, Sam, and there is no veil between me and the wheel of fire."[287] When Sam sees in vision Frodo fighting against Gollum, he discerns Frodo as a figure robed in white with a wheel of fire at his breast. Frodo, the carrier of inner fire, recognizes the counterfire—the fire of devastation and ruin that emanates from Sauron, and that is at its strongest on Mount Orodruin.

At Mount Doom fire fights against fire. The fire that Frodo carries is the one of sacrifice and of an individuality becoming more and more selfless—all the contrary of what Sauron embodies. Frodo's fire sheds

---

[287] Tolkien, *The Two Towers*, 916.

light in the darkness. Sauron embodies the fire that wants to dominate, enslave, and ultimately destroy.

Of all the Hobbits Frodo is the most individuated, the most able to stand on his own. Sam walks the path of complete service and dedication to Frodo, whom he calls master. He becomes like the ground under Frodo's feet. A sturdy ground and a fire of sacrifice meet the landscape of scorched, hard earth and belching fire of Mount Doom. It is no wonder that all of this is reflected in the gifts of Galadriel to the two: the phial to Frodo as a light in the darkness and the earth to Sam. For the picture of the Hobbits to be complete, we will turn next to the minor pair. Together with Pippin and Merry, Frodo and Sam constitute a higher unity.

## The Minor Pair

What Pippin and Merry say towards the end of the odyssey seems an apt characterization of the contrast of this pair with the major pair. Pippin says to Merry, "We Tooks and Brandybucks, we can't live long in the heights." And Merry replies: "Not yet at any rate. But at least, Pippin, we can now see them, and honour them. It is best to love first what you are fitted to love, I suppose. . . . I am glad that I know about them [things deeper and higher] a little."[288]

The first trial of size for the two Hobbits comes through the Orc abduction through the lands of Rohan. Tolkien tells us that for Pippin and Merry, "Evil dreams and evil waking were blended into a long tunnel of misery, with hope growing ever fainter behind."[289]

The second apparent sign of the growth of the two is made even outwardly apparent in the Fangorn adventure. Treebeard gives the Hobbit a special water. Gimli is later surprised because he believes that Pippin and Merry have grown. And Legolas knows that they must have drunk the Ent draughts. Merry and Pippin later return to the devastated Shire, where they will act with great boldness and scare the other Hobbits sent to stop them. Their apprenticeship is finished; they are now able to initiate and lead others. Let us look first at Pippin, then at Merry.

---

[288] Tolkien, *The Return of the* King, 852.
[289] Tolkien, *The Two* Towers, 440.

Pippin's Took ancestors tended to be bolder and more adventurous than other Hobbits, and tended to become leaders or chieftains. Pippin's curiosity and impulsivity is revealed for the first time when he creeps to the edge of the well in Moria and drops a loose stone to the bottom of it, with a resulting sound that is amplified through the space and angers Gandalf, since it will alert the Orcs of their presence. Pippin's is a particular kind of curiosity; we will see it somehow enhanced once more.

Pippin's consciousness first awakens in the ordeal of the Orc abduction. He is then able to act out of the intuition of the moment, and of taking calculated risks, as in the episode in which he purposefully drops his Elven brooch to offer a clue to his pursuing companions; or in the event that leads to the two Hobbits' release from the Orcs. It is during this adventure that Pippin expresses regrets at having come along for the adventure.

After rejoining the other members of the fellowship, Pippin seems utterly unable to restrain his curiosity and resist the temptation of looking into the *palantír*. Gandalf knows that Pippin has had a narrow escape, though Pippin also saved him from looking into the Stone himself. Pippin disingenuously tells Gandalf that he had no idea of what he was doing, but Gandalf rebukes him that he was perfectly aware of his choice, and even so did not refrain. With the test of the *palantír* Pippin has a little parallel experience to that of Frodo at the seat of Amon Hen.

Later Gandalf introduces Pippin to Denethor in glowing terms. In debt to Boromir's valiance in his defense, Pippin offers his services to Denethor and is knighted. When Denethor turns to Gandalf, Pippin sees a similarity between the two. "Yet *by a sense other than sight* Pippin perceived that Gandalf had the greater power and the deeper wisdom, and a majesty that was veiled. And he was older, far older" (emphasis added).[290] And what this "sense other than sight" could be emerges soon after. When Denethor refers to the power of the *palantír*, Pippin intuits what Denethor has left unsaid. Pippin notices a peculiar expression in Denethor when he mentions the Stone; he can vaguely intuit that Denethor knows more about the Stone than he is letting on. Pippin

---

[290] Tolkien, *The Return of the King*, 740.

knows through intuition the curiosity of someone who has after all acted similarly to him. It seems to resonate inwardly.

At the siege of Gondor, Pippin has renewed regrets of having come. He expresses this to Gandalf, who sternly reminds him that he has brought this upon himself. When, soon after, Pippin is introduced to Faramir, he is moved by a new feeling. He can intuit the grandeur of the man, whom he sees in many ways similar to, though less remote than, Aragorn. And in both of them he recognizes "the wisdom and sadness of the Elder Race."[291]

When dread and despair spread through Minas Tirith, Pippin sees Faramir wandering in a feverish state. This is one of the darkest trials of soul for the Hobbit, obliged to witness Denethor's growing insanity. And in a sense the danger that could threaten Pippin's soul is here made manifest to his eyes. This is the trial of soul of Pippin, having to place duty above the comfort of obedience. When Denethor, assailed by grief and regret, starts preparing the pyre for Faramir and himself, Pippin wants to see Gandalf and counters Denethor's wishes, having to break his vows of fealty. Pippin communicates to Gandalf that something frightening is happening with Denethor and Faramir, motivating the wizard to abandon his priorities to attend to the urgent need.

The final test to Pippin's mettle comes when the Black Gate swings open and out pour myriads of Orcs and Men, leaving the Gondor army trapped. At that moment Pippin can only think of his coming death. But it is also at this moment that he gains understanding for Denethor, and hence for himself. Pippin is crushed by a Troll, experiencing overwhelming pain and falling into inner darkness.

Merry's first trial takes place in Bree, when he comes close to the Black Riders, though he can only hear them indistinctly and is not recognized by them. Soon after he has a frightful dream, of which he says: "I went to pieces. I don't know what came over me."[292] Strider recognizes that it is the power of the Black Breath that terrified and overpowered Merry. A next step occurs for Merry as for Pippin in the Orc abduction through Rohan, though in this one it is Pippin who takes most of the initiative.

---

[291] Tolkien, *The Return of the* King, 792.
[292] Tolkien, *The Fellowship of the Ring*, 170.

Merry has spent some of his time in Rivendell studying, among other things, the maps of Middle-earth. Whereas Pippin awakens during the Orc abduction, Merry truly awakens in the Fangorn forest. He can make his way forward because he remembers the maps he studied in Rivendell, and he is not afraid.

In Isengard, after Saruman's demise, we can recognize another significant trait of Merry. He is the one able to recognize that among the people of Saruman there are "some others that were horrible: man-high, but with goblin faces, sallow, leering, squint-eyed."[293] And these remind him of a "Southerner at Bree." Aragorn is in agreement with Pippin's insight. Here we see in Merry the element of curiosity, but a curiosity different from that of Pippin. In fact, soon after Pippin expresses a morbid interest in the *palantír*, it is Merry who warns him to stay out of the affairs of wizards. He points out that he, a Brandybuck, is no match for inquisitiveness, but that this doesn't apply in relation to the *palantír*, because of its nature.

Aragorn intuits that Merry's path lay with Théoden. And soon the king wants Merry as his esquire. Merry kneels in front of him, putting himself at his service, suddenly filled with love towards the king. When Merry first hears Éowyn saying she is doing well, he believes she has been crying. And it turns out that her distress comes from Aragorn choosing to go the Paths of the Dead.

Merry fights the idea of being left behind in Rohan. And it is Éowyn who lets him foresee that there may be a way for both of them to reach Gondor. When all the riders are assembled, Merry's gaze falls on a "young man" and he recognizes the face of one without hope, going to his death. Merry resists again the orders to stay behind, but the king is resolute. Éowyn, disguised as man, takes him on her horse and hides him under her cloak.

Like Pippin, now Merry wonders why he has been so eager to come, when he had been given every opportunity to remain behind. The city draws near and the Rohirrim are still unchallenged. Merry struggles in his soul between horror and inner doubt, and with the fear that it is too late and all their efforts are in vain. Then he feels a change in the wind and in the light. After Théoden's death Dernhelm/Éowyn challenges

---

[293] Tolkien, *The Two Towers*, 552.

the Nazgûl, and unveils that she is a woman. Merry remembers the face of the sad youth without hope that he saw in Dunharrow. Pity, awakening in him, moves him to courage. He cannot resist the idea of Éowyn dying in the flower of her youth and in such a desperate mood of soul. Then the Black Captain falls upon Éowyn, who cleaves his Fell Beast's neck with a skilled stroke, but the Black Rider shatters her shield and breaks her arm. Merry, unseen by the Nazgûl, has stabbed him from behind, his sword hitting between head and mantle; his crown rolls to the ground. Those present hear a cry going up into the air and fading, the cry of one utterly defeated. Merry stands close to the king and to Éowyn, whom he believes dead. It seems it is Merry's fate to further know the Black Breath that he was the first of the Hobbits to experience in Bree.

After the flight of the Nazgûl Merry realizes that his arm has been numbed and he has lost use of the left hand. And he sees that his sword's blade is fading and withering away, completely consumed by the strength of the opponent. It was the same sword, taken from the Barrow-downs, that had fought on the side of the Dúnedain in the battles against the forces of Angmar and its sorcerer king. The deathless sorcerer king has now come back as a Nazgûl; in between times he had been a Black Rider. It seems the Black Breath follows Merry's being with persistence.

In the Houses of Healing Merry's mind is going dark and his arm is being drained of its life, a little like Frodo at Weathertop. When Aragorn turns to Merry, he is optimistic and says: "These evils can be amended, *so strong and gay a spirit is in him*. His grief he will not forget; but it will not darken his heart, it will teach him wisdom" (emphasis added).[294] And in fact Merry awakes with desire for a meal and a pipe.

When everything is settled, Éowyn gives Merry the gift of an ancient horn set with "runes of great virtue." And she tells him, "He that blows it at need shall set fear in the hearts of his enemies and joy in the hearts of his friends, and they shall hear him and come to him."[295] In fact, back into the devastated Shire, Merry can now blow the horn of Rohan and people come to his help, almost compelled to do so.

---

[294] Tolkien, *The Return of the* King, 851.
[295] Tolkien, *The Return of the* King, 956.

In Merry and Pippin we find two complementary kinds of knowledge; in Merry the conscious knowledge of day consciousness, the one that comes from the air of day; in Pippin the intuitive knowledge coming from the waters of sleep. And the way the two look at the world complements each other. Merry wants to face the outer dangers. He meets with the Black Breath at Bree and again in Minas Tirith. He wants to be in the thick of action. He is a champion of inquisitiveness, and that is what he says about himself; and above all he is a gay spirit. Pippin holds much closer to his inner world. He faces the danger of the *palantír* that threatens his peace of mind. He faces the same danger in Denethor, and he is thrust into the thick of action when he is forced to leave the comfort of the sidelines and call on Gandalf's help. We see that Merry and Pippin face the same danger but in complementary ways: Merry the external threat of the Black Breath and the confrontation with the Nazgûl; Pippin the compulsion of the hidden powers of the *palantír*, which brings him dangerously close to Sauron.

It is emblematic of these differences how the two perceive the change between Gandalf the Grey and the new Gandalf the White. Merry says: "He has grown, or something. He can be both kinder and more alarming, merrier and more solemn than before."[296] In contrast Pippin expresses:

> The sound of [his] laughter had been gay and merry. Yet in the wizard's face he saw at first only lines of care and sorrow; though as he looked more closely he perceived that under all there was a great joy: a fountain of mirth enough to set a kingdom laughing, were it to gush forth.[297]

Whereas Merry notices with care the external behavior, Pippin penetrates in the inner life of the wizard, his life of feelings. Merry has studied the wizard through an analysis of the external impressions he has received. Pippin has let his inner responses guide him; he senses what resonates in his inner being, causing comfort or discomfort.

---

[296] Tolkien, *The Two Towers*, 576.
[297] Tolkien, *The Two Towers*, 742.

Merry lets surface what outer impressions bring to light through ideas he can formulate from them; Pippin works through the more enigmatic waters of intuition. The two Hobbits are to each other like air is to water. Pippin is more intimate and reserved. Merry is a gay spirit; the horn Éowyn offers him matches his joyous nature by calling on the joy of others.

## Four Hobbits and Four Temperaments

The four Hobbits illustrate what in many spiritual traditions of the world have been called the four temperaments. It is because they encompass all aspects of the temperaments that the four Hobbits can complement each other so fully.

The temperament is found at the intersection of the line of heredity (physical and etheric bodies) and what has developed in the individual's karmic trajectory of reincarnations (soul and ego); that which is most general belonging to the human species, and that which is most individual and unique that will never appear again in the same form. The temperament in fact stands right in the middle: "The temperament balances the eternal with the transitory."[298] And it relates to the four bodies already described earlier in the chapter: the physical body, the ether body that sustains life, the soul element that animates it, and the ego.[299]

The four constituting bodies of the human being find their physiological expression in different parts of the human organism: the expression of the ego is in the blood and its circulation; the soul element in the nervous system; the ether body in the glandular system (pineal, pituitary, thyroid, parathyroid, thymus, pancreas, adrenals, ovaries and testes); the physical body in the sense organs. The temperament finds its expression according to which physiological function predominates

---

[298] Steiner, *Mystery of the Human Temperaments.*

[299] The exact term that Rudolf Steiner uses for what I call "soul element" is "astral body," which designates "the union of the soul body and the sentient soul" or the lower elements of the soul, closest in their expression to the physical body (*Theosophy*, 59). This is a matter that occupies much of chapter 1 of *Theosophy* and would take us too far afield into spiritual science within the limited confines of this work.

and impresses itself upon the whole; it arises from the way the four bodies interact.

When the ego dominates the other bodies through the circulation of the blood, the choleric temperament shines forth; when the soul element dominates the other bodies through the nervous system, the sanguine temperament arises; when the etheric body dominates the other bodies through the glandular system, the phlegmatic temperament is expressed; when the physical body dominates the other bodies through the sense organs, we see the melancholic temperament. We can now return to the major and minor Hobbit pairs in relation to these concepts.

In Sam we see the temperament of earth, the melancholic. Like many of his temperament he knows deeply inside what it means to suffer, and has a natural capacity for offering support and empathy. He is able to hold himself to very high standards and is deeply loyal to his friend, whom he calls master. It is thanks to his thorough and methodical outlook that Frodo can stand on solid ground; and it is thanks to his humor and sense of perspective that Frodo can release the tension of his determined and single-minded pursuit. Without Sam, Frodo would be consumed.

Frodo displays what can be called the fiery choleric temperament. He is suited to fight against all odds; once he takes on the challenge, he does not let go; new challenges only confirm the call to get the job done. He is naturally fitted for leadership, and the others have recognized it long before the quest started. He values courage and trust, and he calls these forth in others. He acts with enthusiasm and has stamina in the most trying of conditions. But it is Sam who has to remind him of his humanity and his limits; he would not see them when left to himself.

Merry has the traits of a sanguine, the temperament of air. He says he is no match for inquisitiveness, and he shows his interest in many new things. He is awakened by the new experiences of Fangorn and Rohan. He seems to delight in everything new that meets him. His is a gay nature with a natural optimism, showing itself in a marvelous way with his prompt recovery and good spirit soon after his trying illness in the House of Healing, when he simply asks for a meal and a pipe. It is quite telling that to Merry Éowyn offers the horn of Rohan, through which people of the Shire will come to his help with joy.

Pippin is facing the inner world of the introvert and of the phlegmatic, related to water. He has deep knowledge and understanding of the inner world. This leads him to the fascination of the *palantír* on one hand and close to the world of madness personified in Denethor. With the *palantír* he narrowly escapes tremendous inner temptations. In Denethor he sees the effect the *palantír*'s use can have even upon one of the strongest minds of Middle-earth. Pippin understands the world of others, but tends to shy away from leadership; in fact he remains on the sidelines almost until the end, though he shows he is a good observer and is a person of patience and tolerance. He who mostly stands behind the curtains of events faces an inner test through a role that is thrust upon him by circumstances. He has to reluctantly break his oath towards Denethor and take an initiative that he has not sought, by calling upon Gandalf.

We have seen that the adventures of a series of characters are densely interwoven in order to form higher unities. We have on one hand three, and on the other four. Gandalf, Aragorn, and Frodo may be the main heroes, the more superhuman of the whole trilogy. Still, their collaboration would come to naught were it not for the presence of the all-too-earthly Hobbits, Frodo's friends.

On one hand Gandalf, Aragorn, and Frodo work collaboratively in awakening and uniting the inhabitants of Middle-earth against the dangers of Sauron's ultimate hidden plans. And on the other hand the same is true about the concrete task of eliminating the threat of the Ring by bringing it back to the fire that created it. Aragorn and Frodo are completely devoted in their task to the vision of Gandalf. Frodo accepts the authority of Aragorn, when Gandalf seems to be lost in the mines of Moria. Then Frodo becomes fully independent in accomplishing the central task of the fellowship.

Gandalf, Aragorn, and Frodo form a higher unity. They act in concert, and their collaboration is essential because it addresses what it means to be fully human. They represent the full dimension of the human being—a being that is known in spiritual traditions as consisting of spirit, soul, and body.

We find the workings of the four Hobbits to intervene at another dimension of what it means to be human. Their collaboration is found at a level closer to earth, at the intersection of terrestrial and divine, in the expression of what was known from Greek culture up to the Middle Ages as the temperaments. It is under this archetypal dimension that they form once more a higher unity. The division of the tasks between the major and minor pairs reflects of the need of collaboration between the temperaments that we all carry within, though they always come to expression unilaterally. The seemingly stronger of the four, Frodo, is still only one-sided, and needs the fullness of the four in order to carry out the central mission of the quest. More could be said if we turn our gaze to the whole fellowship. It is not the intent of this book to look at what the Elven element in Legolas, the Dwarf element in Gimli, or the purely Man in Boromir, add to the whole.

We have completed this look at the constitution of the spiritual human being and outlined how deeply the archetypal realm has inspired all of Tolkien's creative effort in *The Lord of the Rings*. We will look now at other aspects of the human condition that render his book such a compelling story for our times. This time we will turn to the objective correspondence of what is known as the microcosm of man; we will look at the macrocosm of the spiritual world that surrounds him, even though it is veiled by the sense perceptions.

# CHAPTER 6

# THE WORLD OF THE SPIRIT

---

> The Other Power then took over: the Writer of the Story [*The Lord of the Rings*] (by which I do not mean myself), that one ever-present Person who is never absent and never named.
> —J. R. R. Tolkien

We will continue now the exploration of the world of archetypes through which Tolkien moves with seeming ease in the trilogy. In *The Silmarillion* and *The Lord of the Rings*, Tolkien leads to what is known in esoteric tradition as the times of Atlantis and what follows after them in Western Europe. He confirms many things that his conscious mind did not pursue; even things that his Catholicism would have abjured. We will first turn to his portrayal of the spiritual ascent that the Hobbits experience from the Shire to Tom Bombadil's domain and into the Elven domains of Middle-earth. Rivendell and Lórien are like enclaves of the spiritual world on earth.

This will form the counterpart to what was presented in the previous chapter. Whereas there we looked at what lies in the inner human being, we will now turn to the archetypes of the world outside, at the dimensions of the larger world in which the human being lives—a world known to spiritual traditions.

The world of the spirit is not one single, homogeneous place. It is a world in which the human soul ascends by degrees. This has been known in all spiritual traditions, as far back in time as the old wisdom of India. Tolkien may not have known these traditions. It is all the more remarkable that he reflected them quite faithfully and exactly.

# SOUL WORLD AND SPIRIT WORLDS

The *Fellowship of the Ring* outlines a remarkable process of ascent into spiritual understanding, or penetration of spiritual reality, on the part of the members of the fellowship. Its major steps are the Old Forest and the Barrow-downs seen as a unity—Tom Bombadil's domain—then Rivendell and Lórien.

## Tom Bombadil's Domain

Tom Bombadil's domain encompasses the Old Forest to the north and the Barrow-downs to the south. From the beginning we are told that the Old Forest has a higher quality of aliveness than other forests: "Everything in it is very much more alive, more aware of what is going on, so to speak, than things are in the Shire."[300]

As they get deeper into the forest the Hobbits feel they are watched closely by an ambivalence growing to enmity. The air becomes hotter and stuffier; the heaviness is more than just an external condition. When Frodo tries to sing, he cannot find his voice; even such a simple thing exacts an energy that he cannot produce out of himself. As they proceed further into the forest, visibility is reduced; and they are drawn inexorably towards what they want to avoid, the center of the forest and the Withywindle River, "the queerest part of the whole wood." It is a river of dark waters lined with ancient willows. The heat increases, and to this are added armies of flies. Sleepiness seems to be the very basic condition of the place, and the state of consciousness it induces.

In the Old Forest Frodo utters the word *fail*. His song ends with the words "For east or west all woods must fail." And the narrative immediately comments "Fail—even as he said the word his voice faded into silence. And Merry comments, "They do not like all about ending and failing."[301]

---

[300] Tolkien, *The Fellowship of the Ring*, 108.
[301] Tolkien, *The Fellowship of the Ring*, 110.

It is Tom Bombadil, the master of this place, who rescues the companions. His songs are ones of seeming merry nonsense. On the way to Tom's house more is revealed about this unusual country that is so familiar to Bombadil: "Strange furtive noises ran among the bushes. . . . They caught sight of queer gnarled and knobbly faces. . . . They began to feel that all this country was *unreal*, and that they were stumbling through an ominous *dream* that led to *no awakening*" (emphasis added).[302]

Before presenting Tom, we will go into the other half of the experience, complementary to the first and key to an understanding of this enigmatic land. Interestingly the Barrow-downs begin immediately beyond Tom's house itself. The house in fact separates the two domains.

In the Barrow-downs there are no trees, nor visible water. The fog distorts the perception of space. Here instead of the heat we have a coolness that the sun does not seem able to warm up. The air is heavy but, unlike in the forest, it is chilly. Just as in the Old Forest here too the Hobbits cannot resist an irrepressible desire to sleep. But here it is not nature that is oppressive; it's the presence of other human souls from the depths of time.

As the companions progress in the new landscape, the mist becomes colder and wetter, the wind ever more chilly. And then a sudden darkness falls. Frodo is overtaken by fear and starts panicking and calling out to his companions. Then he is met by the tall and ominous figure of a Wight, who starts conversing with him. And the theme of cold is reemphasized: "He thought there were two eyes, *very cold* though lit with a pale light that seemed to come from some remote distance. Then a grip *stronger and colder* than iron seized him. The *icy touch froze* his bones and he remembered no more" (emphasis added).[303] And now Frodo sees his three companions dressed in the garb of men of arms of other times. Then his consciousness is challenged by a song, a "*cold* murmur . . . far away and immeasurably *dreary*." He hears strings of "grim, hard, *cold* words, *heartless* and *miserable*" (emphasis added).[304] In this instance, as in the whole episode of the Barrow-downs, Tolkien is emphasizing soul coldness.

---

[302] Tolkien, *The Fellowship of the Ring*, 119.
[303] Tolkien, *The Fellowship of the Ring*, 137.
[304] Tolkien, *The Fellowship of the Ring*, 137.

Frodo hears a chilling song from a remote voice, which becomes an incantation. It keeps emphasizing cold: "Cold be hand and heart and bone, and cold be sleep under stone: never more to wake on stony bed, never till the Sun fails and the Moon is dead, . . . till the dark lord lifts his hand over dead sea and withered land."[305] As it is a nature being who traps the Hobbits in the Old Forest, so now it is a human form that attacks them (a crawling arm) and a human artifact that binds them (the sword). It is at this moment that Frodo remembers Tom's promise and words, and calls on him. After freeing the companions, Tom proceeds to break the spell of the mound to prevent the return of other Wights. Tom qualifies the ghosts as "sons of forgotten kings walking in loneliness, guarding from evil things folk that are heedless."[306] The Hobbits do not fully understand; they are in a dream state in which "they had a vision as it were of a great expanse of years behind them, like a vast shadowy plain over which there strode shapes of Men, tall and grim with bright swords, and last came one with a star on his brow."[307] We saw earlier on that these inner experiences correspond to a dreamy reliving of previous lives.

Tom Bombadil is one of the most enigmatic figures in The Lord of the Rings. To Goldberry Frodo asks, "Who is Tom Bombadil?" And Goldberry simply answers, "He is." But she is not answering Frodo in the sense of the "I am" of selfhood. She adds: "He is the Master of wood, water and hill."[308] And Frodo misunderstands that everything in Tom's domain belongs to him, to which she replies negatively, and comments: "The trees and the grasses and all things growing or living in the land belong each to themselves. Tom Bombadil is the Master. No one has ever caught old Tom walking in the forest. . . . He has no fear. Tom Bombadil is master."

Master, as Verlyn Flieger points out, does not denote desire for possession; it is intended as "teacher" and "authority." Then Frodo asks directly to Bombadil, "Who are you Master?" And Tom answers, speaking in the third person:

[305] Tolkien, The Fellowship of the Ring, 138.
[306] Tolkien, The Fellowship of the Ring, 142.
[307] Tolkien, The Fellowship of the Ring, 143.
[308] Tolkien, The Fellowship of the Ring, 122.

> Eldest, that's what I am. . . . Tom was here before the river and the trees. . . . He made paths before the Big People. . . . He was here before the kings and the graves and the Barrow-wights. . . . He knew the dark under the stars when it was fearless [the time of the song of creation]—before the Dark Lord came from outside.[309]

Talking about Bombadil, Gandalf says that his original name was Iarwain Ben-adar, "oldest and fatherless." And Gandalf adds that Tom could not have been summoned to the Council because he would not have been interested; nor would he be able to grasp the power of the Ring and the stakes at play.

Tom is ushering the Hobbits into another level of consciousness; he is leading them beyond the threshold of the senses. At his table Hobbits drink plain water, "yet it went to their hearts like wine and set free their voices. The guests became suddenly aware that they were singing merrily, as if it was easier and more natural than talking."[310]

When Frodo asks Tom if he rescued them after hearing their calling, Tom indicates it was not the case, that he was simply busy singing, but then he adds:

> Just chance brought me then, if chance you call it. It was no plan of mine though I was waiting for you. We heard news of you, and learned that you were wandering. We guessed you'd come here ere long down to the water: all paths lead to Withywindle. . . . But Tom had an errand there, that he dared not hinder.[311]

And Tom concludes his speech as if he just were about to fall asleep, then continues to speak in a singing voice.

The next day Tom tells them stories. He speaks to them as if he were speaking to himself, often mixing speech with song, or interrupting himself to stand up and dance. Tom leads the Hobbits into a world in

---

[309] Tolkien, *The Fellowship of the Ring*, 129.

[310] Tolkien, *The Fellowship of the Ring*, 123.

[311] Tolkien, *The Fellowship of the Ring*, 123.

which he "laid bare the hearts of trees and their thoughts, which were often dark and strange, and filled with a hatred of things that go free upon the earth, gnawing, biting, breaking, hacking, burning: destroyers and usurpers."[312] He indicates to the friends that within his domain the Great Willow is the most dangerous creature, to whom all other trees submit. Quite tellingly, at the end of his tales, Tom once more nods as if he were falling asleep.

Tom's domain is one of singing, sleeping, and dreaming; we are right into a world of dreams, in which the images have qualities of a dream. The two domains—Old Forest and Barrow-downs—awaken a consciousness similar to dream, a deeper world than that of the senses. One is in the realm of warmth and growth and related to natural processes; the other, equally dreamy, takes us into coldness and decay and is related to deceased human beings and events of the past.

The relationship to time is also different in Tom's house than in the rest of Middle-earth, as it will later be in Rivendell and Lórien: "Whether the morning and evening of one day or many days had passed Frodo could not tell. He did not feel either hungry or tired, only filled with wonder."[313] And the weather in this order of reality changes constantly.

The four Hobbits awaken differently to the new order of reality that is Tom's domain. Whereas Merry and Pippin have what are basically nightmares, in his dreams Frodo is not a participant but a witness. His dream of the Orthanc tower and the captive Gandalf leads him beyond past experience to something objective, though not immediately understandable. He is objectively seeing Gandalf in another place. Only later does Gandalf confirm to him that his dream was true. Flieger calls this a "dream-vision" and an "out-of-body experience," which allows the dreamer to experience objectively another time and another place.[314] Frodo is waking to deeper aspects of reality than anything experienced before. After dreaming of Gandalf at Orthanc, he then has a vision of the ending of his journey, the sailing off from the Grey Havens. Of this last dream we are told that it was a vision and that it "melted into

[312] Tolkien, *The Fellowship of the Ring*, 127.
[313] Tolkien, *The Fellowship of the Ring*, 129.
[314] Flieger, *A Question of Time*, 189.

waking." In addition, in Tom Bombadil's domain the Hobbits have access to the whole field of time, as we have seen in the experience that touches most significantly Merry, with a hint of a previous life recollection.

In Tom Bombadil's domain we find ourselves in what is known in spiritual tradition as the astral or elemental world, the first stage of the spiritual world; and in terms of consciousness we enter what Steiner calls the "imaginative consciousness," or Imagination.

Imagination comes in to replace the sensations from the physical world. Images are produced in the same way as an outer object would produce a sensation, but this time completely inwardly—they do not depend on an external object. Imaginations are as real as those produced by physical senses, but they have a soul-spiritual origin. The world in which we enter through Imagination is in fact more real than what comes to us through our senses, as Tolkien points out. In Imagination we are approached by certain trials and dangers. In a certain sense the pupil loses the ground under his feet. When one starts having Imaginations, they look like perceptions without causes; from an external perspective, the imaginative world would be one of hallucinations and illusions. The mix of earthly and soul-spiritual is visible in the way Frodo relates to Goldberry. It is very different from what he will experience later in relation to Galadriel: "The spell that was now laid upon him was different: less keen and lofty [than the one of the Elves] was the delight, but deeper and nearer to mortal heart; marvelous and yet not strange."[315] Goldberry represents for Frodo a mix of sensual/instinctual and otherworldly.

The source of confusion and danger at this stage is that the human being perceives only the manifestations of spiritual beings, not the beings themselves. The imaginations express qualities of the beings, not the beings themselves. Therefore the pupil doesn't know the meaning of the images. This is why it is important to develop a strong sense of self. In effect, in the elemental world, what we have as feelings, desires, yearnings, wishes, and passions present themselves to us from the outside, coming towards us. We stand before them as we do in front

---

[315] Tolkien, *The Fellowship of the Ring*, 121.

of physical objects and beings in our world, but in a much more puzzling way. Our sense of self allows us to withstand the onslaught.

In the soul world there is an inversion of what comes to us in physical perception. First of all what comes from us seems to move towards us. In addition an inner experience we cherish (a feeling, desire) appears to us as something that is attacking us. Our thoughts, wishes, and desires are transformed into images, and the neophyte cannot distinguish these from objective spiritual happenings. Images disguise their true reality; they deceive. A debasing feeling like vanity or lust can appear not only charming but completely trustworthy, something that calls us to great heights and offers us great rewards. And the reverse can be true of positive soul qualities.[316] There is a possible danger to remain in this state of confusion for a long time. Tolkien seemed to know the dangers present at this stage. Witness what Ramer says of his experiences in the world of dream in *The Notion Club Papers*: "There's lying in the universe, some very clever lying. I mean some very potent fiction is specially composed to be inspected by others and to deceive, to pass as record; but it is made to the malefit of Men."[317]

The soul has basically two polar attitudes toward everything it meets in life that are greatly prominent in the astral world: sympathy and antipathy. These concepts are larger than the usual meaning of these words. Sympathy signifies acceptance of what comes toward the soul. It is what allows us to live within the other being, or object. Antipathy is necessary in order to experience oneself in separation from the world. It is the motion of the pendulum that awakens self-consciousness. We need antipathy, no less than sympathy, in order to develop faculties of understanding and acceptance. In the Old Forest we find excessive sympathy and endless growth; in the Barrow-downs excessive antipathy, cold and dying. One is the experience of the elemental world in nature, the other the elemental world of the soul. In both realms we find forces that can be both benevolent or malevolent, with a predominance of the latter.

At the center of the experience of Tolkien's elemental world we find the encounter with Tom Bombadil himself. He is called the trickster

---

[316] Steiner, *The Stages of Higher* Knowledge, 26–27.
[317] Tolkien, *The Lost Road and Other Writings*, 196.

in Jungian interpretation; the Lesser Guardian of the Threshold in spiritual science. Let us look at what we can learn from one and the other.

In her Jungian analysis Pia Skogemann sees the Old Forest and Tom Bombadil's kingdom as "the frontier between consciousness and the unconscious."[318] For her Bombadil represents "those forces in the unconscious that support the growth of consciousness."[319] And Tom is the one through whom the four Hobbits receive weapons and become "knights" on a quest. Before that the four had naively neglected to consider that fighting could have been their lot. Thus, through Tom Bombadil the four become the equivalent of knights on a spiritual quest.

The Old Forest represents both the positive and negative aspects of the unconscious. It's only in Tom Bombadil's house proper that no evil enters. And Skogemann also calls Tom a trickster figure: The "trickster turns the world upside down by pulling things into the light that are hidden in the dark."[320] He wants to bring light to humankind. It seems that Tom doesn't have the malicious aspects that are usually associated with a trickster in many cultures. However, these aspects surround the house on both sides—towards a warm and a cold pole.

Jung calls the trickster "the product of an aggregate of individuals ... welcomed by each individual as something known to him, which would not be the case if it were just an individual outgrowth."[321] In this sense Bombadil has much of a Hobbit character—or appears to the Hobbits thus—and has those very same qualities that render the Hobbits somehow more immune to the lure of the Ring. Tom looks at the Ring and peeps through it as if to mock Sauron's eye. He is not made invisible by the Ring but can make it disappear. Frodo puts on the Ring in Tom's house and becomes invisible to his friends but not to Tom, who jokingly cautions him against using it.

The trickster, this guardian between two worlds, that has traits of the individual, is what is known to spiritual science as the Lesser

---

[318] Skogemann, *Where the Shadows Lie*, xiii.
[319] Skogemann, *Where the Shadows Lie*, 20.
[320] Skogemann, *Where the Shadows Lie*, 82.
[321] C. G. Jung, Collected Works, Vol 9i, in Skogemann, *Where the Shadows Lie*, 84.

Guardian of the Threshold. He guards the entrance to the spiritual world from those who are not prepared to forego the habits of life on the material plane. He is the first figure that we must meet when we enter the spiritual world in earnest and in a lawful manner. He shows us the reality of who we truly are, which is hidden from us for our own good until we are ready to step across the threshold. The Guardian is the one safe guide into the world of the spirit, allowing us to first enter it without an inflated appraisal of ourselves. Inner strength and genuine humility are essential in order to cross the threshold consciously. We may remember that Frodo has been much humbled before arriving in Tom's domain, and continues to be soon after.

The Guardian is a being that the individual has collaborated at fashioning. When we meet the Guardian, he reveals that the powers that presided over ourselves, up to that time, determined the individual's happiness and unhappiness in life, based on the tenor of his or her life in previous incarnations.[322] Now the individual has to take up a part of the work that they did on his behalf.

The Guardian reveals that the blows of fate were brought upon the person as the consequence of harmful deeds in earlier incarnations. In a full encounter with the Guardian, all aspects of previous lives—good or bad—are visible to the individual: "Your past actions are separating themselves from you, stepping out of your personality. They are assuming an independent form, one that you can see. . . . I am that self-same being, who made a body for itself out of your good and wicked deeds."[323] In the Barrow-downs the companions meet this level of experience in the awakening of previous life memories, hinted at in a half-veiled fashion. We can now see that Tolkien's insertion of previous life memories in this part of the narrative corresponds to deeper archetypal reality.

The threshold stands in place thanks to all our fears and our recoiling back from taking responsibility for thoughts, feelings, and actions. The Guardian warns us not to cross the threshold until we have conquered our fears and feel ready to take on new responsibilities for the spirit. Frodo masters fully his courage in the presence of the Wight; he finds

---

[322] Steiner, *How to Know Higher Worlds*, 195.
[323] Steiner, *How to Know Higher Worlds*, 186.

a determination he did not know he possessed. He is now invested of a new task for the spirit.

The Guardian shows us the safest entrance to the spiritual world. Before meeting the Guardian we are, so to speak, the instruments of family, nations, and races. After meeting the Guardian we start to understand our own tasks and also know how we can help accomplish the tasks of the groups around us, our people and our race. This is because after meeting the Guardian we are left alone by the spirits of nation, tribe, and race. The Guardian in fact reveals these spirits to us. We receive a sense of a newly acquired freedom and we take on new responsibilities in a natural fashion. This is the baptism of the spirit that Frodo has received through Tom Bombadil; he has steeled his resolve for a spiritual quest that will serve all Hobbits and all inhabitants of Middle-earth. He carries through the ordeal the other Hobbits, though they themselves have not lived the experience as fully.

After the elemental world the soul enters into the spiritual world proper; these are the stages portrayed as Rivendell and Lórien. Each of the Hobbits undergoes these experiences with varying degrees of awareness, Frodo most consciously of all. Rivendell and Lórien give the Hobbits the inner strength for delving into deeper and deeper levels of trials of the soul. In fact we will hear of Galadriel, queen of Lórien, accompanying Frodo and Sam almost to the very last stages of the Mordor experience.

## Rivendell, the House of Elrond

In Rivendell live some of the Eldar "from beyond the furthest seas." Having lived in the blessed realm they have no fear of the Ringwraiths, because they live at once in both worlds and can exert power above the ordinary. And Gandalf reveals that the power that is present in Rivendell can allow it to resist Sauron's constant encroaching, but only for a while.

Elrond, the master of Rivendell and a ring-bearer himself, has witnessed all the three Ages. Elrond's parents were Eärendil and Elwing. Eärendil was the child of the mortal Tuor and the Elf Idril; Elwing, the grandchild of Beren, a human, and Lúthien, (daughter of the Elf-king Thingol and the Maia Melian). Elrond descends from all three lines of the Elves (Vanyar, Noldor, and Sindar).

Because of his Half-Elven heritage the Valar give Elrond the choice of whether to be counted among the kindred of Elves or of Men. Elrond chooses to belong to the former. During his stay in Middle-earth he develops to a high degree the art of healing and knowledge of Middle-earth's past. Skogemann qualifies Elrond as a sort of guardian of all things of beauty of the last three thousand years. And she judges that Rivendell is like a relic of the past, equivalent to a library, albeit a spiritual library.[324]

The text lets us know that "merely to be [in Rivendell] was a cure for weariness, fear and sadness."[325] The future members of the fellowship recognize that there is such a power in the land of Rivendell that all their cares and anxieties seem to vanish. This does not mean that the trials that lay ahead are now forgotten; for the moment they simply have no power to weigh on their minds. The companions find themselves inspired and hopeful, living fully and enjoying every moment, in fact building the strength for darker days to come.

We are not told of any ordinary dreams in Rivendell. Rather, something else takes the place of the dream, at least for Frodo. When Frodo listens to the music and poems in the Hall of Fire, he is held in a spell, even though he does not understand much. It seems that words have the magic power to evoke visions of distant lands and bygone times. And the physical surroundings look as if transfigured "like a golden mist above seas of foam that sighed upon the margins of the world."[326] More and more Frodo feels transplanted into a living dream that engulfs and overwhelms his consciousness. Frodo reveals to Bilbo, who had been reciting his poem, that his words seemed to connect to something about which he himself was dreaming. In the listening he had lost awareness that it was Bilbo who was speaking until almost the end. Bilbo recognizes that it is difficult to remain awake in Rivendell until one builds strength and habit. It seems we are moving into a realm

---

[324] Skogemann, *Where the Shadows Lie*, 124.

[325] Tolkien, *The Fellowship of the* Ring, 219.

[326] Tolkien, *The Fellowship of the* Ring, 227.

beyond the threshold, a realm that is otherwise challenging to ordinary consciousness.

We are told that the Hobbits spent almost two months in the House of Elrond. But time in Rivendell—as in Bombadil's domain, even though differently from it—does not flow as in the ordinary world. When Frodo asks how long he is supposed to stay in Rivendell, Bilbo, who has long dwelled there, replies: "Oh, I don't know. I can't count days in Rivendell."[327]

In Rivendell the meaning of prophecies and dreams is revealed. Boromir talks about the dream that came to his brother (Faramir) and himself. In the dream "the eastern sky grew dark and there was a growing thunder, but in the West a pale light lingered, and out of it I heard a voice, remote but clear, crying:

*Seek for the Sword that was broken:*
*In Imladris it dwells;*
*There shall be counsels taken*
*Stronger than Morgul-spells.*
*There shall be shown a token*
*That Doom is near at hand,*
*For Isildur's Bane [the Ring] shall waken,*
*And the Halfling forth shall stand."[328]*

After hearing this prophecy Elrond produces Isildur's sword, Narsil, that was broken and has been reforged. And he introduces Aragorn, son of Arathorn, descendent of Isildur, chief of the Dúnedain (Rangers) of the North to whom the sword belongs by right. Immediately after, Elrond calls unto Frodo to show everyone the Ring.

In Rivendell Frodo remembers his dream from Tom Bombadil's house, in which he saw Gandalf captive atop the tower of Orthanc. "'I saw you!' cried Frodo. 'You were walking backwards and forwards. The moon shone in your hair.'"[329] At that moment Frodo can realize

---

[327] Tolkien, *The Fellowship of the* Ring, 266.
[328] Tolkien, *The Fellowship of the* Ring, 240.
[329] Tolkien, *The Fellowship of the* Ring, 254.

that what felt "was only a dream" had a ground of reality, because this is now possible in Rivendell.

In Rivendell Elrond and Gandalf primarily, but others also, offer what we could call occult teachings: matters of good and evil upon which depends the future of Middle-earth become clear; a veil of illusion is torn from consciousness. The history of Middle-earth is perceived from its deeper foundations, beyond the smoke-screens of everyday life. A new threat is perceived coming from the East. Boromir describes it "like a great horseman, a dark shadow under the moon. Wherever he came a madness filled our foes, but fear fell on our boldest, so that horse and man gave way and fled."[330] Aragorn talks about the role the Rangers have played. They are the ones who relentlessly pursue and hunt down the servants of the Enemy. They have protected the North because evil creatures fled from the Rangers, and peace was preserved. Outwardly the Rangers perform an ungrateful task. They live a hidden life, and withstand the elements bound to the duty they have embraced. They are protecting the inhabitants of Middle-earth from dangers about which they cannot speak, and they are exposing themselves to suspicion and ingratitude from the very same people they protect.

The revelations grow under the lead of Gandalf, who explains how he went into the Necromancer's realm in Dol Guldur, where he discovered that the old Enemy, Sauron himself, was gaining new strength and power. He goes on to say that at the time in which Saruman consented to take action against Sauron, the Council drove the Necromancer out of Mirkwood and the Ring found its way into the open again. Gandalf concludes, "a strange chance, if chance it was." Gandalf recounts his encounter with Saruman and the treason of the latter. Drawing lessons from the betrayal of Saruman, Gandalf concludes, "It is perilous to study too deeply the arts of the Enemy, for good or for ill."[331]

In Rivendell plans are made for the future of Middle-earth. The ways of the spirit that take shape in Rivendell could not be further away from ordinary common sense. Throwing the Ring into the Fire of Mordor responds to a higher order of necessity that only Gandalf and

---

[330] Tolkien, *The Fellowship of the* Ring, 239.
[331] Tolkien, *The Fellowship of the* Ring, 258.

Elrond can apprehend. About the choice of throwing the Ring into the fire, which the Elf Erestor calls "folly," Gandalf replies:

It is wisdom to recognize necessity, when all other courses have been weighed, though as folly it may appear to all those who cling to false hope. Well, let folly be our cloak, a veil before the eyes of the Enemy! For he is very wise and weighs all things in the scales of his malice. But the only measure that he knows is desire, desire for power; and so he judges all hearts. Into his heart the thought will not enter that any will refuse it, that having the Ring we may seek to destroy it. If we seek this we shall put him out of reckoning.[332]

And further, "Yet such is oft the course of deeds that move the wheels of the world; small hands do them because they must, while the eyes of the great are elsewhere."

In Rivendell personal destiny becomes a clear and conscious choice for those who have a role in the future of Middle-earth. The nine Ringwraiths of Sauron are opposed by the nine in the fellowship of the Ring, who have all found their way to Rivendell, responding to a call of destiny. Elrond recognizes it thus: "You have come and are here met, in this very nick of time, by chance as it may seem. Yet it is not so. Believe rather that it is so ordered that we, who sit here, and none others, must now find counsel for the peril of the world."[333] Frodo accepts the challenge from a place in himself that he still does not fully know. Though feeling a call to stay in Rivendell with Bilbo, he hears himself say: "I will take the Ring . . . though I do not know the way." Elrond, who has been hoping for Frodo to take up this task in complete inner freedom, responds: "I think this task is appointed for you, Frodo; and that if you do not find a way, no one will. This is the hour of the Shire-folk. . . . Who of all the Wise could have foreseen it?"[334]

In Rivendell we find an oasis in Middle-earth in which the spiritual world is still active. The same will be only more so in Lórien. We have moved from the astral world and the imaginative consciousness to the spiritual world—or lower Devachan of spiritual tradition—and the stage of inspirational consciousness, or Inspiration. Here evil has no

332 Tolkien, *The Fellowship of the* Ring, 262.
333 Tolkien, *The Fellowship of the* Ring, 264.
334 Tolkien, *The Fellowship of the* Ring, 264.

access; Rivendell, like Lórien, is protected from it. Interestingly, only after Rivendell does Frodo meet his double—Gollum—and is able to claim him as his own.

After the world of colors of the astral world comes Devachan, which is in a certain sense a "world of sounds." The archetypes, which are the reality of this world, resound: everything lives in what could be called a spiritual music.

> To an observer, it is like being in an ocean of sounds and tones in which the beings of the spiritual world are expressing themselves. Their interrelationships and the archetypal laws of their existence reveal themselves in the chords, harmonies, rhythms and melodies of this spiritual "music," which reveals to our spiritual "ear" what reasoning in the physical world perceives as an idea or natural law.[335]

This is reminiscent of what Frodo experiences in the Hall of Fire.

In the spiritual world we perceive the archetypes, the idea of a being on earth, the "living thoughts" and spirit beings. In the spirit world the idea of any animal on earth—cat, dog, cow, sheep, or other—acquires as full a concrete and visible order of reality, as its physical counterpart does on earth. And this level of reality represents a great enhancement in relation to physical perception. Everything appears all the more real, but different from what we experience through physical senses, because the archetypes are in constant motion; they can take countless forms.[336]

In Lower Devachan we move from Imagination to Inspiration. Steiner tells us of Inspiration in relation to Imagination: "The world of Inspiration is placed within the Imaginative world. When the Imaginations begin to unveil their meanings in 'silent speech' to the observer, the world of Inspiration arises within the Imaginative world."[337] With inspiration the experiences of the higher worlds that first unfolded themselves in Imagination reveal their meaning. And

---

[335] Steiner, *Theosophy*, 125–26.

[336] Steiner, *Theosophy*, 123–24.

[337] Steiner, *The Stages of Higher* Knowledge, 47.

this is exactly what happens during the Council of Elrond in Rivendell. Everything that lies hidden in the background of Middle-earth's cosmic fate is unveiled. The deeper causes of the surface events lie in the confrontation of spiritual powers; Elrond and Gandalf know it. Once we know of the deeds of Sauron, Saruman, and Gollum and the fate of the Ring itself, we know most of what is essential to the future of Middle-earth. We are looking behind the curtains of the world stage, and we can intervene on the affairs of Middle-earth with greater insight and more precise impact.

Tolkien shows us that he understood the nature of the realm of Imagination and its limitations before we reach the stage of Inspiration. Imagination is not yet the place for a full understanding of the revelations of the spirit. Tolkien realized that beings make us hear and see them

> in some appropriate form, by producing a direct impression on the mind. The clothing of this naked impression in terms intelligible to your incarnate mind is, I imagine, often left to you, the receiver. Though no doubt they can cause you to hear words and to see shapes of their own choosing, if they will.[338]

And the narrative of the trilogy follows suit. An example: Frodo has a dream of other place, other time, in relation to Gandalf atop the Orthanc tower; only in Rivendell is the meaning of the dream fully revealed. Furthermore, Frodo steps into a new stage of consciousness in the Hall of Fire, though he also acknowledges that it is difficult for him to maintain awareness.

Through inspiration we are further separated from the instrument of the senses, and no representation, such as the image in the stage of Imagination, arises. Since there is no influence upon the will from this side, it is all the more important to develop a higher feeling for truth and falsehood, for right and wrong. There must be the capacity to develop strong feelings of pleasure in the attainment of truth and goodness; displeasure and pain in the presence of logical error.

---

[338] Tolkien, *The Fellowship of the Ring*, 202.

Esoteric students must learn to live through the whole gamut of emotions, from grief to enthusiasm, from afflictive tension to transports of delight in the possession of truth. In fact they must learn to feel something like hatred against what a "normal" person experiences only in a cold and sober way as "incorrect"; they must enkindle within a love of truth that has a personal character—as personal and as warm as a lover feels toward the beloved.[339]

Steiner indicates that hearing the revelations of what the seers have initially received through Inspiration serves as an awakener of inspiration in the recipient if this is done in great earnestness: "One's own Inspiration is stimulated by hearing an account of the Inspirations of others."[340] It is thus that we can strengthen our capacity of intellectual discrimination—which allows us to see hidden relations concealed in the facts—and deepen our determination for action. This is what happens mostly through Elrond and Gandalf's intercession at the Council of Elrond. The future fellowship is fired for its future task by hearing the tales of Elrond and Gandalf, two of the ring-bearers. The next ring-bearer, Galadriel, will appear in Lórien.

It is no wonder that in Rivendell the fellowship is formed; the call of destiny finds its confirmation. Nine individuals, each from their own side, have been inspired to converge. Frodo hears the voice of his higher self as a surprise, calling him to rise beyond himself, even if his lower self says that he doesn't know how. A further step has been achieved in rising beyond the bonds of race and blood. Now all of the representatives of Middle-earth have found their universal task: Elves, Dwarves, Hobbits, and Men.

## Lórien and Galadriel

Lóthlorien, or Lórien, the Golden Wood, is placed at the heart of Middle-earth and the heart of Elven kingdoms on Middle-earth. It is hidden from ordinary sight, defended through magic and Elf

---

[339] Tolkien, *The Fellowship of the Ring*, 33.
[340] Tolkien, *The Fellowship of the Ring*, 41.

warriors. At the center of the Golden Wood lies the circular city of Calas Galadon. A fountain is placed in front of the largest tree at the center. From the center our attention moves upwards to the top of the highest *mallorn* tree.

Upon coming to Lórien, it seemed to Frodo

> that he had stepped over a bridge of time into a corner of Elder Days, and was now walking in a world that was no more. In Rivendell there was memory of ancient things; in Lórien the ancient things still lived on in the waking world. Evil had been seen and heard there, sorrow had been known . . . but on the land of Lórien no shadow lay.[341]

Entering into the hill of Cerin Amroth, at the center of Lórien, Frodo experiences that all his eye apprehends is vibrant, with shapes that seem as fresh as something just formed for the first time, but also seeming to have endured forever. The colors are the same ones he always knew, but they appear to the eye as if he was perceiving them for the first time. There is no winter in Lórien, nor disease or deformity; in short, none of the suffering and death of the external world reaches Lorien.

Recalling the experience, Sam says, "I feel as if I were inside a song."[342] Frodo realizes that he is in a timeless land that does not alter, fade, or fade from memory. He knows that after leaving he can still recall the experience of Lórien and hold himself in its presence. Laying his hand upon a tree, Frodo's sense impressions of its texture are heightened, and he can also feel united with the life within it. The intense delight he experiences is not his own; it's the delight communicated to him by the tree. And in the middle of the trees he can hear the call of the sea and its birds, for which he has been longing.

After leaving the enchanted land the Hobbits realize that in Lórien time flows differently than in the rest of Middle-earth, and Frodo surmises that this is an experience that must have been common in the

---

[341] Tolkien, *The Fellowship of the* Ring, 340.
[342] Tolkien, *The Fellowship of the Ring*, 342.

past and that now only survives in Lórien. Going down the Great River Anduin, Sam, judging from the cycle of the moon, is led to believe that the company barely spent any time in the Golden Wood. He carries the memory of three nights with certainty, but also the feeling of having spent there a full month. And Frodo adds that he has no memory of any moon in Lórien, only sun alternating with stars. For his part Aragorn confirms that they were in Lórien longer than they thought, because now winter is upon them. Frodo realizes that part of Lórien's magic has to do with the power of Lady Galadriel, and of the ring she wears. Galadriel is associated with the element of water, whereas Elrond is with air. They have the respective ring: Nenya for Elrond and Vilya for Galadriel.

Verlyn Flieger points out that besides taking place outside ordinary time, Lórien is experienced by the party beyond ordinary consciousness. Nor does the narrative convey any dream from the Hobbits, or any of the other fellowship members. In fact the narrative specifically states that "no sound or dream disturbed their slumber."[343] This is why Treebeard translates Lothlórien as "Dreamflower," or a state of elevated dream. Flieger further indicates that Olofantur, the earlier true name of Lórien, is the name of the Vala who was "master of visions and dreams."[344] This makes Lórien a land of dream, and the fellowship is thus inside a dream, confirming Sam's feeling of being "inside a song." Lórien represents more than a dream, an expansion of consciousness beyond the confines of time. It is no coincidence that in Galadriel's mirror Frodo and Sam travel backward and forward in time. Frodo sees Bilbo in Rivendell, and travels far into the past of Númenor and its destruction by the Great Wave, and into the future, witnessing the siege of Gondor.

When the experience in Lórien is over, Merry affirms that it was like a dream fading away; not so Frodo. To him the dream has been more real than anything he has experienced before or after, and he has the impression of "falling asleep again." Returning to the old life now becomes the real test, because it invites a diminution of consciousness.

It is not surprising then that, like Rivendell, Lórien provides regeneration to all of the companions, most noticeably in the weary

---

[343] Tolkien, *The Fellowship of the Ring*, 379.
[344] Tolkien, *Unfinished Tales*, quoted in Flieger, *A Question of Time*, 192.

Aragorn, as Frodo notices: "For the grim years were removed from the face of Aragorn, and he seemed clothed in white, a young lord tall and fair; and he spoke words in the Elvish tongue to one [Arwen] whom Frodo could not see. *Arwen vanimelda, namarië!*"[345]

From Lórien the fellowship can see Southern Mirkwood, and in the midst of it upon a stony height Dol Guldur, where Sauron used to dwell. It is probably occupied again by his armies, since a black cloud can often be seen hovering over the place. Haldir remarks: "In this high place you may see the two powers that are opposed one to another; and ever they strive now in thought, but whereas the light perceives the very heart of the darkness, its own secret has not been discovered."[346] It is understandable that in Lórien Gollum, who had been following Frodo, once again has no access, because the forest is guarded from all evil. And although Frodo sees the eye of Sauron in Galadriel's mirror, he is in no danger.

We may ask then, "Who is Galadriel?" Skogemann sees in her an "Anima Mundi" (Soul of the World) and a "mistress of initiation . . . who mediates between the archetype of the Self and consciousness."[347] The light of the phial that Galadriel gives Frodo comes from the light of the last Silmaril, from which derives the light of Eärendil's star. Galadriel is thus able to place Frodo in touch with Middle-earth's ancestral source of light.

Galadriel is of Noldor descent, one who remembers the early days of Valinor, land of the Vala, and she was the last to reach Middle-earth; she is one of the most powerful of the Elves that have come to Middle-earth. She knows past, present, and future; and of her and Celeborn, her husband, it is said "no sign of age was upon them, unless it were in the depths of their eyes."[348]

It was Galadriel who convened the White Council, wishing Gandalf to be its leader. Galadriel knows that Gandalf is alive even before everybody else, and it is she who orders Gwaihir to carry him to Lórien for regeneration after his trials. However, she does not reveal

[345] Tolkien, *The Fellowship of the* Ring, 343.
[346] Tolkien, *The Fellowship of the* Ring, 343.
[347] Skogemann, *Where the Shadows Lie*, xiv, 23, 111.
[348] Tolkien, *The Fellowship of the* Ring, 345.

this knowledge to the fellowship in Lórien. Later on she follows the fate of the fellowship by conveying messages to Aragorn through the Dúnedain and the sons of Elrond. As we have seen before, Galadriel will be especially present in Frodo and Sam's trials in Mordor, directly with the light of her phial and indirectly through the inspiration she offers especially to Sam at critical points.

In the presence of Galadriel, Sam feels as if he were completely vulnerable and transparent to her gaze; she seems to test him for his strength while at the same time offering him the chance to relinquish the quest. In fact the other members of the fellowship likewise feel as if they were presented a choice between an arduous path ahead and something else they desired, a chance to leave behind the hardships of the war against Sauron. Boromir feels as if he had been offered a temptation by her. And Aragorn offers a foreboding answer to the riddle in response to Boromir, whose heart is restless: "There is in her and in this land no evil, unless a man bring it hither himself. Then let him beware!"[349]

The Old Forest is a mixed dream/nightmare. In Rivendell the dream/vision is called forth in Frodo by the bards and singers. In Lórien Frodo lives fully in the dimension of dream/vision. When we look at these realms with the insights of spiritual science, we can recognize the stages of the planetary ascent through the spheres of the planets after death, or the stages of a complete initiation while in the body.

The realm of Tom Bombadil is the one that the soul meets relatively early after death. Its boundaries are marked by the Earth and the spiritual Moon, and the process of reviewing earthly life called kamaloka. In conscious initiations on Earth this corresponds to crossing the Gate of the Moon and living in the world of Imaginations, the awakened thoughts teeming with life. Perceiving this level of reality means one has entered into the first stages of the spiritual world, but just because now one is exposed to a world of Imaginations does not mean that one knows how to interpret them. Tolkien talks pointedly about this conundrum in his *The Notion Club Papers*.

Rivendell represents the next stage; it is guarded from all evil, even if precariously through the power of Elrond and his Ring of Air. Elrond

---

[349] Tolkien, *The Fellowship of the Ring*, 349.

is the one who preserves all knowledge of the history of Middle-earth. It is through this that the lurking evil of Sauron can be countered. It is a real deed of knowledge to form the fellowship that can confront the power that would enslave the whole of Middle-earth. Rivendell is like a library in which is preserved all knowledge of Middle-earth. No evil can get past its gate. In terms of spiritual science it forms the threshold of the Gate of the Sun and the entrance into the pure spiritual world, the lower Devachan of Indian tradition.

As Skogemann points out, Elrond's residence is a house of stone; Elrond preserves culture and all the knowledge that allows Middle-earth the strength to withstand Sauron's plans. Galadriel lives atop the highest *mallorn* tree of Lórien, a step closer to the Sun, so to speak. She can fashion new culture as it were; she has no need of books since she can look into past, present, and future. The step from Rivendell to Lórien is significantly indicated by Tolkien: "In Rivendell there was memory of ancient things; in Lórien the ancient things still lived on in the waking world."[350] We are entering the higher spiritual world, past Saturn and the spheres of the planets, the higher Devachan of Indian tradition, though Lórien is simply an oasis of an earlier stage of human consciousness. And Galadriel truly can be called "a mistress of initiation . . . who mediates between the archetype of the Self and consciousness" as Skogemann indicates.[351] In the language of spiritual science, she is the Higher Guardian of the Threshold who asks of the one wanting to penetrate the higher spiritual world a further step of sacrifice.

In terms of spiritual science in Lórien we are entering the higher Devachan (spiritual world) and the intuitive stage of knowledge and consciousness, or Intuition. At this stage also Inspiration ceases, and one has the experience of no longer being outside of things and events, but within them: "What now lives in the soul is in reality the object itself. The 'I' has flowed forth over all beings; it has merged with them."[352] This complete merging into another being occurs without loss of self-consciousness. For this to be possible, the I needs to be strengthened to

---

[350] Tolkien, *The Fellowship of the* Ring, 340.

[351] Skogemann, *Where the Shadows Lie*, 23, 111.

[352] Steiner, *The Stages of Higher* Knowledge, 7.

a very high degree. This experience of complete communion is hinted at in Frodo's experience:

> All that he saw was shapely, but the shapes seemed at once clear cut, as if they had been first conceived and drawn at the uncovering of his eyes, and ancient as if they had endured for ever. He saw no colour but those he knew, gold and white and blue and green, but they were fresh and poignant, as if he had at that moment first perceived them and made for them names new and wonderful.[353]

Entering into a circle of white trees, Frodo hears the sound of the sea and of sea birds. Laying his hand upon a tree, "never before had he been so suddenly and so keenly aware of the feel and texture of a tree's skin and of the life within it. He felt a delight in wood and the touch of it, neither as forester nor as carpenter; it was the delight of the living tree itself."[354]

In Galadriel we find a moving portrayal of the meeting with what spiritual science calls the Higher Guardian of the Threshold. This figure of light is the one that tells the evolving human being something like the following:

> Until now, you have worked only to free yourself, but now you are free you can help free all your fellow beings in the sense world. Up to now, you have striven as an individual. Now you must join yourself to the whole, so that you may bring with you into the supersensible realm not only yourself, but also all else that exists in the sensible world.[355]

The Lesser Guardian of the Threshold shows us how much we are still tied to the world of the senses through our instincts, drives, desires,

---

[353] Tolkien, *The Fellowship of the Ring*, 341.
[354] Tolkien, *The Fellowship of the Ring*, 342.
[355] Steiner, *How to Know Higher Worlds*, 203.

passions, and all forms of selfishness. After a time the Greater Guardian accompanies the Lesser one. This Greater Guardian is a magnificent form of light, and we only meet him when we have completely freed ourselves from the world of the senses.

Before the encounter, we have worked at perfecting ourselves; now we realize our duties towards other human beings. At this point the very real temptation arises of rising to the spiritual world alone and leaving behind those who are still enslaved to the senses, and severing our destinies from theirs. But this would condemn us to inhabit only the lower regions of the spiritual world. The Higher Guardian stands in fact between the lower spiritual realms and the higher ones.

Deciding to put our newly acquired powers exclusively at our own personal service is the choice of black magic. And this is a very great and alluring temptation. The Guardian asks us to renounce the fruits of what we have earned and to place ourselves at the service of the whole of humanity. This choice seems deprived of all appeal. The companions experience each in their way that Galadriel gives them a choice; it would be more correct to say that she leaves them free to choose.

The pupil has had to know his true self before entering the world of the spirit through the Lesser Guardian of the Threshold, or Jung's trickster. Now he has to offer his life's work in service to the rest of his fellow human beings. This is such a tremendous step and requires such resolve that many will turn back from it; or in a further step away from it, will keep their knowledge for their own apparent benefit, and exert it over their fellow human being. This is what we will see of Saruman, whom Gandalf keeps equating to himself with good reason. Galadriel, as the Higher Guardian, reveals with no need of words that the choice lay in embarking in an arduous, seemingly merciless task, or having the choice of returning to normal life and abandoning the quest. Those who bring evil intentions to the Guardian project their own shadow upon her; such is the case of Boromir, who does not want to relinquish the power the Ring could offer his father or his realm. This split of soul ultimately leads him to his death.

# ASCENTS AND DESCENTS

Tom Bombadil's domain, Rivendell, and Lórien are stages along the journey in which the forces of the spirit are bestowed upon the company to strengthen them in the trials to come. *The Fellowship of the Rings* is framed around a structure of ascents and descents: descents into the experience of trials, ascents into oasis in which the spiritual world can grace the fellowship with new strength. The theme that has been set in motion in the succession between Tom Bombadil's domain and Rivendell is repeated in various ways. Let us look at these in relation to the major Hobbit pair.

After the Old Forest comes the test of the meeting of the Ringwraiths, the envoys of Sauron. They throw their strongest challenges at Weathertop and at the Ford of Bruinen. Then the company retires for rest and regeneration at Rivendell.

After Rivendell comes the mountain Caradhras. This is an evil that is not allied with Sauron. It was called "the Cruel" by the Dwarves. The snow that threatens the fellowship was sent by Caradhras because it fell only along their path, not further away. Here we have a repetition of the elemental domain of the Old Forest, but now in the cold of a high mountain rather than the sultry heat of the forest. After Caradhras the company enters into the bowels of Middle-earth and faces an otherwise formidable foe. Here appear the Orcs and Uruk-hai and, most formidable of all, the Balrog, sent directly by Sauron. Here occurs the initiation of Gandalf, and the severe loss of his guidance that affects the company very deeply. It is natural that such a sobering test be followed by the light of Galadriel's realm and Galadriel's phial.

When Frodo and Sam are separated from the rest of the company, in the Emyn Muil they face a similar challenge to that of the Old Forest. Frodo and Sam turn in circles in a landscape that seems to have the intention of disorienting them and sucking them towards its center, much like the Withywindle River in the Old Forest. Once past the mountains the Hobbits find themselves in the putrid marshes where no animal form stirred, only snakes and worms and other undesirable creatures. Here they also face the spectral ghosts of dead Elves, Men, and Orcs in what Gollum calls the "Dead Marshes"; we are told that they are of a period even more ancient than the ghosts that haunted the Barrow-downs.

Frodo, who looked into the specters, says: "I saw them: grim faces and evil, and noble faces and sad. Many faces proud and fair . . . I know not who they are."[356] Gollum shows knowledge of a great battle of which he had heard before acquiring the Ring. This is a trial all in all equivalent to what they have found in the Barrow-downs, another aspect of the soul elementals.

Finally the two Hobbits face in full force the realm of Sauron in the no-man's-land before the Black Gate. The landscape becomes bleaker:

> Even to the Mere of Dead Faces some haggard phantom of green spring would come; but here neither spring nor summer would ever come again. Here nothing lived, not even the leprous growths that feed on rottenness. The gasping pools were choked with ash and crawling muds, sickly white and grey, as if the mountains had vomited the filth of their entrails upon the lands about. High mounds of crushed and powdered rock, great cones of earth fire-blasted and poison-stained, stood like an obscene graveyard in endless rows, slowly revealed in the reluctant light.[357]

The two Hobbits have come to the desolation that lay before Mordor, "a land defiled, diseased beyond all healing—unless the Great Sea should enter in and wash it with oblivion."[358] Even the light of the sun seems to be deprived of all healing quality. Hiding in a circular pit, Frodo sees various spectral figures coming out of the past. He loses knowledge of time, and the boundaries between sleep and waking are blurred. Here the test of the Ringwraiths is intensified to a new height.

---

[356] Tolkien, *The Two Towers*, 614.
[357] Tolkien, *The Two Towers*, 617.
[358] Tolkien, *The Two Towers*, 617.

After the regeneration of Ithilien the theme repeats itself anew and reaches a climax. Shelob's realm is even darker than what they had experienced in Moria:

> Here the air was still, stagnant, heavy, and sound fell dead. They walked in a black vapour of veritable darkness itself that, as it was breathed, brought blindness not only to the eyes but to the mind, so that even the memory of colours and of forms and of light faded out of thought. Night always had been, and always would be, and night was all.[359]

The two lose all notion of time and perspective of space and distances. Shelob too is the expression of an ancient primeval evil, one that does not submit to the will of Sauron. She serves none but herself and was there long before Sauron started his work. Gollum is under her spell, obscuring his will from the light of consciousness and the possibility of regret. This is the effect of his promise to her.

From Shelob's Lair the two reach the desolation of Mordor, where nothing else than scorching heat, dryness, and parched earth can survive. In the last part of the journey are added the fumes of Mount Orodruin. The two could not survive were it not for the spiritual presence of Galadriel, materialized in her phial; they are facing the dark night of the soul. To this can only follow the absence of all spiritual succor and sheer annihilation, or a turning point of time, inaugurating a new aeon.

The fellowship advances in its quest in two parallel ways. On one hand it has to face hostile powers and overcome them. This is the very stuff of all epic quests. It is the most accessible dimension of adventure. The counterpart is hidden from our obvious understanding in those interludes that we can access as welcome periods of rest and regeneration in an otherwise relentless and harrowing descent into deeper and deeper trials.

These moments of rest are something more than absence of action; we could call them moments of inner growth—a different kind of opportunity than the one offered by the heat of action. It is in their

---

[359] Tolkien, *The Two Towers*, 701–2.

receptivity, openness, and inner maturity that the members of the fellowship receive a draught of forgetfulness and of healing.

In Tom Bombadil's domain, in Rivendell and Lórien, the four Hobbits are offered new forces with which they can confront the formidable opponents who work for Saruman or Sauron. They travel first through the soul world—what most traditions knew as the underworld, and Christian doctrine still called Purgatory—before it became the caricature that some of us were taught in catechism. There are tests in the underworld, which look deceptively similar to those undergone in the rest of Middle-earth.

In Rivendell and Lórien the differences with the rest of Middle-earth are accentuated. We are told that we have to do with islands, as it were out of time and space, in relation to Middle-earth. Here the tests of the fellowship are different: they are tests of wakefulness and learning. We can perceive how the different members of the fellowship fully integrate the experiences—Frodo foremost in this group—or hesitate and doubt, as is the case for Boromir. We witness how in their retrospective reflections about the two spiritual oases, some have understood more, some less.

There is nothing simple or simplistic in the structure of *The Lord of the Rings*. This is part and parcel of the enduring power of the trilogy. In it are reunited Tolkien's medievalistic tastes and his deeply modern outlook. The enduring power of Tolkien's masterpiece lies in positing the core questions lying at the end of all things, at the end of times, or turning points of history. And we live at the end of times, as practically all spiritual traditions agree to when referring to the present. What more does Tolkien offer us from this perspective?

# CONCLUSIONS

## *THE LORD OF THE RINGS* IN PRESENT TIME

In the trilogy we are not confronted with the troubles of a distant
past; we are, indeed, presented with the issues of today.
—Pia Skogemann

You can make the Ring into an allegory of our own time,
if you like: an allegory of the inevitable fate that waits
for all attempts to defeat evil power by power.
—J. R. R. Tolkien (from the interview at the
Rotterdam "Hobbit Dinner" of March 28, 1958)

We have reviewed what *The Lord of the Rings* offers in terms of a deeper
understanding of the human being and of the spiritual dimensions, or
worlds, of which he is part. Indirectly we have also pointed to Tolkien's
views about the ages of humankind and history. We will conclude, as
it were, by turning from the past to the future. How does *The Lord
of the Rings* concern modern human beings now? How does it inform
them about the nature of present challenges, and about those lying in
the future?

# LIVING IN A TURNING POINT OF HISTORY

There is a surface parallel between the situation of Middle-earth as described in *The Lord of the Rings* and our own, now that the future of our planet stands in the balance from an ecological, economic, social, cultural, and practically any other perspective. Before the time that will mark the end of Middle-earth's Third Age, the odds seem stacked against civilization. Sauron's enslavement of Middle-earth is perceived as a fait accompli. Great individuals like Saruman, Théoden, and Denethor have fallen directly, or indirectly, under his clutches. Frodo's attempt to get rid of the Ring seems to stand at a one in a million chances of success. Common sense would dictate there is nothing more to do than wait for the obvious denouement. And what could a party of nine, with four unexperienced Hobbits, offer anyway to the future of Middle-earth? At one point in the book Tolkien offers us a poignant image.

From Lothlórien the fellowship beholds Southern Mirkwood and a black cloud hovering above the heights of Dol Guldur, which seems to indicate that Sauron's armies have occupied once more the place where he used to dwell. This leads the Elf Haldir to remark, "In this high place you may see the two powers that are opposed one to another; and ever they strive now in thought, but whereas the light perceives the very heart of the darkness, its own secret has not been discovered."[360]

What is it that the Dark Lord cannot perceive? This is best stated in the words of Gandalf:

> Indeed [Sauron] is in great fear, not knowing what mighty one may suddenly appear, wielding the Ring, and assailing him with war, seeking to cast him down and take his place. That we should wish to cast him down and have no one in his place is not a thought that occurs to his mind. That we should try to destroy the Ring itself has not yet entered his darkest dream. In which no doubt you will see our good fortune and hope.[361]

---

[360] Tolkien, *Fellowship of the Ring*, 343.
[361] Tolkien, *The Two Towers*, 485.

Here in artistic form is predicated a change of paradigm. What evil fights against us and in us can only be countered creatively, not fought against. We have to find another place from where to leverage, another paradigm from which to operate. We have to subvert the values that perpetuate the Ring, both in society and within the human being.

In the middle of rising ecological, social, economic, and financial catastrophes, what are the prospects for planet earth? Just looking at climate change, rising seas, earthquakes, tsunamis, and the melting of glaciers spells sobering prospects for the human race. Extinction of species, extinction of whole fishing populations, loss of land to desertification, loss of ecosystems, rising sea waters, unbearable heat—the list goes on and on. Everywhere there is hopelessness and powerlessness, as if we live under Sauron's spell. Untreatable problems are faced ineffectively or accelerated even in spite of desires and efforts to the contrary. Not to speak of outright denial and the attempt to return to a highly idealized, and completely unreal, past, as we witness today in many nations.

To elevate our perspective we can turn to world religious and spiritual prophecies. World traditions speak of a great watershed coming around our times. Christianity has its apocalyptic predictions, upon which minor, fanatic sects prey for Armageddon scenarios. Indian tradition announces the end of Kali Yuga. The Maya predicted major global changes around the year 2012. And we live in this great collective anxiety towards the future. Tolkien felt it very tangibly, and imaginatively too: "If anguish were visible, almost the whole of this benighted planet would be enveloped in a dense dark vapour, shrouded from the amazed vision of the heavens! And the products of it all will be mainly evil—historically considered."[362] He tempered his often pessimistic views about the present by explaining that what works for the good is not equally visible. In a letter to his son Christopher, where he reasserts his historical views, he adds, "And at the same time one knows that there is always good: much more hidden, much less clearly discerned, seldom breaking out into recognizable, visible beauties of word and deed or face—not even when in fact sanctity, far greater than

---

[362] Carpenter, *Letters of J. R. R. Tolkien*, 76.

189

the visible advertised wickedness, is really there."[363] We will look for that hidden good in the pages of *The Lord of the Rings*.

A lot has been already said about *The Lord of the Rings* here and elsewhere. But another view could be briefly sketched to add another challenge, though it is a view that this research cannot prove or disprove. In the draft of a letter to a certain Miss Batten-Phelps, Tolkien wrote about his book:

> It was written slowly and with great care for detail, and finally emerged as a Frameless Picture: a searchlight, as it were, on a *brief period in History*, and on a *small part of our Middle-Earth*, surrounded by the glimmer of limitless extensions in time and space. Very well: that may explain to some extent why *it "feels" like history*; why it was accepted for publication; and why it has proved readable for a large number of very different kinds of people. (emphasis added)[364]

The letter was not sent, and therefore this was not known in Tolkien's time.

In the same letter looking back "on the wholly unexpected things that have followed [*The Lord of the Rings*'s] publication" Tolkien says:

> I feel as if an ever darkening sky over our present world had been suddenly pierced, the clouds rolled back, and an almost forgotten sunlight had poured down again. As if indeed the horns of Hope had been heard again, as Pippin heard them suddenly at the absolute *nadir* of the fortunes of the West. But *How?* And *Why?*[365]

Note how here Tolkien lives in two levels of experience at the same time; at one level what could have been something of historical reality, and

---

[363] Carpenter, *Letters of J. R. R. Tolkien*, 80.
[364] Carpenter, *Letters of J. R. R. Tolkien*, 413.
[365] Carpenter, *Letters of J. R. R. Tolkien*, 413.

at the present level of reality. The past continues to be felt into the present. It may be said that this was a prevalent mood of soul for the English author.

Tolkien then relates the episode of a man visiting him in Oxford who felt that some old pictures seemed to be designed to fit the narrative of *The Lord of the Rings*. He was wondering whether Tolkien knew them and had used them for his own inspiration. When he realized Tolkien had no possible knowledge of the pictures, he was silent for a time, then added, "Of course, you don't suppose, do you, that you wrote all that book yourself?" Tolkien responded:

> No, I don't suppose so any longer. I have never since been able to suppose so. An alarming conclusion for an old philologist to draw concerning his private amusement. But not one that should puff any one up who considers the imperfections of "chosen instruments," and indeed what sometimes seems their lamentable unfitness for the purpose.[366]

Pressing more deeply about the possible historical dimension and the "small part of our Middle-Earth," Tolkien writes in another letter:

> The action takes place in the North-west of "Middle-earth," equivalent in latitude to the coastlands of Europe and the north shores of the Mediterranean. But this is not a purely "Nordic" [term that Tolkien uses instead of Northern in borrowing it from his correspondent] area in any sense. If Hobbiton and Rivendell are taken (as intended) to be about the latitude of Oxford, then Minas Tirith, 600 miles south, is at about the latitude of Florence. The mouths of Anduin and the ancient city of Pelargir are at about the latitude of ancient Troy.[367]

A fascinating set of perspectives emerge from these lines all at once. Could *The Lord of the Rings* refer to events that occurred in Europe some millennia before our time? Tolkien was open to the idea. On this matter the jury is out. We enter here a mystery that Tolkien certainly had not

---

[366] Carpenter, *Letters of J. R. R. Tolkien*, 413.
[367] Carpenter, *Letters of J. R. R. Tolkien*, 376.

definitely elucidated, nor do we intend to press further. Suffice to say that if the book discusses events that did occur, it would do so in the imaginative language of legends, not in the historical reports to which we are accustomed in the present. In other words, the story would be an imaginative rendering of historical events to which humanity was still used up to the time of the Middle Ages. Nobody expected the events of the legend of the Holy Grail to be literal; rather, it represents events that occurred at a historical level, but so charged with meaning that they could only be portrayed from the higher perspective of the images of a legend.

## THE LONG VIEW

Let us return to the quality of *The Lord of the Rings* as perceived by Tolkien's contemporaries. Addressing himself to Ms. Batten-Phelps, Tolkien continues:

> You speak of "a sanity and sanctity" in the L. R. "which is a power in itself." I was deeply moved. Nothing of the kind has been said to me before. But by a strange chance, just as I was beginning this letter, I had one from a man, who classified himself as "an unbeliever, or at best a man of belatedly and dimly dawning religious feeling . . . but you," he said, "create a world in which some sort of faith seems to be everywhere without a visible source, like light from an invisible lamp." I can only answer, Of his own sanity no man can securely judge. If sanctity inhabits his work or as a pervading light illuminates it, then it does not come from him but through him. And neither of you would perceive it in these terms unless it was with you also. Otherwise you would see and feel nothing, or (if some other spirit was present) you would be filled with contempt, nausea, hatred.[368]

This note aptly addresses the power of *The Lord of the Rings* over his readers. The imagination must be awakened, or on the point of

---

[368] Carpenter, *Letters of J. R. R. Tolkien*, 413.

being awakened, for the book to take hold of the reader and lead her to unexpected places.

We want now to shed more light on *The Lord of the Rings*'s "world where faith seems to be everywhere without a visible source." I have attempted to capture in this book much about the deeds of Gandalf, Aragorn, Frodo, and his Hobbit companions. But much else still lies beyond the scope of their actions, and yet feels just as real; it is a true "light from an invisible lamp." *The Lord of the Rings* is more than the affair of the inhabitants of Middle-earth; it involves in subtle ways the whole of the cosmos, or in Tolkien's terms the invisible presence of the Valar and the Maiar. These are the lessons that present-day new cultural and spiritual warriors, and all change agents, can most benefit from.

Everywhere in Middle-earth the moving events unleashed by the fellowship emanate wonder. During the tragic days of the Third Age, a few individuals call upon all their strength, and the Valar and Maiar of Middle-earth's firmament respond as if by magic.

The first step in shaking the complacency of decadent times lies in evoking wonder. Thus in seeing the members of the fellowship, Éomer pronounces, "These are indeed strange days. . . . Dreams and legends spring to life out of the grass." And a rider standing next to him echoes: "Halflings! But they are only a little people in old songs and children's tales out of the North. Do we walk in legends or on the green earth in the daylight?" Aragorn replies: "A man may do both. . . . The green earth say you? That is a mighty matter of legend, though you tread it under the light of day!"[369] Théoden expresses his wonder at the sight of the Ents, and evokes the sense of loss of his race that has trivialized the content of ancient songs and legends. "And now the songs have come down among us out of strange places, and walk visible under the sun." And Gandalf replies, "You should be glad, . . . for not only the life of Men is now endangered, but the life also of those things which you have deemed the matter of legend. You are not without allies, even if you know them not."[370]

A time when everything is facing danger, a time in which anything worth living for is made more present, is what clearly presents itself

---

[369] Tolkien, *The Two Towers*, 423–24.
[370] Tolkien, *The Two Towers*, 536–37.

to us in *The Lord of the Rings*. And many could feel this is a strong similarity with what we live in at present. Is not our time mired in loss of meaning and wonder? What are times of global decadence other than a collective descent into the ordinary? Tolkien knows how to awake in us the antidote: a sense of wonder in every page of his legendarium. This is the power that keeps us returning to the pages of *The Lord of the Rings*, that feeds our imaginations ensnared in a collective sense of loss.

But there is more. Tolkien doesn't tire to remind us that the world conspires to come to our help, but we fail to see it if we do not take time. The instances are too numerous to be enumerated here. When Frodo is rescued from the Black Rider by the seemingly casual arrival of the Elves, their leader, Gildor, drops this innocent remark: "Our paths cross theirs [Hobbits] seldom, by chance or purpose. In this meeting there may be more than chance; but the purpose is not clear to me, and I fear to say too much."[371] It is also Gildor who, in this casual encounter, advises Frodo to leave the Shire that is no longer safe for him, and to take with him trusted and willing friends. And the same Gildor alerts Tom Bombadil about the arrival of the Hobbits. Thus, such a small meeting carries tremendous importance and consequence. When Frodo asks Tom Bombadil if he rescued them after hearing their calling, he responds absentmindedly: "Just chance brought me then, if chance you call it. It was no plan of mine though I was waiting for you. We heard news of you, and learned that you were wandering."[372]

Synchronicity is commonplace in all of the fellowship's adventures, small or great. Gandalf indicates that he had visited Dol Guldur to meet the Necromancer, and discovered that this was the old Sauron, gaining new strength and ready to strike again. And Saruman, who led the White Council, reluctantly consented to drive Sauron out of Dol Guldur in the same year in which the Ring had been found by Gollum. Through the latter character, so instrumental to the denouement of the story, Tolkien quietly invites us to be open to constantly see more than meets the eye, to be open to it in the book as he himself was open to it in life and as he would ask us to be in our own. It is a mark of our time to have lost all reverence and awe for the workings of the universe,

---

[371] Tolkien, *Fellowship of the Ring*, 83.
[372] Tolkien, *Fellowship of the Ring*, 123.

and for its reflection in the apparently mundane synchronicities of the everyday. Everything conspires to have us rush from one thing to another in a frenzy, maybe guided by the importance that everything must acquire in times of great need, but in the process, robbing us of those forces through which true change can be achieved. Things that will never be too trivial to be enumerated: commitment generated from the heart, devotion, ability to develop true friendship, complete focus on what we are interested, attention to the small things as to the large ones—those simple things that are most compromised when our minds are under great pressure. And yet who has not been touched by Sam's wholehearted devotion to Frodo? His is the epitome list of very small things done with great love.

So much for the simpler aspects of synchronicity. The greater ones reach a whole other level, as when we are talking about the passage from the Third to the Fourth Age, what could be called a "turning point of time." Our attention is tested to the extreme in the intricacies of these synchronicities. No wonder that Tolkien stopped for quite some length of time on all matters of synchronicity, which tested his need for accuracy and almost maniacal precision, and yet for good reason. We will refer to the day that in the appendices corresponds to March 10, or more precisely from the sunset of March 9 to sunset on March 10.

On March 9 Gandalf reaches Minas Tirith. Aragorn sets out from Erech (where stands the Stone) and comes to Calembel. At dusk Frodo reaches the Morgul-road. Sauron's Darkness begins to flow out of Mordor. March 10 begins in darkness, as the "Dawnless Day." Faramir is rescued by Gandalf outside the gates of the city. Frodo passes the crossroads and sees the Morgul-host set forth out of Minas Morgul.[373]

On the evening of March 9 Pippin and Beregond are speaking of hope and how little they have of it, when th e sun is obscured by a passing Nazgûl. The two hear a faint, cruel, and cold cry in the distance, and fear paralyzes them for a spell. Then the sun shines again. A gloom descends upon Pippin, and he now very much seeks Gandalf's presence. Gandalf announces what Pippin has somehow unconsciously sensed, that the next day will have no visible sunrise because the Darkness has begun. All day long Pippin is oppressed because of the Darkness, and

[373] Tolkien, *The Return of the King*, Appendix B, 1068.

of Denethor's erratic behavior. Then only in the evening does the sun briefly shine through the darkness to send a "brief farewell gleam."

Sam and Frodo have been saved from the attacks of the southern men by Faramir, who intuits that the impending storm is coming and that the hobbits need to hasten on their way. The major pair travels for two days in the direction of Mordor. During the second day everything in nature around them seems to spell out an ever-present, oppressive feeling. And Gollum now reminds the Hobbits that they must walk in the dark, and hide during the day. In the evening of March 9 the Darkness starts engulfing the stars. No dawn appears, other than a murky twilight; the Darkness has begun. Sam is disoriented, thinking it's evening, while Frodo realizes this is something very unusual. The Hobbits are travelling in open territory but are providentially shielded from sight by Sauron's Darkness. By evening, however, all of a sudden the light of the setting sun returns to illumine a surreal scene. The two see a huge, defaced statue of a solemn king of old. The head has been replaced in mockery with a round, roughly shaped, stone. The head itself rolled away, not far off, and its forehead is crowned in silver and gold. The brows are graced by the small, white star flowers of a vine reverently winding around it; and yellow stonecrop sparkles in between the nooks of the hair. The light of the setting sun is the same sun that Pippin saw send out a "brief farewell gleam" before the night.

On his side Merry is fighting against the idea of being left behind. When he wakes up, it is dark. The messenger brings him the gloomy news that the sun will not rise on that day, nor ever again. The air is murky and heavy. Théoden tells him this darkness comes from Mordor; it started during the night and it is getting thicker. The king announces "the great battle of our time." The Darkness sent by Sauron is heaven-sent to the Rohirrim, who are riding towards Minas Tirith. They can travel undercover, and the city's outer wall, that could have held them back, has providentially been destroyed by the Orcs.

During the first night of the Darkness, Aragorn announces he is going to Pelargir upon Anduin, and promises the Dead that, when the land is free of Sauron, he will fulfill his promise to release them. And the next day no sunlight is visible, and the company slips away from sight, followed by the Dead. Aragorn and his host can travel under the protection of Sauron's Darkness, and pass unnoticed towards the lower course of the Anduin to prevent the Corsairs of Umbar from reaching Minas Tirith.

In all the above events, which are just a small excerpt from the whole tapestry of the book, things proceed in ways that no clever human mind could possibly devise, not even Gandalf for all his wisdom. Tolkien wants to show us that there is much more than meets the eye; that only Providence in his Christian terms, or the help of the spirit in more general terms, can account for what happens in our world.

Another, more pointed event, comes forth at the most crucial turning point of time. Sam, climbing Mount Orodruin, intuits the need for haste. "Suddenly a sense of urgency which he did not understand came to Sam. It was almost as if he had been called: 'Now, now, or it will be too late!'"[374] And Frodo is resolved to crawl if needed. In a moment the light pierces through the clouds to reveal the Tower of Barad-dûr, which fills the Hobbits with dread. Fortunately Sauron's Eye is looking elsewhere and the vision fades. The Eye of Sauron is turned to the Captains of the West and to the Black Gate, where the armies are engaged in battle. The Captains of the West are distracting Sauron from the most real danger to his reign; but only Sam and Frodo are in the position to rescue the Captains of the West, and Aragorn the future king, from being annihilated by the armies of Sauron, provided Sam hears the call of urgency.

The above examples bring up not only the power of the spiritual world to send help to the genuinely striving various inhabitants of Middle-earth. It also highlights a central point of Tolkien's cosmology. In Eomer's words, "Our enemy's devices oft serve us in his despite," to indicate that it is through the Darkness of Sauron and the destruction wrought by his Orcs that the Rohirrim can best assist Minas Tirith; the same is true for Aragorn.

Earlier on Saruman acts as a distraction, confusing Sauron. Between the two, acting at cross-purposes, they manage unwittingly to bring Pippin and Merry to Fangorn faster than the two could ever had done on their own; the Hobbits manage to alert the Ents, who will consequently attack and destroy Saruman's Isengard. Consequently,

---

[374] Tolkien, *The Return of the King*, 921.

Sauron fears Isengard as much as Minas Tirith. But Saruman has condemned himself because he cannot find Sauron without the Ring. Translated in modern terms, not everything that seems to be oppressing us will work against us; it may very well destroy much else against which we are set. We may be helped in ways we cannot foresee or fathom.

Human beings and the earth itself seem at present in the position to have to know the depth of powerlessness and despair, succumb to it, or be numbed by it. Only an innate, strong gut feeling, or a conscious understanding of the presence of the spirit, can counter this constant sapping of energy. When we encounter individuals endowed with such strengths—such that can remain calm and hopeful in the midst of all adversity—we all may wonder at how, and from where, their energy comes. This echoes Tolkien's intent when he said that he wrote his most important book to illustrate the need to accept "hope without guarantees."[375] Gandalf speaks Tolkien's mind before the final confrontation with Sauron, "And better so [walking towards Mordor with the slim hope of Frodo accomplishing his task] than perish nonetheless—as we surely shall, if we sit here—and know as we die that no new age will come." And he sums it up thus: "We come now to the very brink, where hope and despair are akin. To waver is to fall."[376]

From the perspective of the plot, this interlacing of forces at battle with each other, and at cross-purposes the one with the other, is what renders *The Lord of the Rings* such a rollercoaster of events and emotions, and makes practically impossible putting down the book. The reader may ask himself how the characters may possibly find a way out of their desperate situation, out of a struggle against all odds. Tolkien himself, in a letter of November 29, 1944, having finished the last two chapters of Book 4, puzzled, "I have got the hero into such a fix that not even an author will be able to extricate him without labor or difficulty."[377] However, none of this is artificial, or something foreign to the consciousness of modern human beings, who at present are wondering how our planet will find a way out. We are in the very same situation of an impossible plot in which

---

[375] Carpenter, *Letters of J. R. R. Tolkien*, 236.
[376] Tolkien, *The Return of the King*, 862.
[377] Carpenter, *Letters of J. R. R. Tolkien*, 103.

we may not see a way out, but some inner hope may tell us that there will be one beyond what we can consciously devise, provided we keep striving.

All of the above could remind us of this passage, inspired by Goethe:

> Until one is committed, there is hesitancy, the chance to draw back—concerning all acts of initiative (and creation), there is one elementary truth that ignorance of which kills countless ideas and splendid plans: that the moment one definitely commits oneself, then Providence moves too. All sorts of things occur to help one that would never otherwise have occurred. A whole stream of events issues from the decision, raising in one's favor all manner of unforeseen incidents and meetings and material assistance, which no man could have dreamed would have come his way. . . . Whatever you can do, or dream you can do, begin it. Boldness has genius, power, and magic in it. Begin it now.[378]

Present-day humanity is fully in the position to test these words of wisdom. Tolkien lived with this certainty and had the courage to act on the above maxim when he embarked on the impossible odyssey, and gamble, of convincing a publisher to invest on a one-thousand-page book, with elaborate appendices, upon which he had spent some twelve years of work. His heroes, likewise, know and act according to Goethe's maxim.

As long as The Lord of the Rings is, for Tolkien it is nevertheless just a little part of a larger story. Tolkien's gaze extends much further in time. His notion of time is not the linear one of modern science; it is the cyclical one known to mythology and to the indigenous mind. Tolkien wants to underline this, and does so in more than one way. His legendarium speaks of ages of Middle-earth, and of previous threats to the survival of humanity. The situation the Hobbits are facing at the end of the Third Age is not unprecedented, though it does present itself in unprecedented fashion. After Gollum throws himself and the Ring into the fire, Sam experiences a brief vision

---

[378] Murray, *The Scottish Himalayan Expedition.*

of swirling cloud . . . towers and battlements . . . upon a mountain throne above immeasurable pits; great courts and dungeons, eyeless prisons sheer as cliffs. . . . Towers fell and mountains slid; walls crumbled and melted, vast spires of smoke and spouting steams went billowing up . . . like an *overwhelming wave*, and its wild crest curled and *came foaming down upon the land.* (emphasis added)[379]

Here Tolkien carries the Great Wave/end of Atlantis dream from his unfinished *The Notion Club Papers* into the heart of *The Lord of the Rings* to give us a perspective of the whole of human evolution. At the end of the Third Age Sam lives an experience that is like an echo of the end of the Second Age, which corresponds to the great flood of Atlantis, a majestic view indeed that can awaken the reader's awe and strengthen his hope. This is moreover a vision that Tolkien carried in his bones, so to speak.

To close, *The Lord of the Rings* tells us that even to us, modern Hobbits beset by incredible odds, it behooves to be able to see the larger picture, appreciate things with detachment, and contemplate with a touch of irony how our apparent enemy is often collaborating with us, unbeknownst to himself. Not a small ray of hope is this!

Larger perspectives, quiet detachment, inner strength, vigorous imagination, tangible hope—these are the gifts of *The Lord of the Rings*. Thus, when we look at the present, we could agree with Tolkien in Gandalf's words: "Yet it is not our part to master all the tides of the world, but to do what is in us for the succor of those years wherein we are set, uprooting the evil in the fields that we know, so that those who live after may have clean earth to till. What weather they shall have is not ours to rule."[380]

---

[379] Tolkien, *The Return of the King*, 925–26.
[380] Tolkien, *The Return of the King*, 861.

# BIBLIOGRAPHY

Bowman, Carol. *Children's Past Lives: How Past Life Memories Affect Your Child*. New York: Bantam, 1997.

Carpenter, Humphrey. *The Letters of J. R. R. Tolkien*, selected and edited by Humphrey Carpenter. Boston: Houghton Mifflin, 1981.

———. *Tolkien: A Biography*. Boston: Houghton Mifflin, 1977.

Flieger, Verlyn. *Green Suns and Faërie: Essays on Tolkien*. Kent, OH: Kent State University Press, 2012.

———. *Interrupted Music: The Making of Tolkien's Mythology*. Kent, OH: Kent State University Press, 2005.

———. *A Question of Time: J. R. R. Tolkien's Road to Faerie*. Kent, OH: Kent State University Press, 1997.

———. *Splintered Light: Logos and Language in Tolkien's World*. Grand Rapids, MI: William B. Eerdmans, 1983.

Grotta, Daniel. *The Biography of J. R. R. Tolkien, Architect of Middle-Earth*. Philadelphia, PA: Running Press, 1978.

Guirdham, Arthur. *The Cathars and Reincarnation*. Saffron Walden, UK: C. W. Daniel, 1970.

———. *The Lake and the Castle*. Saffron Walden, UK: C. W. Daniel, 1976.

———. *We Are One Another: Astounding Evidence of Group Reincarnation*. Saffron Walden, UK: C. W. Daniel, 1974.

Hammond, Wayne G., and Christina Scull. *J. R. R. Tolkien, Artist and Illustrator*. New York: Houghton Mifflin, 1995.

Hardo, Trutz. *Children Who Have Lived Before: Reincarnation Today*. Saffron Walden, UK: C. W. Daniel, 2000.

Helms, Randel. *Tolkien's World*. Boston: Houghton Mifflin, 1974.

Hutton, Ronald. "Can We Still Have a Pagan Tolkien? A Reply to Nils Ivar Agøy." in *The Ring and the Cross: Christianity and the Writings of J. R. R. Tolkien*, edited by Paul E. Kerry, 90–105. Lanham, MD: Rowman & Littlefield for Fairleigh Dickinson University Press, 2011.

———. "The Pagan Tolkien." In *The Ring and the Cross: Christianity and the Writings of J.R.R. Tolkien*, edited by Paul E. Kerry, 57–70. Lanham, MD: Rowman & Littlefield for Fairleigh Dickinson University Press, 2011.

Murray, W. H. *The Scottish Himalayan Expedition*. London: Dent, 1951.

Pearce, Joseph. *Tolkien, Man and Myth: A Literary Life*. San Francisco, CA: Ignatius, 1998.

Riley, Betty. *A Veil Too Thin: Reincarnation Out of Control*. Malibu, CA: Valley of the Sun, 1984.

Skogemann, Pia. *Where the Shadows Lie: A Jungian Interpretation of* The Lord of the Rings. Wilmette, IL: Chiron, 2009.

Steiner, Rudolf. *How to Know Higher Worlds: A Modern Path of Initiation*. Hudson, NY: Anthroposophic Press, 1994.

———. *Theosophy: An Introduction to the Spiritual Processes in Human Life and in the Cosmos*. Hudson, NY: Anthroposophic Press, 1994.

———. *The Mystery of the Human Temperaments*, lecture of January 19, 1909.

———. *The Stages of Higher Knowledge: Imagination, Inspiration, Intuition*. Great Barrington, MA: Steiner Books, 2009.

Stevenson, Ian. *Children Who Remember Previous Lives: A Question of Reincarnation*. Charlottesville: University Press of Virginia, 1987.

Tolkien, J. R. R. *The Fellowship of the Ring; The Two Towers; The Return of the King*. New York: Houghton Mifflin, 1994.

———. *The Lost Road and Other Writings: Language and Legend Before "The Lord of the Rings."* Edited by Christopher Tolkien. Boston: Houghton Mifflin, 1987.

———. *The Monsters and the Critics and Other Essays*. London: Harper Collins, 1983.

———. *Sauron Defeated: The End of the Third Age*. Edited by Christopher Tolkien. Boston: Houghton Mifflin, 1992.

———. *A Secret Vice: Tolkien on Invented Languages*. Edited by Dimitra Fimi and Andrew Higgins. New York: Harper Collins, 2016.

———. *The Silmarillion*. New York: Ballantine, 1977.

West, Richard C. "The Interlace Structure of *The Lord of the Rings*." In *A Tolkien Compass*, edited by Jared Lobdell, 75–92. Chicago: Open Court, 2003.

Printed in the United States
By Bookmasters